"In this tour de force, Tad D⟨...⟩ temporary white evangelicalis⟨...⟩ misogyny, and heteronormati⟨...⟩ ing back this curtain, he show⟨...⟩ ⟨...⟩ commonly confused for white evangelical hypocrisy is actually perfectly consistent with the white evangelical desire for domination and destruction. This book is a must read for all those who wish to better understand the hidden motivations of contemporary white evangelicals, as well as those who recognize the urgent responsibility of resisting what white evangelicalism has become in this day and age."

—**PHIL SNIDER**
Editor of *Preaching as Resistance* and *Justice Calls*

"Tad DeLay's remarkable *Against* represents a pathbreaking psychoanalysis of the evangelical movement. Each page has an arresting new insight into the structure of the evangelical appeal and the damage that it's doing. In lucid prose, DeLay lays out the case for why we need psychoanalysis to understand the recalcitrance of evangelicals when confronted with obvious facts. Rather than condescending to them or parroting the liberal line about the need for more education, DeLay's book articulates the immense enjoyment that derives from the evangelical denial of common sense—including, most importantly, the burning up of the planet. It is an urgent plea for recognition of a problem that threatens everyone's survival and is simply a must-read for anyone concerned about where things are headed."

—**TODD McGOWAN**
University of Vermont

"People wonder why secularism has not yet domesticated American Evangelicals. They wonder why 'pro-life' people cannot see the climate crisis as life-negating. They wonder why godly people support Donald Trump. Such persons should read Tad DeLay's vital book, and temper their fantasies about reason. Today's threatening mode of reason is a powerful 'resonance machine' positing the perpetual absence of absolute self-sovereignty as an injunction to punish. We are, DeLay argues, being punished into apocalypse."

—**PAUL JOHNSON**
University of Pittsburgh

Against

Also by Tad DeLay:

God Is Unconscious: Psychoanalysis & Theology (2015)
The Cynic & the Fool: The Unconscious in Theology & Politics (2017)

Against

What Does the White Evangelical Want?

Tad DeLay

FOREWORD BY
Clayton Crockett

CASCADE *Books* · Eugene, Oregon

AGAINST
What Does the White Evangelical Want?

Cascade Books
An Imprint of Wipf and Stock Publishers
199 W. 8th Ave., Suite 3
Eugene, OR 97401

www.wipfandstock.com

PAPERBACK ISBN: 978-1-5326-6846-3
HARDCOVER ISBN: 978-1-5326-6847-0
EBOOK ISBN: 978-1-5326-6848-7

Cataloguing-in-Publication data:

Names: DeLay, Tad, author. | Crockett, Clayton, foreword.

Title: Against : What does the white evangelical want? / Tad DeLay.

Description: Eugene, OR: Cascade Books, 2019 | Includes bibliographical references.

Identifiers: ISBN 978-1-5326-6846-3 (paperback) | ISBN 978-1-5326-6847-0 (hardcover) | ISBN 978-1-5326-6848-7 (ebook)

Subjects: LCSH: Whites—Race identity. | Race relations—Religious aspects—Christianity. | Evangelicalism—United States—20th century.

Classification: E184.A1 .D325 2019 (print) | E184.A1 .D325 (ebook)

Cover design by Jesse Turri.

Manufactured in the U.S.A.   08/12/19

For Deven

Contents

Foreword

Clayton Crockett

At the 1997 Religion and Postmodernism conference on "God, the Gift, and Postmodernism," held at Villanova University, Jacques Derrida felt it necessary to clarify his connection to Jean-Luc Marion. Derrida said of Marion, "He was not my student." This was in response to a certain confusion about the relationship between Marion and Derrida as Marion's work gained more attention in the English-speaking world. This was not only a question about their personal interaction, but it also addressed the filial relationship between deconstruction and Marion's religious phenomenology. Derrida wanted to clear the record of any confusion, but he was also making two additional points. First of all, he said that he meant this in a positive way; that he could not take any credit for Marion's philosophy and its importance. Marion's success was not indebted in any way to Derrida's influence. At the same time, Derrida wanted to disassociate himself from Marion, to disavow any direct responsibility for what Marion was writing and saying.

This conference on the gift not only addressed theories about the gift in phenomenology and deconstruction, not to mention religion and theology, but it also resonated in and with the academic and professional genealogies that shape many of these discussions and debates. This is a long and complicated way for me to say that Tad DeLay was not my student. He graduated from the University of Central Arkansas, where I teach, and he took courses in the Department of Philosophy of Religion with many of my colleagues. But he did not take any of my classes. He was not my student, and I cannot take any formal credit for his future accomplishments and success.

However, there was a retroactive relationship between us, after he left UCA and went to California. At the study group organized by Barry Taylor at Fuller Theological Seminary, DeLay read my book *Interstices of the Sublime*. When he realized that I was at UCA, he got in touch and we established a strong and positive connection. So much so that I was able to be proud of and share in his successful doctorate from Claremont Graduate University, as well as his burgeoning career as a writer and thinker. This is his third book, after *God Is Unconscious* and *The Cynic & the Fool*. DeLay is the most effective and accomplished theorist of the critical intersection of psychoanalysis and conservative Christian politics. He is able to do something I cannot, which is to synthesize complex ideas and apply them to important situations and explain them in clear and accessible ways. In this vein he follows another person who was not strictly his teacher, Peter Rollins. But where Rollins uses jokes, parables, stories, anecdotes, experimental rituals, and other methods to upset orthodox theology, DeLay analyzes and lays bare the underlying structures of evangelical desire.

This is most apparent in this book, which asks: what do white evangelicals want? The short answer is that they want to destroy us, if us includes anyone who is invested in human flourishing and sustainable life on our planet. This book hits hard at the underbelly of evangelical desire, with its themes of climate denial, white racism, anti-intellectualism, theocratic control of sexuality, and a populism that verges on fascism. The core argument DeLay makes here is that all of these desires are not incidental or marginal to what is happening in the world today, but they are at the heart of everything that is occurring, shaping and distorting our reality in profound ways to create an evangelical-resonance machine that we ignore at our peril.

Desire does not work the way that reasonable people want to think that it does. Desire is much more complicated and ambivalent. White evangelical desire *intends* to generate turmoil in our world because it is the acting out of a profound fantasy of what it means to be the chosen people favored by God. This acting out targets and attempts to destroy the Other, by whatever means necessary, whether the Other is the atheist, the nonwhite, the liberal, the democrat, the Muslim, the socialist, the immigrant, or the poor person. We know that these efforts cannot succeed, because the Other lies at the heart of our self, but this turmoil is destroying our world, with the backing of American nationalism and corporate capitalism. DeLay, himself a convert from white evangelicalism, understands the uncomfortable truth—liberalism will not save us.

We need tools to analyze, diagnose, and understand what is happening. We need the resources to confront this evangelical desire at its own level, which is the level of fantasy and desire. This is a tumultuous task, but DeLay's urgency is evident. Here is not the neutral mask of academicism or moral relativism, but an intervention into the heart of the dark fantasy itself. We are running out of time because the turmoil is building upon itself in positive feedback loops across the globe. Militarism, corporatism, racism, environmental devastation, and proto-fascism converge and ramify each other. These exist under the sign of evangelical Christianity, especially in the United States, even if that is not the only form it takes.

My definition of American fascism is that it is the bundling together of three phenomena—white evangelical Christianity, American exceptionalism and nationalism, and corporate capitalism. These are bundled together in such a way that the links are not always apparent, and sometimes one or another of the three is more evident. But when they work together, as they too often do, they constitute a form (or *the* form) of American fascism. We need to understand, render visible, and disable these links, if there is still time. The consolidation of them makes it stronger and more effective, as dissenters are marginalized or they are crushed by scandal, poverty, or hate.

White evangelical Christianity is just the tip of the iceberg, but it is not simply what it appears on the surface. It functions according to a powerful desire, and its appeal to our desires animates it and makes it work. We want to intervene on the level of interpretation, but we need to shift our analysis and intervention to the level of desire as sketched out by Freud and Lacan. We need to know something about desire, not just their desires but ours, and how ours feeds into and sustains theirs. According to DeLay, white evangelical desire "is moralizing where it should be ethical, individual where it should be collective, hegemonic where it sees itself cornered, and demonic where it sees itself the savior." If we simply oppose these desires with our own, then we become a mirror of and for this twisted desire, and nothing changes. To truly intervene into the field of desire is to distort the symbolic nature of desire itself. We must refuse to continue to affirm our own desires in their moralistic, individualist, hegemonic, and demonic forms. Here DeLay gives us tools to refashion desire, not only of the white evangelical, but our own. We should read this book with fear and trembling.

Introduction

"Truth is not in desire's nature."
—Jacques Lacan

A grim dream followed the tragically early death of a young boy. Deep in grief and fatigue after keeping watch over the sick child for days and nights, the father retired to the adjacent room and fell asleep. In his dream state, he saw his boy draw near beside him. How very happy he must have felt to see his son again.

Up in the real world, a candle lighting the boy's room fell over and set the body ablaze. The smoke billowed up and seeped into the next room, filling the father's nostrils and intertwining with his dream state. The vision collapsed as the boy leaned in to whisper: "Father, don't you see that I am burning?"

What will result once our consciousness is fully organized around trauma and turmoil? As Western democracy careens toward a cliff's edge, we must not presume our institutions will inevitably stabilize or save us. As right-wing authoritarianism roars with aggression unseen for decades, and as we are instructed to tolerate violence, misogyny, or xenophobia as legitimate perspectives, we haven't the time to pretend we all desire some vague "common good." As climate change extinguishes countless species and pushes human civilization to the verge of collapse, we haven't the time to pretend all is well.

Don't You See Turmoil?

This book intervenes in one force of degeneration today, white evangelicalism, which we must not casually dismiss as the irrelevant, revanchist faith of a dying generation. Perhaps our crises today will resolve them-selves by natural processes when one generation ends and another takes the reins, but that's a risky gamble. The old secularization hypothesis told us the world would keep learning and progressing beyond theism, but this proved desperately shortsighted well before 9/11 fatally wounded secular optimism. After the slaughter and our immeasurably worse retaliation, a grotesque violence drenched in our theological desire, we cannot pretend religion will slumber and fade. We're at a pivotal moment today, for no perversion of any faith in the past ever held a candle to the destructive po-tential of white evangelicalism. After all, the fantasy of a sexual encounter leads people to destroy their families every day—why shouldn't a divine fantasy occasionally lead to the destruction of civilization? I'm tempted to invoke Hannah Arendt's notion of the banality of evil, for mass evil today happens not as a killing spree but as a program invoked as a throwaway campaign slogan. Mass evil today is bureaucratic, indifferent, and deadly efficient, though it means well.

What is the genesis of this book? It's not about a particular moment that shall pass but about a plague of turmoil that will persist long after a particular administration or movement concludes. The plague needs analysis. I was politically formed within three historic moments during my graduate studies, and they form the background of the book you hold. First was the Great Recession along with its inadequate resolution. It was a catastrophic loss of the future, the incomprehensible trap of debt and the obliteration of possibilities, and the counter-pressure of Occupy Wall Street, where the taboo against publicly speaking ill of capitalism seemed briefly broken. I saw just how little concern the Boomer generation felt for the prospects of Millennials like myself, and it told me something about the accidentally banal cruelty possible without any hint of malice. Second, a more visceral awakening came as I watched the Black Lives Matter move-ment following the murder of Trayvon Martin, Michael Brown, and so very many others. I caught the slightest glimpse of my privilege. I learned things that could only come from listening rather than trying to see things I couldn't possibly see, and I learned how my very existence was caught up in systems of advantage and harm. I also saw white crowds justify murder, and I watched acquaintances and relatives expressing their hopes that those of us marching in traffic would be run down. I saw how truly controversial white people could find a simple request that a black life matter equally to any other life where officers of the state are concerned. The final moment is still unfolding, and it continually teaches me that no evil is too much for the culture in which I was raised. In 2016, I wrote my dissertation on psychoanalysis, religion, and theories of populism in the midst of a presidential campaign. It was a peculiar time to discuss such a topic, given the United States hadn't had a genuine populist movement in so very long and yet had vigorous developments simultaneously on the center Left and Far Right. I had presumed my research would yield nothing but a theoretical footnote to a bizarre period. In the early evening of Tuesday, November 8, 2016, we felt a collective shock as we realized the polls and forecasts were wrong. Suddenly my work took on a new meaning.

Against a technocratic neoliberal—highly qualified and predictable in equal proportion to a program of mildly uninspiring centrism—a bellicose game show host with no experience would now take the reins. There had never been a campaign drawing more appropriate examples of Godwin's Law. He'd run a campaign born in bigotry that had drawn the support of the Ku Klux Klan and neo-Nazis, mocked the disabled, and proposed using the military machine to kill children; he was as brutal as he was racist, but still the white evangelicals did not protest. He promised to deport eleven million people, called for a Muslim ban, and faked conversion to their faith; he was deceptive as he was empty, but still they did not protest. He called climate change a hoax, encouraged violence at rallies, and bragged of sexual assault; he was as vulgar as he was cruel, and still they did not protest. His constituency was the tribe in which I was raised, for they found in his vacuous soul a mirror of their own. After everything that should have disqualified him, still they did not protest.

In the aftermath, I heard a familiar series of questions about white evangelicals. Do they not grasp the notion of hypocrisy? Why the praise for charlatans? How could they not accept evolutionary or climate science? Why do they mock expertise and defund education? How could anyone inflict their children with conversion therapy? Why do they find the widely popular act of sex a threat? Whence comes the desire for fascism? To each of these questions, my response was a complicated historicization of problems impossible to analyze in the abstract. These apparent contradictions are networked, reinforced, and doing precisely what they are designed to do. The reactionary liberal's fantasy supposes conservatives are dupes in need of education. This deep miscalculation on the part of the liberal misses the point, and liberalism will not save us.[1] Sadism and masochism invigorate a destruction machine

1. Immediately after the election, we saw the Democratic party, never one to take

resonating with neoconservative militarism and neoliberal economics, and such invigoration cannot be resolved by fact-checking. Nothing from the social media infographic to universal college education will save us; information is impotent against this machine. Cruelty operates not at the level of information but at the level of desire.

Don't You See Anxiety?

A fundamental axiom of my work is that we are not subjects who desire to know but instead subjects who desire (full stop).[2] You would think turmoil should be avoided. On the contrary, what happens when turmoil is enjoyed? My methods employ a mix of psychoanalytic theory, political philosophy, history, and survey data, each of which have strengths and weaknesses. My topic is the white evangelical in the United States, specifically their desires and fantasies, but I won't propose a strict definition. Why the subcategory of the *white* evangelical? One need only glance at survey data or read the news to see how the subsection operates with drastically different commitments and stands as a consistent outlier.

Today, seven in ten people in the United States are Christian. Around a quarter identify as evangelical. White Christians account for 43 percent of the population, and white Protestants account for 30 percent. How many Americans self-identify as white evangelical Protestants? Estimates on the percentage vary between the mid-to-high teens. So far as I am aware, Public Religion Research Institute provided the lowest estimate at 17 percent in 2017, a significant drop from 23 percent in 2006.[3] Understand this:

---

advantage of an opportunity, move against the first Left-leaning populism in generations. Instead it called for neoliberal normalcy. It took aim at "norm erosion" and sought a return to hegemonic capitalism with the kindest smile. "America First" nativism will not die of shame it cannot feel, and liberalism will not save us from enemies it cannot or will not name. No matter what becomes of this time of turmoil—whether it is a step toward fascism or instead resuscitates a liberal-centrist order—we can no longer deny that we've seen a glimpse of sadistic desire. We need innovative and even risky hypotheses engaging the fantasies underwriting such rampant, cruel desire. This book is a step in that direction.

2. I'm indebted to Todd McGowan for shaping the way I think about the capitalist subject of desire. See McGowan, *Enjoying What We Don't Have*.

3. "White evangelical Protestants were once thought to be bucking a longer trend, but over the past decade their numbers have dropped substantially. Fewer than one in five (17%) Americans are white evangelical Protestant, but they accounted for nearly one-quarter (23%) in 2006. Over the same period, white Catholics dropped five percentage

white evangelicalism is not entirely unjustified in its paranoia—it is a faith that's dying, and it knows it.

Just how quickly it is dying is more difficult to gauge than the poll above suggests, because holding certain commitments does not necessarily mean someone self-identifies. For example, research on the "nones" indicates a resilient piety among those who claim no religious affiliation (many still pray daily and claim to have a personal relationship with Jesus), and many beliefs incubated within the faith proliferate well beyond evangelical confines. We know that well over a third of whites identify as "born again," so there seems to be a specific revulsion associated with the term *evangelical*. In other words, when we say that only 17 percent of the population is white evangelical, understand there is almost certainly a far larger part of the population inflected with evangelical sentiment that will prove more difficult to measure. I cannot claim to know the scope of such influence. And just as the Republican party holds onto control as a minoritarian power, white evangelicalism exerts an amplified power through the Republican party. Though white evangelicals are only one in six of the population, over a third of Republicans are white evangelical.

Finally, there's an optimistic hope I must quickly dismantle, namely, there's now a repetitive subgenre of journalism in which young evangelicals are highlighted and their beliefs interrogated as if to suggest the next generation will moderate. There's a massive generational gap, given that 26 percent of older Boomers are white evangelicals while only 8 percent of younger millennials identify similarly. Each time these prophecies of moderation erupt, the structure is just the same and the predictions just as futile as the previous iteration of the argument. I have no data to back up my claim here, but I will confidently make it all the same: white evangelicalism will not moderate. It may die off, but no new generation will moderate a religion built on whiteness, nostalgia, and chosenness. If this faith continues to decline and this book becomes irrelevant in the years ahead, I will consider it a welcome mercy.

White evangelicalism is also a practically young faith, a fact its practitioners would surely reject. It is not quite a different religion, but it is more than a different denomination; it is a new sect. It is a reactionary, theological improvisation around whiteness. By calling its religious features a reactionary improvisation I am claiming its enduring commitment is to supremacy

---

points from 16% to 11%, as have white mainline Protestants, from 18% to 13%." Cox and Jones, "America's Changing Religious Identity."

rather than to evangelism, moral values, or whatever else people wish were the defining features of the faith. As a political project in current form, it stretches back no further than the mid- to late-twentieth century.[4] In the latter half of the twentieth century a coalition formed between neoliberal capitalist interests, segregationists, and conservative Christians such that the desires merged into a novel iteration of the faith. The first hint of this coalition in political production was the failed Goldwater campaign, its emergence as a powerful force was the Religious Right of the Reagan era, and its perfected form is today's Trumpism. Aside from the disposable window dressing of doctrines quickly abandoned, all that binds this faith to anything historic is its commitment to whiteness. I commit this book to underscoring how whiteness curates commitments they genuinely believe to be rooted in faith. The faith covers for something more nefarious, and those who disagree with me on this point needn't read any further.

I won't delve laboriously into psychoanalytic theory throughout the book, so I should clarify my scope in the introduction. We will psychoanalyze turmoil and fantasy to examine coalitions of racism, populism, faith, and capital. We will refuse to listen too closely to justifications and instead read actions as evidence of desire.[5] All the religious activities we'll discuss are locations of enjoyment, though the enjoyment will often incur turmoil and anxiety. Shame-heavy rhetoric can be boasting in disguise. For example, when Calvinists tell us they're sinners saved by grace, they don't

---

4. I do not know how to fully credit the array of influences which drove me to this conclusion about white evangelicalism as a young and distinct type of faith, but surely the most prominent influence is the historian Darren Dochuk, who is cited heavily throughout this book. Later, another influence in this direction was Adam Kotsko, and there are surely others. Yes, the leaders to which white evangelicalism would look, e.g., Billy Graham, were always political conservatives and often activists (however much their history is revised as apolitical). And of course, the whiteness underneath it was never apolitical. Still, it was precisely these disavowed political desires that served to activate a practically new iteration of faith over the latter half of the twentieth century. It's not the same evangelicalism of the American revival period, and it's certainly not the same evangelicalism out of which many abolitionists worked in the nineteenth century. The term *evangelical* designated several groups in Christian history and American history, but the evangelicals of the Great Awakenings or the post-fundamentalist era are not the same as the white evangelicals of today. They share similarities, affinities, and occasional authorities, but the evangelical today is not yesteryear's.

5. Psychoanalysis looks at the subject split between conscious and unconscious. A subject may say "I believe X," while actions bear witness to their unconscious belief in not-X. It matters less whether someone consciously perceives their belief in X, Y, or Z. What matters is the attestation of their belief in their material reality.

experience shame but instead turmoil. Far from shame, they are boasting! If they feel the turmoil of God's judgement, they enjoy it alongside confidence in predetermined salvation. This narcissism justifies indifference at best, cruelty at worst. In turning inward to obsess over her standing with God, the believer never need ask whether she's destroying everything else around her. The unconscious will speak, and we must listen.

The French psychoanalyst Jacques Lacan (1901–1981) is my primary point of reference. Lacan located anxiety and turmoil as outer limits of frustration.[6] Because they lend a sense of security or clear standing, I wager anxiety and turmoil are actually sources of enjoyment rather than something subjects prefer to avoid. There is a precise order to the relationship. Lacan put it up on the blackboard for us:

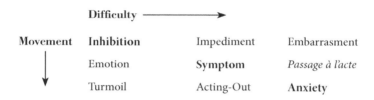

The early Freud believed anxiety was a response to repression. Later in *Inhibitions, Symptoms, and Anxiety*, Freud argued anxiety arrived first such that repression was a response to (rather than a cause of) anxiety. Put differently, repression is the (attempted) solution, and the symptoms that result from repression are the "return of the repressed." Symptoms proliferate and gather even more anxiety. Inhibition, symptom, and anxiety are part of a triad always found together. The subject begins to enjoy the trap they've laid, then the cycle launches again.

For Lacan, anxiety was intractably linked to a question we ask the Other: *Che vuoi?* (*What do you want?* or *What's bugging you?*). This is only one half of the relationship. We also feel anxiety when the Other asks the same of us. When we ask another—a parent, a significant other, a boss, a god—what they want, anxiety rises precisely because we don't know what they will desire. When the same question is asked back to us, we feel doubly anxious if we don't yet know what we want. If a faith is built around submission to a big Other, anxiety blends seamlessly into feelings of security.

6. I use the word *turmoil*, which is used in the standard translations for Lacan's term *émoi*. Others have translated it as "commotion" and "dismay." Table modified for clarity from Lacan, *Anxiety*, 13, 77.

When a believer prays the question "What do you want?" and no answer returns, the believer externalizes her own narcissistic desire as a God telling her what to desire. Fidelity and security are rooted in turmoil and anxiety, which turn out to be a curious mode of (self) co-dependence.

Turmoil shifts back and forth, sometimes appearing as angst or other times as security. Turmoil is "the evocation of the power that fails you, the experience of what you lack in need."[7] If the believer hopes to stay included in her community, she must continually do more to balance her lack. She must listen to a new sermon, attend to a Bible study, add a spiritual discipline, etc. She's sure she's never good enough. As Lacan's graph suggests, turmoil can actually be the goal if we believe we should feel distressed. She is the symptom of her dependence. Or, as Freud simply put it, guilt is preferable to anxiety. In the turmoil of guilt, there's a clear debt owed to the Other. If you know you're guilty, you don't have to wonder anymore. Just knowing you're guilty can be a relief. However, in anxiety you don't know what the Other wants—but you're on the hook for it nonetheless. My thesis claims white evangelicalism is a faith organized around fantasies curating the enjoyment of—not the flight from—turmoil and anxiety.

Don't You See There Is Only One Doctrine?

What's the role of fantasy? Fantasy is part of desire, and figuring out what we desire—especially if it's a question of doubting what we "should" desire—is a venture riddled with anxiety.[8] Psychoanalysts read anxiety as an affect: it signals a problem, and it doesn't deceive. Anxiety doesn't get repressed, but instead the various signifiers mooring anxiety in its place get repressed.[9] For example, when I'm anxious, it will display as various symptoms even though I won't necessarily know precisely why I'm anxious. The affect is on the surface, but the signifiers attached to it submerge. If the Other's question "What do you want?" (or What should you desire?) leads into anxiety, then we're exploring a very obscure relationship between anxiety and desire. Anxiety is in the interval between desiring something

7. Ibid., 77.

8. As Lacan put it, "Anxiety is not doubt, anxiety is the cause of doubt." Ibid., 76.

9. "On the other hand, what I said about affect is that is isn't repressed. Freud says it just as I do. It's unfastened, it drifts about. It can be found displaced, maddened, inverted, or metabolized, but it isn't repressed. What are repressed are the signifiers that moor it." Ibid., 14.

on the one hand and enjoyment (*jouissance*) on the other.[10] The catch, of course, is that one never desires without fantasy.

A few banal fantasies float across white evangelicalism. It seldom tires of arguing over hell, substitutionary atonement, or biblical inerrancy, and it never misses an opportunity to judge women or non-heteronormative sexuality. But if my claim is that white evangelicalism (as a political project) is quite recent, then I'm also claiming these older ideas are utterly irrelevant to the vacuous believer wishing to argue now. This faith holds only one doctrine: an already forgiven and shameless chosenness. They saw a story of Abraham's blessing and coveted that story; in their hands the story mutated into a Christianized simulacrum cobbled together from election, gratuitous pretentiousness, and white settler colonialism. Every other doctrine is improvised and disposable. Chosenness is its ultimate fantasy. Chosenness captures so many more specific doctrines—atonement, afterlife, perspicuity, predestination, the inability to lose one's salvation, and so on. Chosenness means the believer has direct access to a divine knowledge that the unbeliever does not. Taking chosenness for its own use was a double-theft committed by its supersessionism and its racism. Theological chosenness bleeds into racial or national chosenness like a manifest destiny. The chosen believer rests assured she's a member not only of the true faith but the correct lifestyle, the blessed nation, and so on. Every other doctrine can and will be shown disposable, and as white evangelicals drop the theological jargon and identify more directly with white nationalism or the alt-right, the true doctrinal core remains. Chosenness means never second-guessing your narcissism or cruelty.

Fantasy isn't a pejorative term in my work. Yes, in a sense fantasy is a *rejection* of the world as such, but it's also a way to *enliven* the world. Fantasy sustains desire; desire requires fantasy.[11] We can fantasize about fictions un-

---

10. Ibid., 178.

11. When we desire, we don't simply desire the object as such. The object of desire is always infused with our projections, expectations, and significations. Even if the desired object actually exists, it's something different in our imaginations. For example, when a lover desires her beloved, she desires an idealized version of the beloved. She doesn't immediately picture the beloved with all the flaws of a human being. The beloved is real but also imaginary. Further, our objects of desire are always handed to us by a network of signification, demand, and expectations that are part of being speaking subjects in a world telling us what to desire. We never simply desire an object without fantasizing something in the object. We desire more (or less) than what is in the object, and for this we deploy fantasies. And occasionally we find "empty desires or mad desires that are based on nothing more than the fact that the thing in question has been forbidden you," as Lacan put it. "By virtue of the very fact that it has been forbidden you, you cannot do

til the imaginary seems more visceral than reality. Fantasy infuses turmoil with the excitement of some divine mission, as if to say: God wants you to feel this way, so be grateful! "Am I saying this to explain the difficulty of his desire?" Lacan asked of the submissive obsessional neurotic who wishes to be told what to desire. "No, rather to say that his desire is for difficulty."[12] When desire begins to fail, or when the fantasy is revealed as a farce, what perverse vicissitude must it take to keep the subject happy in her turmoil?[13] What does it mean when one increasingly defends the indefensible with the acknowledgement-excuse structure of "Yes, but even so . . . "?[14] Fantasy justifies cruelty, entices with a sense of loss, and ignites a drive for revenge. The Right loves loss. This is the serious lesson, for conservatism and fundamentalism thrive when they feel they are losing. The fantasy of loss lets them kill and feel righteous while killing.

The result is acting-out posing as the *passage à l'acte* (passage to the act).[15] These are two ways to think about a response to tension in terms of whether we want our response to be seen. One person acts because they feel compelled to flee some unwelcome intrusion from the world (*passage à l'acte*). Another acts because they want to display themselves for attention on the world's stage (acting-out).[16] It's at the moment of embarrassment or some other situation demanding response that we act, and the *passage à l'acte* commits us on a new path in the world. It isn't necessarily

otherwise, for a time, than think about it. That too is desire." Lacan, *The Four Fundamental Concepts of Psychoanalysis*, 243.

12. Lacan, *Écrits*, 529.

13. "[T]he neurotic makes use of his fantasy for particular ends. What one reckoned one could make out, beneath the neurosis, to be perversion . . . the neurotic's fantasy is entirely situated in the locus of the Other. The support the neurotic finds in the fantasy is what, when it's met, presents itself as perversion." Lacan, *Anxiety*, 49–50.

14. A claim throughout this book, which mostly works as a subtext rather than something on which I spend much time defending, is the idea that we are exploring a faith comprised of broadly neurotic individuals who feel compelled to take up increasingly perverse language to defend themselves against the recognition that their faith fails them. "Yes, but even so . . ." is a perverse defense at its simplest, for we have the ego's acknowledgement "Yes" followed by the immediate disavowal of what it knows to be true with "but even so . . . " For this observation, I'm indebted to Krips, *Fetish*.

15. For a more sophisticated treatment of these terms, see Lacan, *Anxiety*, 114–30.

16. "This is precisely why it was so useful to set out in the first phases of this disquisition on anxiety the essential distinction between these two registers—on one hand, the *world*, the place where the real bears down, and, on the other hand, the *stage* of the Other where man as subject has to be constituted, to take up his place as he who bears speech, but only ever in a structure that, as truthful as it sets itself out to be, has the structure of fiction." Ibid., 116.

well-calculated, but it puts us on a trajectory. Perhaps it's ending a relationship or deconverting from a faith. It might be a slap for one who's wronged us, or it might be a pledge of loyalty. It's a moment of commitment that might be, but usually isn't, well calculated. The *passage à l'acte* commits us on a path when we must make a fateful choice.

On the other hand, acting-out displays angst as if it's an actor on a stage. It's showing off and seeking attention. The child acts out to display frustration, the adult has a midlife crisis to show himself virile or less dull, and the liberal technocrat declares himself a member of the #Resistance. Acting-out might produce real effects in the world, but its purpose is to display, to justify, and to express itself. What becomes of a faith ostensibly beginning as genuine conversion (*passage à l'acte*) before devolving into flippant, ridiculous, narcissistic, and callous behavior (acting-out)? Its fantasies are a rejection and enlivening of the world, but its harmful masochism and sadism is always a display for the big Other. The masochist enjoys suffering because he imagines the big Other is enjoying, or, to put it in Christian language, he must suffer because God is testing his faith. If it turns into sadism, what the sadist is seeking is not the other's suffering but the other's anxiety.[17] For instance, don't we see a lot of talk now on the Right that gloats over triggering the other with some racist or misogynist slur? This is the sadistic intention of one who cannot formulate their desire. When a faith aims not for the benefit of the world but for the approval of a big Other, acting-out turns into its chief virtue.

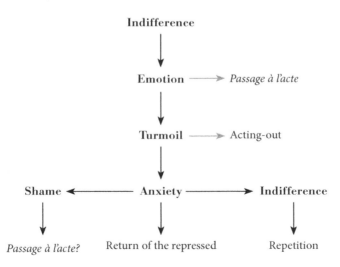

17. Ibid., 104.

In effect, this is my claim: the subject prefers turmoil or anxiety and wraps themselves up in these states as a protection against the shame they couldn't bear. The interesting thing is that shame and indifference can manifest the same on the outside. Shame doesn't defend itself but instead shuts down. Shame is the sense that I am seen *too much* by the world. Indifference likewise doesn't defend itself, because indifference recognizes no need to do so. Shame is the worst of feelings; even death is preferable. People will do anything to avoid it. However, isn't shame a good thing on occasion? Isn't the problem not that religion creates zones of shame but instead that it invests shame unwisely? White evangelicalism says you should feel ashamed of sexuality, but actually they should really feel ashamed of, for instance, locking the immigrant child in a cage or destroying breathable air for future generations.

Deserved shame is the opportunity for a new master signifier,[18] but shame is typically avoided like the plague. Those without eyes to see nor ears to hear must avoid reckoning with their sins. So then, my modified graph suggests the theory underneath all I will suggest in the chapters ahead: the subject is doing all she can to avoid shame, and that is why she enjoys the (comparably easier) state of anxiety and turmoil. It's true of all human subjects, but white evangelicalism seems particularly adept at propping up shamelessness. Fantasy justifies shamelessness and moves them back toward the true goal, which is to be completely free of and indifferent to the trauma of the world.

This book is not an exhaustive history of white evangelicalism, nor does it detail each and every problem demanding analysis. The first four chapters examine the past, while the final chapter, a study of reactionary movements which could stand alone as an independent study, considers the faith's troubling ambitions for the future. If the reader wishes me to

---

18. My point here is drawn from Lacan, who describes shame as a heightened affective state out of which a new signifier is possible. It feels odd to promote the value of shame, but I take Lacan to have an important point here. Masters today certainly prefer those doing their bidding never feel shame nor even consider the harm they commit against the powerless for the sake of the master's profit or power. To ask "What have I done?!" and feel deep revulsion might be precisely what's needed to rotate away from the master's trap. "Today I have brought you the dimension of shame," says Lacan at the end of a seminar. "It is not a comfortable thing to put forward. It is not one of the easiest things to speak about. This is perhaps what it really is, the hole from which the master signifier arises. If it were, it might perhaps not be useless for measuring how close one has to get to it if one wants to have anything to do with the subversion, or even just the rotation, of the master's discourse." Lacan, *The Other Side of Psychoanalysis*, 189.

follow a more amiable definition of evangelicalism such as Bebbington's,[19] or if the reader thinks the faith could not possibly decay into the hierarchies of contempt I explore in the final chapter, or if the reader finds it ostentatious to suggest desire in humans is often filled with fantasies of self-harm and sadistic cruelty, or if the reader wishes me to talk about something other than what white evangelicalism in the United States plainly is today, then read no further. I aim to trace key moments, figures, and ideas reflecting the ethos and fantasies of a most dangerous faith. Truth be told, it feels odd expending academic energy researching such an improvised and regularly ridiculous religion. However, we live in dangerous times and cannot afford to ignore the threats around us.

Don't You See the World is Burning?

If climate change is indeed the greatest threat civilization has ever faced, then a faith aiding and abetting it must face analysis. If it desires an emperor, it threatens democracy. If it fantasizes the eternal torment of its foes, merciless policy shall follow. If it covers a xenophobic genesis, its future will be ever more cruel at worst and indifferent at best. If it holds power within the most powerful military and economic apparatus the world has yet seen, the danger is magnified. It is like what W. E. B. Du Bois called the "new religion of whiteness"[20] desiring to own the earth with a strut and arrogance hinting it felt ownership was its birthright. A century after his claim, has it not proven capable of destroying the inhabitants of the world it owns? My claim is nothing short of this: white evangelicalism is far and away the most dangerous faith the world has yet known. Let us consider its justifications, appetite, seduction, and catastrophe.

---

19. David Bebbington's quadrilateral defines evangelicalism through conversionism, activism, biblicism, and crucicentrism. I don't disagree entirely, but rather I find the underside of each of them to be where helpful analysis begins. For example the underside of conversionism and crucicentrism is chosenness, and the underside of activism and biblicism is the hegemonic or supremacist desire to conform the world to one's wishes. A fundamental lesson of psychoanalysis is that the descriptor one evokes for oneself is already an effort to censor the truth. We need to listen to self-descriptions, but they tell us the truth in disguise.

20. Even worse, isn't the white evangelical's chosenness so very similar to the white soul which believes "The one virtue is to be white"? See Du Bois, "The Souls of White Folk."

In the vision of the burning son from Freud's *The Interpretation of Dreams*, the father woke up at a precise moment. But why? A simple and fair explanation might suggest the body's response to threat. Yes, but what if a dream is indeed a wish?[21] Don't we awake from nightmares when they're too much to handle, when the anxiety reaches a threshold? In a sense, does he not wake up in order to remain asleep—to flee from the horror of loss? However much he desired to see his son again, the sight was too much to bear. Let's take seriously the notion that this father awoke with a consciousness organized around the turmoil. When a culture sees real trauma—from common cruelties to the possible extinction of humankind—how does it opt to ignore the real and prefer the fantasy?

The father looked away. This is the emergency of our moment, for we cannot afford to look away. If democratic civilization survives, it will be for lack of competence on the part of its opponents, not a lack of their desire. We have seen the unmasking of authoritarian desire in our neighbors, and we must analyze those fantasies underwriting the sadism.

We must not look away. We live in a time of racism, xenophobia, and rampant misogyny; a time of nationalism, demagogues, and open bigotry; a time of climate collapse and mass extinction that may well count us among its casualties. So many of us are adherents or former adherents of a most dangerous faith the world has yet known. My friends, don't you see the world is burning?

---

21. Freud's interpretation of this dream emphasized the desire to see the child again. Lacan's interpretation took a much more troubling turn: "If Freud, amazed, sees in this the confirmation of his theory of desire, it is certainly a sign that the dream is not a phantasy fulfilling a wish. For it is not that, in the dream, he persuades himself that the son is still alive. But in the terrible vision of the dead son taking the father by the arm designates a beyond that makes itself heard in the dream. Desire manifests itself in the dream by the loss expressed in an image at the most cruel point of the object. It is only in the dream that this truly unique encounter can occur. Only a rite, an endlessly repeated act, can commemorate this not very memorable encounter—for no one can say what the death of a child is, except the father *qua* father, that is to say, no conscious being. For the true formula of atheism is not *God is dead*—even by basing the origin of the function of the father upon his murder, Freud protects the father—the true formula of atheism is *God is unconscious.* The awakening shows us the waking state of the subject's consciousness in the representation of what has happened—the unfortunate accident in reality, against which one can do no more than take steps!" Lacan, *Four Fundamental Concepts of Psychoanalysis*, 59.

1

Against Future

Apocalypticism and Climate Collapse

"What the climate needs to avoid collapse is a contraction in humanity's use of resources; what our economic model demands to avoid collapse is unfettered expansion. Only one of these sets of rules can be changed, and it's not the laws of nature."
—Naomi Klein

"In fantasy, the subject experiences himself as what he wants . . . in the place where he is truth without consciousness and without recourse. It is here that he creates himself in the thick absence called desire."
—Jacques Lacan

The Optimist and the Pessimist

Halfway between the world wars, Albert Einstein dispatched a letter on behalf of a new project with the League of Nations. The International Institute of Intellectual Cooperation in Paris was founded in 1925 to foster intellectual and cultural exchange between scholars, artists, scientists, and teachers. Humanity's march to extinction might be routed if the higher faculties of reason could generate cooperation. Perhaps a global coterie of genius might chasten the tribal impulses which careened into the Great War.

In the summer of 1932, Einstein pleaded for a public debate with an appeal to his reader's idealism. He'd seen his correspondent's awful account of human aggression, and Einstein felt such pessimism revealed a deep devotion to liberation.[1] Only experts could decipher the perplexing vagaries

1. "You have shown with irresistible lucidity how inseparably the aggressive and

15

rooted in complex psycho-social phenomena driving our self-destruction, he reasoned. Einstein figured a global government would resolve the drive for war, but we were doomed until archaic notions like sovereignty were exorcised from national consciousness. The ruling class already controlled the masses via the press, the church, and the schools. "How is it that these devices succeed so well in rousing men to such wild enthusiasm, even to sacrifice their lives?," he asked. "Only one answer is possible. Because man has within him a lust for hatred and destruction." His ultimate question was so very simple: "Is it possible to control man's mental evolution so as to make him proof against the psychosis of hate and destructiveness?" He sent this open letter to the psychoanalyst who discovered the death drive.

Sigmund Freud's response cheered on the physicist's optimism while lamenting our self-destruction. On Freud's wager, humanity enjoyed repetition. It was the whole reason his clinical practice was full of patients who had every opportunity to change and yet refused. The impulse to destroy was present in animalistic prehistory, cemented with property ownership, and ritualized with law and class divisions. Attachment to an object actually required bipolar affections such as love and hate. We couldn't hold one without the conditions for the other, for love and hate (or progress and destruction) were two vectors of desire. Ridding society of violence would require we first rid ourselves of caring enough to fight. Destruction was not a mistake of evolution. It was practically the point.

While reading the exchange, I can't help but wonder whether Freud secretly hoped Einstein would prove him wrong. Did he see Einstein as a naive physicist out of his element with social analysis? Or did Freud suspect his goal of "transforming neurotic misery into common unhappiness" might express itself in Einstein's project? But the object was the prevention of war, not the excavation of the psyche. "The upshot of these observations," the psychoanalyst concluded, "is that there is no likelihood of our being able to suppress humanity's aggressive tendencies."[2]

---

destructive instincts are bound up in the human psyche with those of love and the lust for life. At the same time, your convincing arguments make manifest your deep devotion to the great goal of the internal and external liberation of man from the evils of war. This was the profound hope of all those who have been revered as moral and spiritual leaders beyond the limits of their own time and country, from Jesus to Goethe and Kant. Is it not significant that such men have been universally recognized as leaders, even though their desire to affect the course of human affairs was quite ineffective?" Einstein, "Why War?"

2. Quotes from Einstein and Freud, "Why War?"

The pessimist proved right when anti-Semitism reached a murderous fever pitch and pressured his evacuation to England. Seven years after the exchange of letters, Freud was still lucid enough on his deathbed to understand the gravity of the German army's invasion of Poland. One believed in an intellectually pacified future which never came. The other foresaw perpetual destruction that has not yet rid the earth of humanity. Neither yet knew of the apocalyptic possibilities of nuclear war or climate collapse around the temporal corner, and neither took seriously enough the religious commitment to realize such vivid apocalypse. They were worlds apart in their visions of the future.

Likewise, the historian Ernest Sandeen once observed, "Ever since its rise to notoriety in the 1920s, scholars have predicted the imminent demise of the movement. The Fundamentalists, to return the favor, have predicted the speedy end of the world. Neither prophecy has so far been fulfilled."[3] Which future do we expect? My argument in this chapter is not so complicated, for a pessimistic account of our dire situation is the only shot we have at an hopeful outcome. Climate collapse is the greatest threat our civilization has ever faced, but those who imagine themselves smart suppose our enemy is ignorance. *If only the duped could see that the world truly is burning*, we reason, *they would vote on a carbon tax*. Such naive optimism is dangerous. Reagan's Secretary of the Interior, James G. Watt, once defended drilling oil and cutting more timber by telling Congress, "I don't know how many future generations we can count on before the Lord returns." It was rare honesty. Apocalyptic fatalism normally keeps its head down. Every day, you cross paths with multiple people who believe God will destroy the world before we reach the next century. What's the point saving what God will surely destroy?

Apocalypse is a peculiar, deadly fantasy linked with climate denial, creating fertile ground for alliances so plainly exhibited between evangelicalism and Wall Street. Why does this alliance exist? What has Christ to do with the Dow? Goals are not identical, but there's a shared ethos of future-denial. Capitalism has little incentive to think beyond the next financial quarterly earnings reports, while evangelicals deny the future in a more literal sense. The political theorist William E. Connolly called it an *evangelical-capitalist resonance machine*. The two parties share affinities—not goals—and they curate their alliance with polyvalent cues across multiple mediating apparatuses: the television in the home, the sermon in

3. Sandeen, *The Roots of Fundamentalism*, ix.

the pulpit, the literature consumed in private, the conversation between friends, the bumper sticker on the gas-guzzling truck, the meme spread across social media, the alternative education of the private or home school, the Bible study in the coffeehouse, and ultimately the political platform. Ideological apparatuses interpellate individuals into haphazardly constructed consciousness, foreign as they seem intuitive. Clandestine radicalization happens completely out in the open, and by the end of it the deregulation of the petroleum industry intertwines itself with heartfelt religion until there's no daylight between the two. In effect, to be a good citizen is to destroy the world. If we wish to postpone the end of the world, we should understand the nature of this resonate machine, its fatalistic fantasies, and its commitment to destroy.

The Desire for the End is Not New

The world was supposed to end so many times already. Far from disillusionment, passing end dates often energize the disappointed faithful. Proliferation of end times thought intensified during the Industrial Revolution. In the northeastern United States, a following grew around the preacher William Miller (1782–1849). The oldest of sixteen children, Miller grew up on the border of Vermont and New York and eventually rejected his Baptist upbringing, preferring deism instead. Something changed during his military service, when he figured the deist God who wouldn't interact with creation couldn't procure an afterlife, so he drew himself back toward the personal God in the Scriptures. He worked a number of jobs while studying the Bible on his own time—self-radicalizing, one might say—until he discovered the world would end in "about the year 1843." He traced his revelation to the same decade of the 1820s during which, over in the United Kingdom, the minister John Nelson Darby claimed to have discovered a rapture in which the faithful would rise to meet Christ in the skies before the Great Tribulation. Each initially hesitated several years before disseminating their revelations publicly. Each supposed there was no public appetite for such a message.

In the early 1830s, Miller committed himself to preaching full-time. It's unclear how many fervent followers he had, but he estimated 50,000 to 100,000. He carried a list of more than seventy signatures from supportive ministers as he traveled thousands of miles back and forth across the northeastern United States and Canada. He purchased a tent to cover

3,000 listeners at a time to hear the prophecy. From the Book of Daniel 8:13–14,[4] he narrowed Christ's return to between March 1843 and March 1844.[5] After April arrived, Miller felt deeply disappointed. However, some followers blamed the Gregorian calendar and drew a new prediction based on the Jewish calendar. Miller's acolyte Samuel S. Snow proposed October 22, 1844. It was the only specific date set during this whole ordeal and a date later called the Great Disappointment. Though evidence is thin, legend has it that followers sold possessions and waited upon the hillsides in anticipation of Christ's arrival.

Why has the global death wish grown in recent centuries? End times thinking wasn't new to Christianity, but its particulars and intensities mutated alongside social factors. Apocalyptic reinvigoration during and after the Industrial Revolution made such pronouncements less than unusual, and Millerites doubtless saw themselves not as a new sect but as committed students within a Protestant tradition. What's interesting is this term *Great Disappointment*. Though Miller was discredited and many abandoned him, his disciples renewed their vigor. One offshoot reinterpreted the "cleansing" as having happened, but in heaven instead of earth. The latter's destruction would have to wait. Disappointing indeed!

Millerites rebranded themselves under the leadership of Ellen White as Seventh Day Adventists, a denomination still in operation today. Darby's rapture was normalized within Protestant and even Catholic circles. Apocalyptic zeitgeist coincided with a surge in missionary activity and mass-produced religious literature, so ideas brewing within American Christianity by the early twentieth century quickly proliferated across the

---

4. "Then I heard a holy one speaking, and another holy one said to him, 'How long will it take for the vision to be fulfilled—the vision concerning the daily sacrifice, the rebellion that causes desolation, the surrender of the sanctuary and the trampling underfoot of the Lord's people?' He said to me, 'It will take 2,300 evenings and mornings; then the sanctuary will be reconsecrated.'" Dan 8:13–14 (NIV).

The Jewish apocalyptic book of Daniel was written as insurrectionist propaganda during the Hasmonean Revolt (167–164 BCE). It aimed to radicalize locals into joining the guerrilla warfare waged by the Maccabees against the Seleucid king Antiochus IV. Miller popularized the practice of reading this book as a work of future-telling.

5. Using a year of flex time for Christ's return actually let Miller argue that he never set a date or time. He was aware of the Scripture's claim that nobody knows the day or hour of Christ's return, and Miller claimed in a letter that his year-long timeframe meant he complied with the Scriptures.

globe. Today only a quarter of American Protestant ministers believe the rapture will *not* be a literal, physical event in the future.[6]

Beyond the mainstream, the cult gives us a vivid case study for apocalyptic desire. Doomsday cults are derided for their insular nature, their suicidal and homicidal violence, and their missed dates. Waco's Branch Davidian siege stands out as an extraordinary case. They were led by their prophet David Koresh (born Vernon Howell), a spiritual searcher who'd joined the commune and successfully consolidated power over time. A splinter group from the Seventh Day Adventists, the Branch Davidians drew federal attention and exchanged gunfire with the Bureau of Alcohol, Tobacco, and Firearms on February 28, 1993. Reports of illegal weapons caches triggered the raid, and the fight left six Davidians and four agents dead. ATF and FBI agents surrounded the compound while negotiators attempted to get children out. After fifty-one days, Attorney General Janet Reno authorized a plan using tanks to deploy tear gas into the compound. A fire engulfed the compound, and though a few Davidians escaped, more than seventy did not. Among the dead were Koresh and twenty-five children. The adults chose to stay and keep children inside when the fire started, and that gruesome fact is what must be reconciled.

In 1997, thirty-nine members of Heaven's Gate committed mass suicide in hopes that a supposed UFO following Comet Hale–Bopp would collect their souls. Its prophetic duo, Ti and Do (Bonnie Lou Nettles and Marshall Herff Applewhite), believed they were two prophets appointed in the book of Revelation to preach a final warning to humankind. Their message benefited from cultural advantages when they began in the 1970s. Several books at the time, including Erich von Däniken's bestseller *Chariots of the Gods?* (1968), claimed aliens represented themselves as gods to ancient people. At the same time, Hal Lindsey's bestseller *The Late Great Planet Earth* (1970), and a film version narrated by none other than Orson Welles, laid the foundation for Dispensational apocalypticism's renewed mass appeal. Heaven's Gate benefited from the UFO and Christian crazes. The group's website still boasts of graduating to the "Evolutionary Level Above Human (the 'Kingdom of Heaven')" and boarding an alien spacecraft traveling to "'Their World'—in the literal Heavens."[7] The duo fully expected to be slaughtered in

6. Lifeway Research, "Pastor Views on the End Times."

7. The homepage reads: "Our 22 years of classroom here on planet Earth is finally coming to conclusion — 'graduation' from the Human Evolutionary Level. We are happily prepared to leave 'this world' and go with Ti's crew . . . We are so very thankful that we have been recipients of this opportunity to prepare for membership in Their

the streets. It was only after Ti's untimely death from cancer that Do hatched the option of suicide. Again, the failure of the message did not diminish the word but, instead, reinvigorated the death drive.

Failure rebirths as success. When radio evangelist Harold Camping predicted the rapture would land on May 21, 2011, he was obsessed with reading the Bible as a codebook. Words indicated numbers calculable as dates, the first of which landed in 1994 when Camping convinced dozens the end was near. He acquired a worldwide audience by the time of the 2011 predictions. He picked the year claiming it was the seven-thousandth anniversary of the great flood in Genesis. Followers left jobs and sold possessions (some donating proceeds to Camping's ministry) as they awaited the day. When the moment passed without incident, Camping followed the Millerite style and argued a spiritual judgment had indeed occurred, while the main event was reprojected for October 21, 2011. He later relented from predictions and passed away without ever being raptured in 2013. Years later, while driving across the deserts of the American Southwest, I saw a billboard warning of the 2011 rapture. It was either a vestige of failure or a reminder of shame's impotency.

There's a danger in making a caricature of the doomsday fool. The cult member isn't uniquely abnormal, and often the mainstream is cultish desire writ large. Many evangelicals found reassurance in Camping's failure, his problem being less the apocalypticism and more the date-setting. *We know that nobody knows the day or the hour!* was the denial deployed.[8] We see this pattern over and over with apocalyptic belief. Just as falling for the small con makes us more susceptible to the large con, failure amplifies the core belief. The cartoonish caricature of the cultish fantasy makes more bland iterations palatable.

We don't recognize the nihilism closer to home. In August 2014, then chairman of the Joint Chiefs of Staff General Martin Dempsey told the press that the relatively new Islamic State should be considered an apocalyptic cult and treated accordingly. "They can be contained, not in perpetuity," Dempsey

---

Kingdom, and to experience Their boundless Caring and Nurturing." See Heaven's Gate, "Hale Bopp Brings Closure to Heaven's Gate."

8. This refrain is taken from Matthew 24:36 (NIV), which reads: "But about that day or hour no one knows, not even the angels in heaven, nor the Son, but only the Father." Earlier in the chapter, the writer of the Gospel of Matthew attributes to Jesus a prophecy of the destruction of the temple and Jerusalem in 70 CE. This verse is now more commonly used to imagine a future apocalypse, which is sure to come but barred from prediction.

reasoned. "This is an organization that has an apocalyptic, end-of-days strategic vision and which will eventually have to be defeated."[9] The irony was totally lost. A general commanding a superpower supplemented by Christian fatalism saw danger only in the Islamist iteration. How much more a danger would the Islamic State hold if it conjoined its vision to an unparalleled nuclear arsenal? Suppose it were capable of raising the seas. Perhaps then we'd call a fledgling band of extremists the most dangerous organization in civilization's history, but this award belongs elsewhere.

We haven't the luxury of avoiding the implications. The most dangerous faith in the world today is white evangelicalism, the most dangerous organization the Republican party,[10] and the most dangerous arrangement global, neoliberal capitalism. Each gladly amplify the most clearly catastrophic threat human civilization has ever faced in climate collapse.

Unfortunately, we'll prefer extinction if survival requires burdensome industry regulations. In June 2017, President Trump announced the nation's exit from the Paris Agreement, joining two other nations. Syria held out due to a prolonged civil war and related sanctions, while Nicaragua argued the provisions were not radical enough. By November, both joined and left the US alone in the world as the sole holdout. The 2015 agreement sought to limit global temperature rise to 1.5–2 degrees Celsius above pre-industrial levels. The target was at once too little to prevent mass extinction and almost certainly too ambitious. It was signed at a point in which American public opinion on anthropogenic global warming (ever lagging behind the world) was finally a majority. At the time of this book's publication, the United States is the sole holdout among the otherwise unanimous signatories. The Paris Agreement was signed in the year our atmosphere reached beyond a staggering 410 carbon parts per million, the highest since the Pliocene epoch some three million years

9. Dempsey, as quoted in Associated Press, "Dempsey Hits Islamic State 'End-of-Days' Vision."

10. Credit lies elsewhere for part of this observation. Both for its support of climate change and for carelessly handing the nuclear codes to a clown, Noam Chomsky called the GOP the most dangerous organization in the history of civilization in a 2016 interview with the BBC. "It's an outrageous statement," he acknowledged, "but it's true." I don't know whether I'm prepared to call it the most dangerous organization in history given the genocides of our past, but certainly the GOP is the most dangerous organization in the world today. When interviewed by Democracy Now! host Amy Goodman, Chomsky did not hedge: "I mean, has there ever been an organization in human history that is dedicated, with such commitment, to the destruction of organized human life on Earth? Not that I'm aware of." Chomsky, as quoted in Democracy Now!, "Chomsky on the GOP."

prior when the oceans were fifty to eighty feet higher. If we look at the broad range of ways we shape our environment—for instance, air pollution alone kills as many as 9 million per year—the catastrophe is already beyond words. But even in the most conservative estimates, the death toll is likely already in the hundreds of thousands per year.[11]

We should read this decision alongside another at the year's end. Evangelicals believe the Middle East will eventually see peace, but it can only arrive at the end of days. In December, President Trump announced the American embassy's relocation from Tel Aviv to Jerusalem. The move pleased long-term goals of Israel, but it was purely a dog whistle to Dispensationalist evangelicals. To this crowd, modern Israel is not a new state instituted by a 1947 United Nations partition plan and attack on Palestinians the following year. Instead, Israel is a reconstitution of a noun recognized from their Scriptures.[12] The embassy opened on the seventieth anniversary of Israel's independence, during which Palestinian angst and its violent suppression by the Israeli Defense Force reassured evangelicals. As if to make the signal clear, the opening was planned for the day before the *Nakba*, the commemoration of the catastrophic loss of Palestinian land. Evangelicals saw a preliminary step toward prophecy in the theatrics. Through his servant Trump, the divine chess master was moving the pieces toward a calculated end without yet announcing checkmate. The violence merely told them they had time left.

It's easy to mistake doctrines and creeds as the primary ingredients of faith, but in many ways these are the least important. Belief is fantasy, but it also serves as a cue retroactively justifying behavior. Desire directs belief and behavior. Belief generally conforms to behavior, not vice versa. So when

11. Estimates on the death toll and future projections vary. The World Health Organization projects an additional 250,000 deaths per year between 2030 and 2050. Other organizations have doubled the projected casualties. See World Health Organization, "Climate Change and Health."

12. It does not seem to matter to them that Jewish identity now traces from a complex and diverse history. The very name "Israel" inscribes the modern state into history. Its record of striving with Palestinians today is read as a continuation of strife two or three thousand years prior. The evangelical today does not think of strife as the result of the 1967 Six Day War or the *Nakba*. The Dispensationalist misreading of Daniel, Ezekiel, and Revelation leads them to believe that strife is from the time of Jacob and Esau or Isaac and Ishmael, and it will continue until a temple is rebuilt. In common iterations of this future-vision such as that of LaHaye and Jenkins's *Left Behind* series, the Antichrist will secure a peace treaty between Israel and its neighbors, forge an agreement to move the Dome of the Rock and/or Al-Aqsa mosque, and allow the temple's rebuilding. Trump's embassy move does none of this and, in fact, produces more strife in the meantime.

we link apocalypticism and climate change denial, we must be careful not to think of resonance as cause and effect. Beliefs, behaviors, and desires cluster in networks to reinforce, disintegrate, amplify, exacerbate, and destroy in haphazard turn. Apocalypticism is *not* a singular cause of climate denial, but the fantasy sends devotees a coded message only they will hear.

We should take a lesson from Robert Schumann's *Humoreske* (1839). The piano piece was written with three staves. The pianist plays the upper and lower staves with the right and the left hands, but the staff in the middle (containing the melody) isn't played. Schumann designed the melody to work like an inner voice furnished by the listener. As historian Frank Ankersmit explained, "the melody . . . will be *listened to* by the listener, without actually being *heard* by him."[13] The question is whether we can listen to things we don't actually hear. Connolly used Schumann's missing melody to suggest something about an evangelical-capitalist resonance machine, and we should be clear on the signal's danger. What the liberal believes to be mishearing is, in fact, something she cannot hear. It is the conservative who hears a melody—a vicious anthem for the end of all things—in the propaganda staves.

Future Denial by the Numbers

We have a poverty of data on future denial, a problem so easy to rectify and yet ignored. We do have sparse reports here and there, and we might at least cast them as a scattered mosaic of nihilistic fantasy. Statistics don't tell us how fervently people believe something or whether it drives concrete effects, but affirmation of future denial in a poll signals something interesting from a psychoanalytic perspective: the respondent's ego feels no need to censor her fatalistic fantasies. Many religious beliefs—and apocalypticism is certainly an example—are not necessarily notions in which the believer is strongly invested, but they don't actually need to be strongly invested in order for the belief to have effect. Even very casual and unimportant beliefs still activate effects or resonate with allied interests. A casual death wish appears in the data, so, granting the limits of data, how many of us believe the end is near?

---

13. Ankersmit, as quoted in Connolly, *Capitalism and Christianity, American Style*, 54.

In 2010, the Pew Research Center released startling results gauging how Americans envisioned the next four decades.[14] Many of the questions were innocuous (will computers be able to converse with humans?) or positive (will cancer be cured?), while others queried the likelihood of an energy crisis or world war. Buried in the back of the report was a fascinating question about whether Christ would return in those forty years. An astonishing 48 percent of Christians agreed,[15] or roughly four in ten Americans overall. This belief was lower for Catholics (32 percent), mainline Protestants (27 percent), and the religiously unaffiliated (20 percent). However, nearly six in ten evangelicals (58 percent) expected Christ's return by 2050. Feel the gravity of this revelation: only one in ten American Christians felt sure Christ *wouldn't* return by mid-century.

We should really keep better track of these views over time![16] Apocalyptic belief has almost certainly dropped as white evangelicalism shrinks as a percentage of population, but our data to prove it is thin. Another survey three years later indicated one in five Americans believed the world will end in their lifetime,[17] while nearly one in seven people worldwide believed the same. What makes the American ideological disposition unique is a fusion of apocalypticism and rampant disbelief in climate science. A third of Americans—including 65 percent of evangelicals—believe that natural disasters are evidence of the end times.[18] Apocalyptic belief correlates negatively with education and wealth as well. If your household makes less than 25 thousand dollars per year, you are over three times as likely to believe the

14. I begin with this older poll partly because of the cluster of other issues it presents for comparison but more importantly because of the clear wording of the survey question on Christ's return. Note especially that the number of white evangelicals (and therefore likely the prevalence of apocalyptic belief in the public) has dropped since 2010. I have adjusted my claims about the prevalence of apocalyptic belief downward to account for the length of time since this poll. See Pew Research Center, "Public Sees a Future Full of Promise and Peril" and Pew Research Center, "Jesus Christ Returns to Earth."

15. Pew Research Center, "U.S. Christians' Views on the Return of Christ."

16. Polling firms don't repeat apocalyptic questions year after year, and groups asking these questions at all inquire with different wording. That is to say, it probably makes a difference when the question is asked abstractly (Will the world end in the twenty-first century?) or personally (Will the world end in your lifetime?). Read these numbers with caution, but see in them the malaise of rampant pessimism.

17. IPSOS, "One in Seven (14%) Global Citizens Believe End of the World is Coming in Their Lifetime."

18. Cox, Navarro-Rivera, and Jones, "Americans More Likely to Attribute Increasingly Severe Weather to Climate Change, Not End Times."

world will end in your lifetime when compared with an over-75-thousand dollar-per-year household.[19] College graduates are less than half as likely as those with no college experience to believe Christ will return soon.[20]

Evangelicals are the outliers in all of these surveys. Nearly eight in ten see violence in the Middle East as evidence of the end.[21] When surveys gauge belief in the approaching end times, evangelical affirmation lies consistently in the high fifties to low sixties. Americans are at least twice as likely as the global norm to believe the end is near, and white evangelicals are roughly twice as likely as the average American to believe the world will end soon with Christ's return. How could they possibly care whether the oceans swallow all coastal cities by year 2500?

In Jewish mysticism, the object of piety is to mend the world (*tikkun olam*).[22] Christianity might have the kingdom of God, but what's the impetus to repair what God shall destroy? Even the term *apocalypse* itself is pertinent given that the word literally means "unveiling." Let us keep these dual meanings in mind. What is truly unveiled if not dissatisfaction with the world and the desire to destroy it?

At the time of this book's writing, only seven in ten Americans believe the world is warming at all. Barely half attribute warming to human

---

19. Lifeway Research, "Many Americans link U.S. military strike in Syria to end times."

20. Pew Research Center, "Jesus Christ Returns to Earth."

21. "Among those who say Christ will return, 73% of Evangelicals say that world events would turn against Israel the closer we get to the rapture or end times compared to 49% of non-Evangelical Christians. 79% of Evangelicals say that the unfolding violence across the Middle East is a sign that the end times are nearer compared to only 43% of non-Evangelical Christians." Telhami, "American Attitudes Toward the Middle East and Israel."

22. According to the Lurianic myth, time began when the *Ein Sof* (the "All in All") was compromised. Of the ten sacred vessels containing the qualities of God, seven shattered and spread the divine light across the universe. In this mystical tradition, one follows the commandments of God not to derive personal benefit but in order to bring these shards back into unity. Every act of submission to God brings creation closer to original unity, the perfection preceding the cosmic shattering of the *Ein Sof*. The Jewish phrase for this process of universal repair is *tikkun olam* (the "mending of the world"). The measure of faithfulness is not right belief or good intent, but instead the critical measure is whether or not one is participating in the project of mending or repairing the world. With such a test for righteousness, it's no mystery why Jewish communities often supported progressive causes. In the early twentieth century, for instance, American Jewish-lead efforts to organize labor unions or drive suffrage and civil rights campaigns was a natural outgrowth of the commitment to mend the world.

activity.[23] In a dizzying display of cognitive dissonance, slightly less than half believe climate scientists agree that global warming is happening. The partisan divide is stark: nine in ten Democrats and half of Republicans believe the earth is warming at all, regardless of whether they believe carbon is the culprit. Nearly eight in ten Democrats believe warming is anthropogenic, while a quarter of Republicans agree.[24] As of 2017, the public saw the Islamic State as a slightly greater danger than climate change,[25] which is somewhere between a genocidal and extinction-level case of misjudged threat calculations.

We've sailed past the 400 carbon PPM threshold, the absolute limit to prevent a sixth mass extinction event.[26] A quarter of the carbon in the atmosphere was introduced in the last fifty years, and we now face feedback loops wherein the retreating ice caps reflect less sunlight back into space. The more the earth heats, the more it will heat. Some changes will lock in irreversible new normals. Even the best-case scenarios project a six foot sea level rise by 2100 (again, on pace for a conservatively estimated fifty feet by 2500). If a large antarctic ice shelf breaks sooner than feared or if the polar ice caps melt entirely, a six-foot rise over decades will seem like nothing. Nearly half of Americans live in counties on the shoreline.[27] Worldwide, about four in ten live within 100 kilometers of the shore.[28] Borders will physically move as coastal lines take new shape, entire cities will evacuate inland, and climate refugees could number anywhere from hundreds of millions to as many as a billion by 2050.

The future is cancelled in the same way the past does not exist for the evangelical. I want to be very clear on this relationship, because we do not understand apocalypticism unless we also see its interconnection with

23. Yale Program on Climate Change Communication, "Yale Climate Opinion Maps."

24. Pew Research Center, "The Partisan Divide on Political Values Grows Even Wider."

25. Pew Research Center, "Globally, People Point to ISIS and Climate Change as Leading Security Threats."

26. The numbers I use on the climate and energy crises are on the middle-to-conservative end of estimates. I intentionally use these projections and estimates so as not to overstate the crises (if that were even possible), but know that the situation is almost certainly far worse that what is presented here.

27. National Oceanic and Atmospheric Administration, "What percentage of the American population lives near the coast?"

28. Socioeconomic Data and Applications Center, "Percentage of Total Population Living in Coastal Areas."

multiple support structures (creationism, market, media, etc.). The relationship of Big Oil, Fox News, Wall Street, and the Republican party to evangelicalism is one of mutual interests or affinities. However, the evangelical denial of the future and past are one and the same. Roughly equal numbers of Americans are apocalyptic and creationist, beholden to an ideology which stitches itself to deregulation. If someone tells me the world was created in seven days, I can guess their opinion on raising the minimum wage to a living wage. This is how the resonance machine works.

Fox News Channel (FNC) provides the clearest, overt justification for these fantasies of denial. We'll explore its history further in chapter 4, but let's begin here for its role in the resonance machine. FNC host Sean Hannity portrayed climate change as left-wing phony science, a waste of time, and a hoax.[29] Greg Gutfeld called climate concern hysteria and feared that those who wouldn't "parrot the panic" might become victims of intellectual bullying.[30] Until his ouster from the FNC main stage, Bill O'Reilly hedged his doubts by telling viewers, "nobody can control the climate except God, so give a little extra at mass or services."[31] O'Reilly suggested staying in the Paris Agreement might buy good will, but he concluded "It doesn't really amount to much anyway. Let it go."[32] O'Reilly's grandfatherly calm and smug indifference ensured the audience there was no need to panic. It might be the end of the civilization, but it's no big deal.

If the climate crisis is ignored, the energy crisis fails to even register attention. For ten thousand years of civilization after the dawn of the agricultural revolution, our main sources of energy were wood and domesticated animals. With the discovery of coal, the steam engine powered the Industrial Revolution by scaling up energy return on energy investment (EROI). Whatever the unit of measurement, any energy source can be calculated by energy yield or return (X) to energy input or investment (Y). The X:Y ratio shows the energy source's efficiency. Globalization was carried on the back of cheaper energy. The advent of oil gave us a source of energy we had never seen before and might never see again. At the high-end estimate, oil's initial energy return on energy investment was as much as 150:1. However, EROI changes over time as extraction becomes more difficult. When the first major domestic oil field was drilled in Pennsylvania in 1858 by Edwin

29. Hannity, on Fox News Channel, "You're Out of Your Mind."
30. Gutfeld, on Fox New Channel, "A Megaphone for Their Master."
31. Media Matters, "O'Reilly."
32. Media Matters, "Bill O'Reilly."

Drake, oil was practically pouring out of the ground. It was an irresistibly lucrative investment, and global markets settled into a state of dependence that proved resistant to changing EROI. Oil's EROI has dropped by at least two thirds (some estimates, including the numbers below, are considerably worse).[33] Drake needed only to drill sixty-nine feet down, whereas the Deepwater Horizon operation drilled nearly seven miles. As crude oil extraction required ever more sophisticated techniques, companies turned to dirtier sources closer to the surface. Credible estimates now peg conventional oil at 16:1 EROI. Tar sands oil (5:1), the dirtiest and costliest of all petroleum alternatives, measures barely within the 5–9:1 ratio seen as the absolute minimum for modern civilization. Though some deliver better returns, many renewable energy alternatives hover just above or just below this threshold. Hydroelectric proves best at 40:1, followed by wind at 20:1 and photovoltaic solar at 6–9:1 as the technology improves. Against these renewable numbers, we can see why coal (18:1) continues to be an attractive source as well as why nuclear power (5:1) will not save us. We have an unnoticed emergency, a critical need for viable alternatives in a world that (outside of the energy sector) does not see there's a problem at all.[34]

As Kevin Mequet explained, "Globalization and the incredible rates of economic and financial growth in the twentieth century have been possible only because of the increased use of cheap energy. Unfortunately, while capitalist economics is premised upon the possibility of infinite growth, you cannot have infinite growth given a finite resource."[35] If we do not quickly improve our alternative fuel sources oil will eventually drop to below the 5–9:1 minimum EROI threshold required for contemporary civilization. At that point, the grand experiment of human civilization as we know it would conclude. Game over.

We are investigating fantasies supplementing desire for game over. The fantasy bides its time until the end in repetition of familiar territory.

33. Guilford et al., "A New Long Term Assessment."

34. EROI estimates vary widely. Even my numbers on oil are open to debate. The existence of EROI ratios is widely accepted, but the specific numbers are disputed and continually changing with technological development. Further, the numbers I present for renewables do not account for energy storage, which would lower them. I have made an effort to place my numbers in the mid to high range of estimates I've seen in order to avoid overstating the gravity of the problem, meaning the situation is likely more dire than I describe. I wish to acknowledge the controversy over specific ratios, so read this with caution. For sources of data I use here, see Inman, "The True Cost of Fossil Fuels," and Inman, "Behind the Numbers on Energy Return on Investment."

35. Kevin Mequet, in Crockett and Robbins, *Religion, Politics, and the Earth*, 95.

It imagines there's no time for progressive labor reforms, for discovering new and renewable energy resources, for military truces, and so on. The world will only collapse a bit further, for humankind cannot ruin what God shall destroy.

Guilt and Shame are Left Behind

Whence comes turmoil and shame? Does the evangelical feel no shame at destroying the job prospects or breathable air for his grandchildren? As psychoanalytic theorist Joan Copjec told us, shame would be proof that our ideological commitments lie in vain. "In shame, unlike guilt, one experiences one's visibility, but there is no external Other who sees, since shame is proof that the Other does not exist."[36] Shame does not attempt to substitute. When the subject feels shame, it's as if she is seen *too much*. The subject wants to hide from the world, for her existence feels exposed and void. Any affective state, including guilt and anxiety, is preferable to shame.

Shame doesn't defend itself, and it shares that characteristic with indifference. There is a world of difference between shame and comfortable indifference, but externally they might manifest identically. It is the middle register between the two—anxiety—which jumps to defend itself. Anxiety is always preferable to shame, so the evangelical rifles through her apologetic arguments and buttresses her faith with propaganda. The aggressive defense is evidence of anxiety. Psychoanalysis reads anxiety as a symptom: something isn't working. The subject knows it isn't working, and that's all the more reason to double down and defend a belief that fails. If the evangelical could see 500 years into the future and learn that the world does not end, she would feel shame at her wasted ideological commitments.

Apocalyptic fantasy is a virtual vindication proving fidelity wasn't wasted. Tim LaHaye and Jerry B. Jenkins's book series *Left Behind* is a microcosm of virtual vindication. With eighty million copies sold, *Left Behind* projects a revealing fantasy of global suffering. It was labeled "prophecy-based fiction," a play on historical fiction likewise envisioning fate's inevitability just as the past is set. The series began with the chaotic rapture. Like unbelievers, clothes were left behind as believing souls were collected to heaven. Aircraft and vehicles driven until moments before by the faithful collided without direction, and the majority of the world—depicted as having no working knowledge of the Bible whatsoever—turned to experts to ask what kind of

36. Copjec, *Imagine There's No Woman*, 127.

new weapon must have been deployed. The plot depended on a reader find-ing it plausible that miraculous world events could perfectly mirror Scrip-ture, yet the unbeliever would remain too foolishly hard of heart to see.

The series depicts the rise of an Antichrist from Eastern Europe who with the aid of demonic influence forces the United Nations to relinquish power. In his new empire, the Antichrist rebrands the UN as a Global Com-munity, a unilateral superpower with nearly omnipotent military force to finally secure peace. Peace is a demonic lure. True to the evangelical fantasy, it is the Antichrist who establishes peace in Israel and rebuilds the temple (which is, again, a reason evangelicals read continuous strife as a positive sign). Jews, Catholics, Muslims, and liberal Protestants, all of whom are adherents of false faiths, are susceptible to the Antichrist's manipulation. Only newly converted evangelicals see through the deception. Chaos is pe-riodically reintroduced by a series of judgments from heaven drawn from the twenty-one judgements in the book of Revelation. The series follows a band of post-rapture converts who brand themselves the Tribulation Force, and their travails deploy every evangelical trope imaginable.

The dialogue of the Tribulation Force and the goals of the Antichrist paint a picture of virtue and vice typical of late twentieth-century white evangelicalism in the United States. The Global Community represents the trap of peace, the danger of a multinational currency, and futility of inter-national cooperation. America plays the part of a flawed nation, but after its eclipse of power the series shows a key feature of the evangelical fantasy: if the singular nation blessed by God with manifest destiny is flawed, any alternative will prove far worse. The series depicts Jews and Muslims as resistant at first to the Antichrist but ultimately compliant. It caricatures Jews and Muslims as hardheaded and defiant—not so much faithful as ir-rationally committed to false faiths.

The Antichrist proposes to limit population growth by advancing abor-tion rights, and when a Tribulation Force member named Chloe becomes pregnant and fears her child might be collected for a children's Antichrist praise choir, she considers and ultimately rejects "infanticide." When Chloe expresses the option of killing her child, her counsel tells her, "You're no better than the abortionists who refer to their unborn babies as embryos or fetuses or pregnancies so they can 'eliminate' them or 'terminate' them rather than kill them."[37] Likewise, the Antichrist promotes abortion both for population control and to eliminate any irregular fetus. Labor camps and

37. See especially LaHaye and Jenkins, *The Indwelling.*

euthanasia are also on the Antichrist's agenda. Thusly so, the culture war tropes of the 1980s (intensified with trite references to Nazi policies) are reprojected as the final line in the sand for the end of all things.

Violence is praised throughout the series, for the Tribulation Force is a combination of a parachurch ministry and a paramilitary organization equipped with home bases, aircraft, and ammunition. It's church and a militia. Global Community troops are legitimate targets, which the Tribulation Force considers unfortunate (the soldier will immediately descend to hell upon death) yet justly deserved for those who pledged themselves to Satan. The Tribulation Force even organizes a food co-op through internet communication and aircraft, ostensibly to avoid taking the "mark of the Beast" which allows the remaining world citizens to participate in commerce. The food co-op model reads much like a Christian homeschooling network. The mass execution of Christians by guillotine alludes to the Reign of Terror. Specifically, the Antichrist's leftists, like the Jacobins of the French Revolution, will surely persecute all those who shall not pledge fealty to secularism ideals or the devil. There's no difference between the secularist and Satanic worship.

The reader must enjoy the specter of persecution. *Left Behind* reads the book of Revelation as a straightforward timeline, but somehow only the evangelicals are able to understand anything. Aside from the recycled Religious Right tropes throughout, the inability to reason or comprehend is what makes *Left Behind* interesting as a projection of the evangelical imaginary. Nobody else sees the bald truth of cataclysms (impossibly global earthquakes, plagues, comets, etc.) mirroring the precise order of Revelation's seal, trumpet, and bowl judgements. Evangelicals hold a monopoly on reason. Their peculiarity is evidence of their righteousness or chosenness, which serves as such a brilliantly adaptive defense against shame. Thus when capitalism looks at evangelicalism, it sees an ally. The two share no creed or savior, but they share in whiteness, smug disposition toward the ideological opponent, patriarchy, a plundering drive to destroy, in chosenness, and a pessimistic ethos of future denial.

The Resonance Machine

In 2011, American Atheists paid for a billboard sign in Huntsville, Alabama. The inflammatory sign read: "You KNOW they're all SCAMS" with signs for Christianity, Judaism, and Islam. The group's leader appeared as a guest with

FNC host Bill O'Reilly to discuss the controversy.[38] In the course of justifying why faith is not a scam, O'Reilly uttered the following wisdom: "I'll tell you why [religion is] not a scam in my opinion. Alright? Tide goes in, tide goes out. Never a miscommunication. *You* can't explain that."

Baffled at his host's audacity, the guest suggested perhaps the tide was caused by "Thor on top of Mount Olympus" [sic]. O'Reilly persisted on the inexplicability of the tide until the guest retorted, "It doesn't matter if I can explain it. That doesn't mean that an invisible, magic man in the sky is doing it."

The host pounced: "And you're free to believe that."

Did the guest expect something beyond disingenuousness? He later acknowledged a missed opportunity to shame his host with a lesson about the moon's gravity. O'Reilly was indeed mocked online for failing to understand the role of the moon, as if that mattered. In reality, the guest's very appearance on the show lent himself as a prop in an unwinnable game. O'Reilly's audience knows, just as the man himself knows, about the moon. The facts simply aren't a factor in the debate. Only smug affect and aggression wins on the Right. On the other hand, liberals display an inverted resistance.

To millions of followers, President Obama recently tweeted out, "If anybody still wants to dispute the science around climate change, have at it. You'll be pretty lonely." He included a certain number alongside his castigation. Over the last decade, the number 97 percent emerged as a fixation for those who wrongly believe the climate battle will be won by critical reflection on scientific consensus. The number ninety-seven was first proclaimed in a 2009 University of Illinois study surveying climatologists with the American Geological Institute, the overwhelming majority of which agreed both that the earth was warming and human activity was a significant cause.[39] In the next year, the National Academy of Sciences published results from a survey of nearly fourteen hundred climate scientists, with 97 to 98 percent agreeing on anthropogenic climate change.[40] John Cook's famously exhaustive 2013 study examined nearly 12,000 abstracts on climate in peer-reviewed journals from 1991 to 2011 and found 97.1 percent in agreement with anthropogenic causes among abstracts

---

38. Oddly enough, both men's careers collapsed in shame due to sexual misconduct within a year of each other.

39. CNN, "Surveyed Scientists Agree Global Warming Is Real."

40. Anderegg et al., "Expert Credibility in Climate Change."

taking a position.[41] A study by James L. Powell, the director of the National Physical Sciences Consortium, showed that global warming research papers published between 2013 to 2014 actually had a higher consensus (only four denials out of 69,406 authors of peer-reviewed articles, or a 0.0058 percent denial rate).[42]

By that point, a numeric meme had been born. John Oliver, the host of HBO's *Last Week Tonight*, conducted a segment on the misleading way that media treats climate disagreement. Oliver argued the point-counterpoint nature of evening news shows misleads the public into thinking there are two equal sides. So he created a skit wherein three climate change deniers were shouted down by ninety-seven men and women in lab coats. This too is fantasy.

How did the number ninety-seven become so loved? Perhaps its close (but not quite full) assent lends more credibility than complete unanimity, as if 100 percent agreement might look too biased. The number exists to be loved or rejected. Liberals rarely consider that the number is, of course, higher now than when it was first announced a decade ago, and the conservatives see a signal of ideological castigation from indoctrinated dupes. The number took on a mythic status for liberals and conservatives alike, and its potency was drained.

We will lose the battle for the climate if we persist in believing we are simply engaging different points of view held in good faith. The death drive cannot abandon its commitment to self-deception without abandoning its enjoyment, so we should take a closer look at Connolly's term *evangelical-capitalist resonance machine*. It designates dynamics in play across social assemblages. There's never direct causation between the two but instead infiltration, metabolization, and expulsion. The world is left digging through the waste.[43] Institutional practices—be they religious or economic—carry

41. Cook et al., "Quantifying the Consensus."

42. Powell, "Climate Scientists Virtually Unanimous."

43. The analogy is crude, but I mean it seriously. Taking the notion of a resonance machine from Gilles Deleuze, Connolly explained: "[N]o political economy or religious practice is self-contained. Particularly in politics these diverse elements *infiltrate* each other, metabolizing into a moving complex. Spiritual sensibles, economic presumptions, and state priorities slide and blend into one another, though each also retains a modicum of independence from the others. Causation as resonance between elements that become fused to a considerable degree. Now causality, as relations of dependence between separate factors, morphs into energized complexities of mutual imbrication and interinvolvement, in which heretofore unconnected or loosely associated elements *fold, bend, emulsify, resolve incompletely into each other*, forging a qualitative assemblage

an ethos vivifying and intensifying their interactions and replications.[44] Connolly's argument resists a strictly causal relationship between the faith and economic imaginations. Neither the crudely Marxian religion-as-symptom nor the pompous "useful idiots of Wall Street" explanations quite work today. Instead, capitalism and evangelicalism share affinities—not goals—which resonate and shore up short-term victories. Only after abandoning efforts to frame one as the stooge of the other might we answer his question: "What is the connection *today* between evangelical Christianity, cowboy capitalism, the electronic news media, and the Republican Party?"[45] It is for this problem that he invokes the piano piece by Schumann wherein the hearer "hears" a melody not found in the written piece. The evangelical hears cues the progressive does not hear, partly because the progressive persists in the illusion of a shared concept of the common good or good faith dialogue. Connolly explains resonance as such:

> The capitalist-evangelical assemblage finds multiple modes of expression, each amplifying the other: in the market apologism and scandal mongering of the electronic news media, in mobilization drives by Fox News, the Republican Party, and campaign ads, in administrative edicts to roll back environmentalism, weaken labor, and curtail minority rights in the name of religious morality, in rightwing appointments to the Supreme Court, in support for preemptive wars, in tolerance or much worse of state practices of torture that negate the Geneva Conventions, and in the propagating a climate of fear and loathing against the Islamic world. The resonance machine that results both infiltrates the logic of perception and inflects the understanding of economic interests.[46]

An existential ethos underwrites resonance. Whiteness and aggressiveness are the most visible factors, but conservatives invariably cling to hierarchy. A fixed hierarchy means that one always knows one's secure place in society. Even low economic birth as a white male ensures a privileged position. Today, the bourgeoisie *know* their admirers desire servitude. They'll protest against higher wages, affordable healthcare, consumer protections, labor rights, and so on. The common man sees himself not as proletarian but as bourgeoisie in waiting. Isn't this a clever perversion of Plato's magnificent

---

resistant to classical models of explanation." Connolly, *Capitalism and Christianity, American Style*, 39–40.

44. Ibid., 2.

45. Ibid., 39.

46. Ibid., 40.

myth in *The Republic*, where he argues a society should be led by those with hearts of gold and crumbles if led by farmers or workers with hearts of iron and bronze? Capitalism needs a mythical submission fantasy. Christianity adds an injunction to submit to authority as well as a promised, heavenly reward even when earthly suffering never ceases.

The Overton Window shifts partly because no commitment evoked as a campaign slogan is ever irreplaceable or even that important. The slogans and causes of the moment are improvised and meant to shore up alliances. Would any Republican today vouch for Nixon's idea for a universal basic income for the poor? Could any conservative call Martin Luther King, Jr. an "outside agitator" after Reagan declared his holiday in January? No, for as the ethos amplifies reverberations, new ideas become master signifiers while older ideas become anathema. Connolly continues:

> I am saying that the partners to the resonance machine in question have an existential orientation that encourages them to transfigure interest into greed, greed into anti-market ideology, anti-market ideology into market manipulation, market manipulation into state institutionalization of those operations, and the entire complex into policies to pull the security net away from ordinary workers, consumers, and retirees—some of whom are then set up to translate new intensities of resentment and cynicism into participation in the machine.[47]

Certainly the affinity for future denial was stoked carefully. Anti-regulation capitalists were lucky that Dispensationalism so thoroughly infected Christianity during the twentieth century. This is not a new concept for readers who've seen my prior work, but when the Irish Anglican minister John Nelson Darby popularized the rapture after his revelation in the late 1820s, he couldn't have imagined the effect he would have on the actual collapse of the planet warmed by carbon. The system of Dispensational theology founded by Darby divided time into seven periods or dispensations, with our location situated in the penultimate dispensation before the end times. Without mass appeal, his theology floundered until Cyrus Scofield footnoted explanations of Dispensationalism and the rapture in his *Scofield Reference Bible* (1909), a widely influential study Bible during the first half of the twentieth century. The Scofield Bible was itself subsidized with funds from oil tycoons Milton and Lyman Stewart, who poured even more money into the distribution of fundamentalist literature. As I've put the ironic relationship elsewhere, "Oil money converted into theology,

47. Ibid., 43.

which converted back into an almost theological trust in oil. The oil warned us of an apocalypse, and we returned the favor by inviting its aid in our demise."[48] Dispensationalism served as one tool disengaging public interest in the discoveries of the latter twentieth century.

By the early 1980s, Exxon was reading the future. When Exxon began discussing the impact of carbon in 1978 and confirmed anthropogenic global warming in 1982, it came amidst a flurry of cutting-edge research exploring the new possibilities for Arctic drilling as the ice caps retreated. For the first two decades after its discovery, 83 percent of peer-reviewed papers and internal documents from Exxon scientists concluded not only that global warming was occurring but that human activity was a cause.[49] Before that, in 1956 the Shell geologist M. King Hubbert projected the ominous possibility of peak oil. In what became known as the Hubbert Curve, United States oil production would peak in the late sixties and global production would peak not long after. Hubbert proved correct domestically when production did indeed peak in 1970 (that is, until new deregulation cleared the way for more petroleum extraction). Exactly when the world oil supply peaks remains the subject of debate, but we are clearly running out of time.

Oil producers saw an opportunity in receding ice caps, but the advantage would disappear if the public learned the truth. Early efforts from environmentalists to raise the alarm in the late seventies and early eighties had little effect outside their communities. The public was first alerted to the reality of global warming when NASA scientist James E. Hansen gave his infamous 1988 Congressional testimony on the threat.[50] The same year saw the first report from the Intergovernmental Panel on Climate Change. Ever after, Big Oil spoke out of both sides of its mouth. Research for the sake of oil exploration continued, as did the new mission of public deceit. A faith with a history of rejecting expertise proved a natural ally.

How Does a Death Cult Enjoy?

Science historians Geoffrey Supran and Naomi Oreskes examined discrepancies between ExxonMobil's in-house data and the public perception simultaneously pushed. The results were starkly incriminating. While

48. DeLay, *The Cynic and the Fool*, 70.

49. Supran and Oreskes, "Assessing ExxonMobil's Climate Change Communications (1977–2014)," 9.

50. Shabecoff, "Global Warming Has Begun, Expert Tells Senate."

the overwhelming majority of its internal documentation supported the reality of anthropogenic climate change, more than eight in ten of its "advertorials" (paid, editorial-style advertisements) in *The New York Times* told a different story of doubt.[51] Supran and Orsekes's study came during scrutiny from Attorneys General in seventeen states and territories, the question being whether ExxonMobil knowingly deceived the public. ExxonMobil defended itself by pointing to a list on its website naming more than fifty articles on climate research. Read for yourself, said ExxonMobil, to which Supran and Oreskes reply, "We stress that the question is not whether ExxonMobil 'suppressed climate change research,' but rather how they communicated about it."[52]

The 1997 Kyoto Protocol on global greenhouse gas emissions presented a revenue threat, so Exxon's advertorials causally suggested, "Let's face it: The science of climate change is too uncertain to mandate a plan of action that could plunge economies into turmoil."[53] Scientists simply couldn't predict temperatures with certainty, so doing nothing was a virtue: "We still don't know what role man-made greenhouse gases might play in warming the planet . . . Let's not rush to a decision at Kyoto."[54] The real apocalypse was shrugged off as no cause for alarm.

ExxonMobil recently backed away from explicitly casting doubt on climate science and instead shifted funds to proxies. Its beneficiaries such as the American Enterprise Institute and the US Chamber of Commerce allow oil money to posture responsibly while affiliates wage the ground war. ExxonMobile funded the American Legislative Exchange Council (a coalition producing legislation templates for Congressional conservatives) until it severed ties in 2018. The company still donates millions to climate deniers in Congress. The company shows no shame in doing all this while calling the Paris Agreement "an important step forward."

Political leaders enliven fantasies by openly parroting capitalist interests. Climate regulations are bad for business, bad for the economy, or bad for America. The base inculcates the cue into a vortex of religious, ethnic,

51. "For example, accounting for expressions of reasonable doubt, 83% of peer-reviewed papers and 80% of internal documents acknowledge that climate change is real and human-caused, yet only 12% of advertorials do so, with 81% instead expressing doubt." Supran and Oreskes, "Assessing ExxonMobil's Climate Change Communications (1977–2014)," 1.

52. Ibid., 2.

53. Ibid., 6.

54. Ibid.

and economic grievances. *I've read the Book*, the base thinks, *and I know how the story ends!* This is virtual vindication. Meanwhile, the capitalist enjoys the deregulation and slashed tax rates for capital gains. The military enjoys budgets boosted by a public that believes war shall only ever end with the arrival of an Antichrist. The effects of future denial also extend indirectly to public education, student loans, wages, policing, inequality, healthcare, and so many interrelated issues that don't matter if the future is canceled. The beneficiary is the capitalist, but the evangelical is not without benefit: in destroying the world, she saves herself from a bit of shame.

Friedrich Nietzsche used the French word *ressentiment* to describe an imaginary revenge taken by those without power. It's a herd instinct for preservation, and if a group cannot take physical revenge due to lack of might or social restrictions, the herd takes refuge in smug self-righteousness and assures itself that God will smite evildoers. For Nietzsche this was the key to morality for those who feel their power restrained. Whereas the powerful considered the opposite of good to be low, the powerless reinvented the dynamic so that the opposite of good was evil. We live in the age of *ressentiment*. Unfortunately, Nietzche was totally wrong about the direction of *ressentiment*: it's now those with the most power who now feel disempowered and lash out with wanton cruelty.

Resonance takes constant pressure and willful partners in self-deception. It sustains itself via hostility. As open animosities toward traditional targets (the African American, the Muslim) become less acceptable, sustaining insular resonance requires new targets: the expert, the university, the scientist, the lawbreaker or protestor (as a metonym for the person of color), and so on. It isn't surprising that between 2015 and 2016, the number of Republican voters who see colleges and universities as a positive social influence dropped 11 percentage points down to 43 percent.[55] Climate denial is part of a broader problem of willful science illiteracy,[56] which is

55. Geiger, "From Universities to Churches, Republicans and Democrats Differ in Views of Major Institutions."

56. I noted above a relationship between denials of climate and evolutionary science. Denial is common enough to serve as a type of social connector. While six in ten Americans believe humans evolved over time, about a third believe evolution resulted from natural processes (rather than guidance from a supreme being). Between 30 and 40 percent believe that humans have always existed in present form. But nearly six in ten evangelical Protestants say humans have always existed in present form. Just as roughly equal numbers of Americans are apocalyptic and creationist, the evangelical numbers for creationism and apocalypticism are in the same ballpark as well (between five and six in ten). Among creationists, 56 percent report most or all of their friends hold their

one node within the an even larger problem of knowledge itself becoming libidinally invested and transformed into a taboo.

It's all just fantasy rejecting and enlivening reality. In the 1933 Marx Brothers film *Duck Soup*, there's an admittedly overused example that I'll nevertheless repeat here. In one scene, a woman turned around in shock to discover a man standing at the other side of the bed while she was undressing. "Your excellency, I thought you left!" she cried while scrambling to cover herself. After he insisted he clearly hadn't left, she persisted, "But I saw you with my own eyes!"

We are then treated to the famous line from the other: "Well who ya gonna believe—me or your own eyes?"

Indeed, what chance has knowledge against the thrust of desire? When in the spring of 1997 thirty-nine members of Heaven's Gate gathered in the beautiful outskirts of San Diego to drink a mix of vodka and phenobarbital, what were they enjoying? Could their demise have been avoided with better information about the likelihood of a UFO trailing Comet Hale–Bopp? Could psychologists have taught them the mechanisms abused by cult leaders? Could we have recognized the value of their strongly held opinions and come to some middle ground or agreement on the need to commit mass suicide?

More to the point, why do we not recognize that self-destruction is a type of enjoyment? Why don't we recognize the same desire for a big Other to reassure us we are right exists across every ideological persuasion, compromising our ability to form judgements about what is best for society? We are living on the verge of climate collapse, a sixth mass extinction event, the displacement of billions of human beings, consequent war over previously plentiful resources, rampant disease, and famine. We careen toward the edge without realizing the destruction is welcomed by those who'd feel vindicated by a world getting worse and worse. Recall the observation from the historian Ernest Sandeen at the beginning of the chapter—neither the prophecy of the end of fundamentalism nor the prophecy of the end of the world has yet reached its conclusion. The joke and its implicit casualty count might catch up to our present day.

.

---

same beliefs about Earth's origins, whereas 37 percent of atheist believers in evolution say the same. See Pew Research Center, "U.S. Public Becoming Less Religious," and Hill, "National Study of Religion & Human Origins," 22.

2

Against Knowledge

Racist Origins of Alternative Education

"I would like to ask you to turn away from your PhD degree . . .
and for a moment consider the BA Degree given to those who are
Born Again by the Holy Ghost."

—FROM A LETTER TO THOMAS ALTIZER

Alternative Histories

Like four in ten Americans, I grew up assuming humankind began within the last ten thousand years in current form.[1] My seventh-grade history textbook told me this. It began with the book of Genesis and blended seamlessly into Sumerian and Babylonian history. In the textbook, I learned of how tribes dispersed across the earth after the Tower of Babel, where languages were confused. It read, "We need guidance because the *dispersion* of mankind, *the scattering of people over earth,* complicates the study of world history. So many people in so many places cannot all be studied at the same time. By focusing on God's plan, we see how history leads to Jesus Christ. God first chose a special nation out of which Christ would come."[2] One of the sites to which people dispersed, Ur, was the Sumerian city from which Abraham emigrated. At the bottom of the page was a timeline stretching from 2300 to 1700 BCE denoting the origin of Sumerian and Egyptian civilizations, Abraham's departure, and Hammurabi's Babylon. The chronology was drawn from James Ussher, who calculated the world's beginning at October 23, 4004 BCE. I learned Hebrew slaves built the great

1. See Swift, "In U.S., Belief in Creationist View of Humans at New Low," and Hill, "National Study of Religion & Human Origins," 1.

2. Combee, *History of the World in Christian Perspective,* 8.

pyramids nearly a millennium after the archaeological record suggests the complex at Giza was built. I didn't learn that Sumerian cuneiform predated the timeframe for the biblical flood, which went strangely unnoticed by cultures with record-keeping abilities, but I learned that global floods were mentioned in other ancient texts. I distinctly recall feeling enthralled at the immersive conjunction of material studied in Sunday school with world history class. It lent a sense of reality to the fantasy, as if the Genesis chronology should be read literally as any other history.

My school was a private Christian institution. Together, Abeka Books (from which I draw above), Accelerated Christian Education (ACE), and Bob Jones University Press print the lion's share of textbooks used in Protestant private schools and homeschools. I wouldn't have been immune to such information had I attended a public school. Nearly a sixth of public high school biology teachers endorse or lend credibility to creationism and/ or intelligent design.[3] As a project director for the National Center for Science Education, Stephanie Keep warned of the problem's scope: "There are about 3 million students taking high school biology in this country in any given year. So we can conclude that somewhere in the neighborhood of half a million students will be presented with a favorable view of creationism/ [intelligent design] this year in their high school biology classes alone."[4] In *Edwards v. Aguillard* (1987), the Supreme Court ruled creationism was a religious belief, so teachers couldn't be forced by the state to teach it, yet many get away with teaching creationism every day. Why is there an appetite for such clairvoyant misinformation?

The textbook above results from multigenerational trends already in motion during the nineteenth century. An alternative history is a denial or disavowal. The ego both knows and denies, and denial is facilitated by a fetishized object (a self-proclaimed authority, a spurious argument, secret evidence ignored by scientists, etc). The creationist knows her argument falls flat, which is why she expends so much energy to claim the contrary. Additionally, repetition generally signals unconscious enjoyment of a pattern, especially when that pattern proves itself in error. Conscious justifications for maintaining a pattern are retrojected. What's primary is the enjoyment of a failing behavioral pattern. In the case of alternative

3. Berkman, Pacheco, and Plutzer, "Evolution and Creationism in America's Classrooms."

4. Keep, "Still Fighting for Evolution in Schools."

histories, the repetition is one of racial animosity perpetually blending into self-deception.

If we desire to uncover the origins of alternative science, gratuitously inept education policy, attacks on the university and expertise, education reform exacerbating inequality, infusion of folk theology, or the rise of the private and home school—as well as the more obvious skepticism toward biology and climate science—we must examine the racial animosity under-writing self-deception. Put another way, if we want to understand why only a fifth of Americans hold a naturalistic view of evolutionary origins, it helps to contemplate why only four in ten are willing to identify slavery as the cause for the Civil War.[5] We must examine the white supremacist history that began its critique of the "government school" in the post-Reconstruction era and rebirthed itself as a Religious Right after schools integrated.

Antebellum to Integration

Prior to the Civil War, comprehensive public education was sparse to non-existent across the South. While states in the northeast proved more open to state-funded and mandated education, southerners viewed education as a family or community prerogative. The education of slaves was largely out of the question, since literacy might be repurposed to absorb Northern abolitionist literature. During Reconstruction (1865–1877) and the years following, southern and northern philanthropists built support for education funding by state legislatures. The situation was dire in the South. As historian Edward Ayers explained, "In 1880, when the national average for white illiteracy was about 9 percent, nearly a third of all whites over ten years old in North Carolina were illiterate, as were about a quarter of the whites in Tennessee, Kentucky, Alabama, South Carolina, and Georgia. The black rate of illiteracy in 1880 ranged from 70 percent in Kentucky to 82 percent in Mississippi. Many children attended school only sporadically if they attended at all, and facilities and pay for teachers were dismal."[6] Increased education expenditure resolved the gap quickly. By 1900, white illiteracy in the South stood at 10 to 15 percent while black illiteracy dropped below half.[7]

5. Heimlich, "What Caused the Civil War?"
6. Ayers, *The Promise of the New South,* 418.
7. Ibid.

There was intense counter-pressure. Many education initiatives were driven by philanthropists and educators seeking to replicate in the South the best practices of the North. Southerners perceived it as cultural replacement. Northern reformers were by no means progressive by modern standards. They sought to reform white education to northern standards, but black education bowed to the needs of industrialization, ensuring the black schoolchild a subordinate future. Such racism still wasn't enough to endear the reformers to the South. As Ayers described the tension, "The philanthropists sold the two reforms as a package, a way to stabilize and modernize a faltering southern racial and class order . . . The reformers thought that prominent southern whites would recognize in the reform a sympathetic attempt to promote the South's best interests. The reformers were wrong."[8] Southern publications warned of two related threats: the white child weakened by education and a black population able to know their rights.[9]

Resistance to education reform from outsiders mirrored the democratic idealism of folk religion during the Great Awakenings. During these periods, circuit preachers in tent revivals took the mantel of authority for themselves and used the seminary-trained clergyman as a rhetorical punching bag. One need not know the Greek and Hebrew nor historical context, the circuit preacher would say, for the pious Christian needed only to read the Bible for him or herself. This doctrine of perspicuity solidified into dogma for American folk theology. Perspicuity meant essential doctrines in the Bible were simple enough to understand without advanced training or knowledge of context. Knowledge and expertise were suspect.

Nevertheless, the philanthropy and reforms continued. From the turn of the century to the Great War, southern illiteracy fell by half again. Southern legislatures grew increasingly comfortable with providing state funds for public education.[10] Still, the racial nature of the fight never concluded.

8. Ibid., 419.

9. "'All that the South asks is that the North will mind its own business and keep its missions to itself,' a Memphis paper testily remarked, while the *Manufacturer's Record* warned that 'the acceptance of such help means the loss of manliness and strength of character.' The Northern philanthropists, fully in sympathy with white Southern desire for white supremacy, found themselves attacked as new abolitionists. The educational crusade threatened the new Southern political order: 'just as soon as all the Negroes in the State shall be able to read and write they will become qualified to vote,' observed a New Orleans paper, 'and it is not to be doubted that they will demand their rights in the primaries with the 14th Amendment to back them up.' A Richmond paper charged that black schools were 'hotbeds of arrogance and aggression.'" Ibid.

10. Ibid., 420.

Former Confederate chaplain Robert Lewis Dabney (1820–1898) ex-emplified post-Reconstruction white supremacy as one of the most influential Presbyterian ministers of the era. Dabney lamented the unrighteous taxation of "oppressed people" or "white brethren" to provide "pretended education to the brats of black paupers, who are loafing around on their plantations." Theft via taxation made his "blood boil with indignation."[11] Another most highly influential Presbyterian theologian, James Henley Thornwell (1812–1862), had previously warned of abolition by framing it as an attack on divine order itself and a slippery slope to communism and atheism. Thornwell saw abolition not as a narrow matter of freeing slaves but as an abstract question "of States to the individual, and of the individual to States; a question as broad as the interests of the human race."[12] But it was Princeton Theological Seminary theologian Archibald Alexander Hodge (1823–1886), a contemporary of Dabney, who gave a warning which lives on today in libertarian circles as well as in Christian private and home-school literature. In his lecture "The Kingly Office of Christ," Hodge warned of "the most appalling enginery for the propagation of anti-Christian and atheistic unbelief, and of antisocial nihilistic ethics, individual, social and political, which this sin-rent world has ever seen." What could be so dangerous? It was the "comprehensive and centralized system of national education, separated from religion."[13] By the end of the century, a new term emerged in the literature: the government school.

The government school isn't simply a synonym for public education but rather a recurring trope used to advance an agenda. Across several decades, it connected multiple conservative affiliates: the white supremacist, the libertarian, and the Calvinist. During the Depression, James W. Fifield, Jr. (1899–1977) created Spiritual Mobilization, a conservative reaction to the New Deal that would serve as a template for later conservative think tanks.[14]

11. These descriptions come from a letter to L. R. Dickinson regarding his 1875 essay "The Public School in Its Relation to the Negro," which Dickinson published under the pseudonym "Civis." Dabney agreed on the danger of state education, which was a rhetorical proxy for the education of black citizens. Dabney voiced praise and told Dickinson, "For some years I have had strong convictions of the falsehood and deadly tendencies of the Yankee theory of popular State education; and I confess that the influence which prevented my lifting up my voice against it was, simply, the belief that so puny a voice could effect nothing against the prevalent 'craze' which has infected the country on this subject." Dabney, "The Negro and the Common School," 177.

12. Thornwell, "Rights and Duties of Masters," 539.

13. Hodge, *Public Lectures on Theological Themes*, 283–84.

14. For further reading, see Toy, "Spiritual Mobilization."

His Christian libertarian magazine *Faith and Freedom* drew the collaboration of the preeminent Calvinist theologian Rousas J. Rushdoony (1916–2001), a leader in the Christian Reconstructionist movement. Rushdoony hoped to replace sectors of secular jurisprudence with biblical law, a system he called *theonomy* rather than the older, less attractive synonym *theocracy*. He founded the Chalcedon Foundation to promote Reconstructionism and eventually published *The Institutes of Biblical Law* (1973), a 900-page tome cataloguing all biblical commands for use in civil law.

Rushdoony despised pluralism, complaining, "in the name of toleration, the believer is asked to associate on a common level of total acceptance with the atheist, the pervert, the criminal, and the adherents of other religions."[15] An activist in the John Birch Society, he felt the American republic was rooted in a combination of economic liberalism and Calvinism, so he saw a libertarian organization like Spiritual Mobilization as an ally in need of intellectual gravitas.[16] Rushdoony's book *The Messianic Character of American Education* (1963) described American education as mired in illiberal, statist issues. In his first chapter, he juxtaposed the fascist education of "state children" and Marxist "passive psychology of man" with the state-controlled schools of the United States. He warned the government school's "statist education" supplanted parental responsibility and made the child property of the state. By the time of the Civil Rights Acts, the government school was a rhetorical trope shared between the white supremacist who overtly desired segregation and the theocrat desiring a version of biblical legal structure. However, a libertarian agenda gave the rhetorical trope its innocuous face.

The twentieth century's leading libertarian Milton Friedman (1912–2006) invoked the government school in his 1955 paper "The Role of Government in Education." It's rare to read a position paper that is so deeply wrong in all its assumptions of its time and (especially) its projections for the future. While government funding of education was acceptable, Friedman argued it shouldn't require government administration, so he proposed a voucher system to separate the two. Parents would be given a sum of money to invest in public or private schools as they saw fit, and the market would work out contradictions. But that came later. The paper actually opened with even more obvious misdiagnoses of the "natural monopoly" and the "neighborhood effect." First, his natural monopoly

15. Rushdoony, as quoted in Balmer, *Thy Kingdom Come*, 65.
16. For further reading, see McVicar, *Christian Reconstruction*.

existed where lack of alternatives led to few educational options. Parents might be "free" to choose from only one school in a given area. Second, the neighborhood effect designated a benefit accumulated by a community as a side effect of the primary beneficiary. The schoolchild would become a good citizen or laborer, which in turn benefitted surrounding markets or neighborhoods. Friedman granted the neighborhood effect of primary and secondary education, so he felt government funding at this level was good. So long as private schools met minimum standards—and here he is woefully inept at defining any such standards on which rural/urban, religious/nonreligious, or black/white differences might agree—they should receive public funding.

Remarkably, Friedman claimed the neighborhood effect diminished the higher one climbed. A student training in vocational school to be a dentist provided little to no neighborhood effect. A college-educated public apparently held little neighborhood effect either, according to the smartest libertarian. Moreover, the lower cost of state colleges gave them an unfair advantage over private universities. Rather than lowering the cost of all, Friedman suggested we cut funding from state schools in order to *raise* prices to private university levels. Students should shoulder this burden through loans, because students only enter higher education to raise future earning potential. Even in 1955—to say nothing of the catastrophically high costs of education today—the argument is disconnected from reality on every programmatic point. Still, Friedman's projections were at their worst when exploring racial implications of privatizing education.

Race entered only as a footnote in this essay, which is remarkable given the Supreme Court's pivotal ruling on segregation a year prior. After telling us he deplores segregation, Friedman forcefully claimed "it is not an appropriate function of the state to try to force individuals to act in accordance with my—or anyone else's—views."[17] Given the choice between forced integration or segregation in the public school, Friedman viewed the former as the lesser of two evils. What of his view on the private school?

> Privately conducted schools can resolve the dilemma. They make unnecessary either choice. Under such a system, there can develop exclusively white schools, exclusively colored schools, and mixed schools. Parents can choose which to send their children to. The appropriate activity for those who oppose segregation and racial prejudice is to try to persuade others of their views; if and

17. Friedman, "The Role of Government in Education," 6.

as they succeed, the mixed schools will grow at the expense of the nonmixed, and a gradual transition will take place. So long as the school system is publicly operated, only drastic change is possible; one must go from one extreme to the other; it is a great virtue of the private arrangement that it permits a gradual transition.[18]

If the public wanted to fund segregated private schools with vouchers, Friedman felt that was fine. It was up to parents to persuade others that segregation or prejudice was wrong. The market and culture would presumably work it all out. This is precisely the naïveté endemic to the individualist, libertarian worldview. No drastic intervention is warranted; people are rational agents acting in their best interests. The drastic increase in southern private schools confirmed Friedman's error. Southern private school enrollment began outpacing the north in the 1940s. Between 1950 and 1965, southern private school enrollment surged more than 120 percent.[19]

The rise of the private school and the homeschool were reactions to integration, which was a delayed and gradual process of ruling and resistance persisting to this day. Desegregation and resegregation occur in ebbs and flows, and the resistance which once disguised itself as administrative feet-dragging reappears in more clever disguise as alternative school experiments today. The Supreme Court decision in *Brown v. Board of Education* (1954) was not the first ruling for integration, and a number of prior Supreme Court decisions had already begun dismantling protections for segregated graduate schools.[20] *Brown v. Board* was the pivotal moment

18. Ibid.

19. It is important to clarify that public school enrollment was also surging in this period due to the baby boom. The surge of private school enrollment itself does not suggest racism so much as the context suggests racism. The period in which private school enrollment in the South began drastically outpacing the North corresponds to the period in which desegregation began in graduate and professional schools, and anyone paying attention could see the direction segregation was headed. From 1910 to 1940, private school enrollment in the South lagged behind the rest of the nation. From 1940 to 1950, the rest of the United States slowed its pace of private school enrollment while the South's enrollment surged 43 percent. In the period of 1950 to 1965, southern private school enrollment jumped to more than 120 percent, while in the rest of the United States enrollment shot back up nearly 100 percent. What is clear is that private school enrollment surged everywhere as a response to integration, though it is equally clear where (and why) enrollment rose most of all. See Southern Education Foundation, "A History of Private Schools & Race in the American South."

20. Ibid.

overturning the so-called "separate but equal" doctrine established by *Plessy v. Fergusson* (1896).

The latter reached the Court after Homer Plessy refused to vacate his train seat on a whites-only car. Plessy was one-eighth African descent, and he volunteered for the action that would lead to his arrest as part of an intentional act of civil disobedience in protest of Louisiana's Separate Car Act. In the majority ruling, Justice Henry Billings Brown concluded, "The object of the [Fourteenth] amendment was undoubtedly to enforce the equality of the two races before the law, but in the nature of things it could not have been intended to abolish distinctions based upon color, or to endorse social, as distinguished from political, equality . . . If one race be inferior to the other socially, the Constitution of the United States cannot put them upon the same plane."[21] Justice John Marshal Harlan was sole dissenter in the case, ironically using the term which would be favored by racists when he wrote "Our Constitution is color-blind, and neither knows nor tolerates classes among citizens."[22] Deciding that Jim Crow laws were weakest in the realm of discriminatory education policy, the NAACP made a tactical decision to focus efforts on denied school admission. A string of appeals and Supreme Court victories from the thirties through early fifties paved the road to *Brown v. Board*.

Linda Brown was the catalyst. As a young girl, she walked six blocks to a bus stop to await transport miles away to Monroe Elementary, which was one of four all-black schools in Topeka. When her father, Reverend Oliver Brown, couldn't enroll her in all-white Sumner Elementary only a few blocks from home, he filed suit with the NAACP against the Topeka Board of Education. By the time the appeals reached the Supreme Court, five similar cases (including several other plaintiffs with children at Monroe Elementary) were consolidated into *Brown v. Board*. Future Justice Thurgood Marshall argued the NAACP's case as he had with several aforementioned suits. The decision might have gone differently had Chief Justice Fred Vinson not died suddenly between arguments and the decision. The new Chief Justice Earl Warren reheard the case in 1953 and sought a unanimous decision. The Court reached consensus, and shortly before the end of term in May of 1954, Warren wrote, "We conclude that in the field of public education the doctrine of 'separate but equal' has no place. Separate

21. *Plessy v. Ferguson*, 163 U.S. 537 (1896).
22. Ibid.

educational facilities are inherently unequal . . ."[23] Initially it was left to state attorneys general to provide plans for implementation; in May of the following year, the Court reversed this leniency and created a plan (*Brown II*) for desegregation with "all deliberate speed."

The South took no deliberate speed. According to the Southern Education Foundation, southern state legislatures "enacted as many as 450 laws and resolutions between 1954 and 1964 attempting to block, postpone, limit, or evade the desegregation of public schools, many of which expressly authorized the systematic transfer of public assets and monies to private schools . . . While none of the new laws specifically mentioned 'race' or racial segregation, each had the effect of obstructing black students from attending all-white public schools."[24] A most effective instrument was the grant, which fueled the rise of the private school. Integration in my hometown of Little Rock, Arkansas stands out as a case study of white supremacist intransigence.

The first African American students enrolled at Central High are known as the Little Rock Nine. On a morning in September 1957, they arrived at school to hear racial slurs from protestors shouting, "Two, four, six, eight, we ain't gonna integrate." Segregationists found support with Governor Orval Faubus, who deployed the Arkansas National Guard to deny the nine students entry. The school district condemned the presence of troops, and Mayor Woodrow Wilson Mann pleaded for President Eisenhower's intervention. Three weeks went by as the students were blocked from joining their peers inside. After the president's warning to Faubus went unheeded, Einsenhower removed Faubus from the equation by federalizing the Arkansas National Guard and deploying the 101st Airborne division to the school to ensure access. One brave student, Carlotta Walls LaNier, later recalled the constant battery of threats and violence: "I considered my tormentors to be ignorant people . . . They did not understand that I had a right to be at Central. They had no understanding of our history, Constitution or democracy."[25] After a contentious school year, Faubus successfully campaigned to close the district's high schools for the 1958–1959 year. Little Rock residents called it the "lost year."

23. *Brown v. Board of Education of Topeka*, 347 U.S. 483 (1954).

24. Southern Education Foundation, "A History of Private Schools & Race in the American South."

25. LaNier, as quoted in Mai, "I Had a Right to Be at Central."

Governor Faubus hatched a plan that is everywhere among us today as a way to penalize Title 1 schools for low marks, erase names of people of color from school buildings, and hand facilities to so-called innovation and privately run charter schools. Faubus supported his call for closure of schools by proposing a replacement, namely, private schools could lease the closed high school buildings. This would ensure segregated education during the lost year. In fact, this plan for private school leases was the tool he used to gain public support in a referendum on school closure.[26] The referendum passed and schools closed, but the private school plan fell apart. This was the lesson: for the white residents of Little Rock, their children's lack of education for an entire school year was preferable to integration.

A coalition was brewing between segregationists, so-called small government libertarians, and Protestant Christians on the Right flank, and I claim they should be read as a resonance machine rather than as independent interests. In between *Brown v. Board* and the Reagan era, the coalition was the fertile ground from which a distinct white evangelicalism grew. The first test run of this coalition in support of a presidential campaign, which would come to fruition with the Reagan administration and the Religious Right, appeared in the guise of the failed Goldwater campaign. In the 1950s and 1960s, Arkansas's Harding College and California's Pepperdine College generated the charge sparking across constituencies by inviting the Goldwater Right (at Harding, Albert Wedemeyer, Fred Schwarz, Clarence Manion, Leonard Read) and leading libertarian figures (at Pepperdine, Friedrich Hayek and Russell Kirk).[27] On to the path to his failed 1964 presidential campaign, Barry Goldwater wrote in *The Conscience of a Conservative* (1960), "Despite the recent holding of the Supreme Court, I am firmly convinced—not only that integrated schools are not required—but that the Constitution does not permit any interference whatsoever by the federal government in the field of education."[28] By this period the ostensibly innocuous cry for "religious freedom" signaled not just anti-black but also anti-union and anti-communist affiliations as well.[29] The coalition was a resonance machine built atop anti-black fantasy. It would prove fruitless to take the various segregationist, libertarian, and theocratic Christian arguments at face value as if they were not marching with similar affinities.

26. See Faubus, "Speech on School Integration."
27. Dochuk, *From Bible Belt to Sunbelt*, 230.
28. Goldwater, *The Conscience of a Conservative*, 28.
29. See especially chapter 6 of Dochuk, *From Bible Belt to Sunbelt*.

Polarization of Evolution

Let us step back and trace the religious polarization of science between antebellum and integration. Nietzsche said it best, for just as modernity unchained the earth from its sun, so too Charles Darwin revealed we were not God's special creatures. When Darwin published *On the Origin of Species* (1859), it was not immediately apparent that Christians would react so negatively. By the 1920s, opposition to evolution was a tenet of faith on par with biblical inerrancy for the conservative American Christian.

Darwin discovered natural selection not long before a key development in biblical studies. Though Jewish theologians had long taken discrepancies in the text as important to the whole, the mid-nineteenth-century Christian scholar sought to reconcile discrepancies through modern investigatory techniques. How could Moses have written the Torah if, for example, he died before its final scene? What might new archeological sciences declare of the famous battles recounted in the Hebrew Bible? In the German academy, Julius Wellhausen (1844–1918) developed the documentary hypothesis to demonstrate distinct voices or agendas reshaping the Torah during its various phases of redaction. The hypothesis proposed a solution to the problem of why there were two creation stories at the beginning of Genesis.[30] It explained why Noah brought a pair of each bird and animal on the ground upon the ark in Genesis chapter 6, but in chapter 7 he brings seven pairs of every clean animal, one pair of every unclean animal, and seven pairs of each bird. The latter list either indicated Noah's working knowledge of temple ritual that wouldn't exist for another millennium, or it indicated the input of later redactors with a priest's agenda. Reading the "plain text of Scripture" no longer worked, so it's no surprise the advance

30. In chapter 1, God created the earth in seven days. Animal life emerges on the sixth day followed by the creation of man and woman as the final act. In chapter 2, God planted a garden (the earth presumably already existed) and placed man there. God then created animals (after man, contra Genesis chapter 1) and commands the man to name each animal; after the task is completed, God creates woman. The two stories are often carelessly read as separate foci on an identical story, but we find these disparities across the Hebrew Bible. The documentary hypothesis scrutinizes markedly different agendas and proposes at least four voices in the text: the Yahwist source (J), the Elohist (E), the Deuteronomist (D), and the Priestly (P). All were active between 1000–500 BCE, but their contexts introduced additional aspects. J source worshipped YHWH while E source worshipped Elohim, and J, E, and D lived in ancient Palestine while P conducted its redactions in Babylonian exile. The writer of Genesis 2 used the name YHWH and could thus be called J source material. Genesis one uses Elohim and models itself after the Babylonian creation myth *Enuma Elish*, therefore it demonstrates E and P agendas.

of European scholarship coincided with an intense Christian pushback against theological scholarship in America.

In the fourth century, Saint Augustine admonished readers to avoid pontificating on matters better studied outside of theology. Attempting to twist observations on heavenly bodies or animal life to fit the Scriptures would ruin the faith:

> Now, it is a disgraceful and dangerous thing for an infidel to hear a Christian, presumably giving the meaning of Holy Scripture, talking nonsense on these topics; and we should take all means to prevent such an embarrassing situation, in which people show up vast ignorance in a Christian and laugh it to scorn. The shame is not so much that an ignorant individual is derided, but that people outside the household of the faith think our sacred writers held such opinions, and, to the great loss of those for whose salvation we toil, the writers of our Scripture are criticized and rejected as unlearned men.[31]

Heresies aren't challenges to orthodox standards. Instead, new orthodoxies grow within veins of prospective heresies. The decision to call one belief orthodoxy and another heresy is always handled in retrospect. Likewise, Darwin didn't challenge an age-old belief in young earth creationism. Instead, biblical literalism and creationism (while surely always present in some form throughout history) were products of print culture, biology, and racism. Literalism couldn't spread until after Gutenberg's printing press. We needed to have affordable Bibles and the ability to read them before we could have possibly uttered the phrase, "But actually the Bible says thus and so." As we'll discuss in chapter 4, historian Mark Noll argued that literalism in American Christianity was a response to slave-holding. The advent of the personal family Bible, the anti-clericalism of American frontier faith, and the need to justify the unjustifiable demanded direct readings of Scripture. Biblical literalism was rooted anti-blackness.

Even among committed Protestants, Darwinism was not immediately a threat. The prominent Harvard botanist Asa Gray (1810–1888), a Darwinian enthusiast who worked to defend *The Origin of Species* in America, saw in natural selection an opportunity to reshape the theological concept of design. Geologist and Oberlin Theological Seminary professor George Frederick Wright (1838–1921) argued scientists and theologians alike walk by faith, and orthodoxy was a type of working theory informed

31. Augustine, "The Literal Meaning of Genesis."

by other fields. Princeton theologian Benjamin Breckenridge Warfield (1851–1921) defended the Bible's inerrancy and yet argued God might work through evolution. Others argued that God worked through evolution for all species except humankind.

On the other hand, the clergyman and scientist Enoch Fitch Burr (1818–1907) found evolution philosophically offensive for suggesting our perceptions (even spiritual feelings) were the result of natural forces. John William Dawson (1820–1899) jumped on the initial lack of scientific consensus and argued Darwin appealed to possibility rather than fact, writing that natural selection was "not a result of scientific induction but a mere hypothesis, to account for facts not otherwise explicable except by the doctrine of creation." Boston Theological Seminary professor Luther Tracy Townsend (1838-1922) echoed concerns about the lack of scientific consensus. Moderate Christian Darwinists split the difference. New Testament professor James Iverach (1839–1922) suggested God worked through processes of natural selection. The highly influential English clergyman Aubrey Lackington Moore (1843–1890) delineated Darwinism from its supposedly implied agnosticism and argued the latter, not the former, was the problem.[32] Just as scientists were initially divided on natural selection, Christian perspectives split across competing agendas and were anything but univocal or oppositional. As the debate between modernists and fundamentalists took shape, it simply wasn't clear whether the Christian should accept or reject the theory.

The Scopes Monkey Trial of 1925 captured public opinion and ossified battle lines. Sectarian shifts plagued American Protestantism at the turn of the new century, and after the ouster of several of its prominent modernist theologians, the 1910 Presbyterian General Assembly became the first to adopt the list of five key beliefs which would soon define fundamentalist wings of Protestant denominations in the second decade. The five beliefs included the inerrancy of the Bible, the virgin conception of Christ, the substitutionary atonement of Christ, the bodily resurrection of Christ, and the historicity of the miracles of Christ (or the second coming of Christ).[33]

32. For the organization of the names in these couple of paragraphs, I should credit Stuehrenberg, "Christian Responses to Charles Darwin, 1870–1900," and BioLogos, "How have Christians responded to Darwin's 'Origin of Species'?"

33. Among the broader fundamentalist community, the truth of Christ's miracles was sometimes switched out for the second coming of Christ. The 1909 *Scofield Reference Bible* helped to drive an interest in end times, but Dispensational apocalypticism was not yet so important at the time of the 1910 Presbyterian General Assembly.

These fundamentals represented the zeitgeist of the anti-modernist position, and while fundamentalists were hostile toward evolution, they attacked it from the flank of biblical inerrancy rather than make creationism a central tenet. It was during the burnout from fundamentalism in the 1920s that evolution became a line in the sand. While fundamentalism decayed into church splits and ruined careers, another option sought to keep the dogma but include a smile. The radio preacher, the first megachurches, new publishing and educational outlets, Pentecostal movements, and so many other novel (often uniquely American) innovations served up less dogmatic alternatives on the west coast and the Bible Belt.

On evolution, the line in the sand was indeed a spectacle engineered for public consumption. The Tennessee state representative and leader in the World Christian Fundamentals Association (WCFA) John W. Butler passed the Butler Act in March 1925 to prohibit the teaching of evolution in public schools throughout the state.[34] The ACLU immediately sought to challenge the case and collaborated with the twenty-four-year-old teacher John Scopes, who was indicted two months later for having assigned his students a chapter on evolution from *A Civic Biology*. Like teachers throughout the state, Scopes was effectively required to teach from a textbook which itself taught forbidden material. Scopes encouraged testimony against himself from students. WCFA founder William B. Riley solicited the aid of William Jennings Bryan, the populist leader to which we'll return in the final chapter. Bryan was a congressman with a habit of failing presidential campaigns, but he was (as literally anything ever written about him will repeat) a gifted orator who so effortlessly tapped the indignation of the common man. Bryan led the prosecution of Scopes, who was defended by Clarence Darrow.

The trial transcript shows Bryan's efforts to make a grand mockery of Darwin. How could anyone claim we were descendants of monkeys? "Not even from American monkeys, but from old world monkeys," Bryan cried out to laughter in the courtroom. "Now, here we have our glorious pedigree, and each child is expected to copy the family tree and take it home to his family to be submitted for the Bible family tree—that is what

34. The wording of the Butler Act is as amusing as it is ridiculous: "Be it enacted by the General Assembly of the State of Tennessee, That it shall be unlawful for any teacher in any of the Universities, Normals and all other public schools of the State which are supported in whole or in part by the public school funds of the state, to teach any theory that denies the story of the Divine Creation of man as taught in the Bible, and to teach instead that man has descended from a lower order of animals." Tenn. HB 185, 1925.

Darwin says."[35] The clown carried on like this until, two days later, Darrow responded in theatrical kind by calling Bryan himself to the stand as a student of the Bible. Bryan deflected questions of whether the days of creation were literal, twenty-four-hour periods and whether the earth is 6,000 years old. Darrow asked whether childbirth is painful because of Eve's sin, and Bryan deflected again: "I will believe just what the Bible says . . . I prefer that to your language. Read the Bible and I will answer."[36] Read the intensity evident in this transcript excerpt, after which the court adjourned:

> **Darrow:** "I will read it to you from the Bible: 'And the Lord God said unto the serpent, because thou hast done this, thou art cursed above all cattle, and above every beast of the field; upon thy belly shalt thou go and dust shalt thou eat all the days of thy life.' Do you think that is why the serpent is compelled to crawl upon its belly?"
>
> **Bryan:** "I believe that."
>
> **Darrow:** "Have you any idea how the snake went before that time?"
>
> **Bryan:** "No, sir."
>
> **Darrow:** "Do you know whether he walked on his tail or not?"
>
> **Bryan:** "No, sir. I have no way to know." (Laughter in audience.)
>
> **Darrow:** "Now, you refer to the cloud that was put in the heaven after the flood, the rainbow. Do you believe in that?
>
> **Bryan:** "Read it."
>
> **Darrow:** "All right, Mr. Bryan, I will read it for you."
>
> **Bryan:** "Your honor, I think I can shorten this testimony. The only purpose Mr. Darrow has is to slur at the Bible, but I will answer his question. I will answer it all at once, and I have no objection in the world, I want the world to know that this man, who does not believe in a God, it trying to use a court in Tennessee—"
>
> **Darrow:** "I object to that."
>
> **Bryan:** (Continuing) "to slur at it, and while it will require time, I am willing to take it."

35. Bryan, as quoted in transcript Scopes, *The World's Most Famous Court Trial*, 176.
36. Ibid., 303.

Darrow: "I object to your statement. I am exempting you on your fool ideas that no intelligent Christian on earth believes."[37]

On the trial's final day, Darrow told the court he wanted a guilty verdict. The issue wasn't of evolution's truth but instead whether or not the defendant violated the Butler Act. The jury found Scopes guilty after deliberating nine minutes, and the judge ordered a fine.[38] The defendant and his lawyer were pleased, for Darrow wanted to appeal the case while Scopes spoke proudly of his commitment to religious and academic freedom. If Darrow and the ACLU desired to overthrow laws prohibiting evolution in the classroom, they'd need to wait four more decades. It was not until the Supreme Court ruled in *Epperson v. Arkansas* (1968) that such bans on evolution in the classroom were finally struck down. The fundamentalist or evangelical would be a creationist after the twenties. Fundamentalists carried on their fighting during the same few decades in which the Jim Crow South busied itself with building monuments to Civil War generals. They were debating evolution during the years with the highest concentration of lynchings. At least in part, these debates were proxy battles for white supremacy. For the southern Protestant, the Scopes trial proved what they suspected all along, that Northerners intended to cripple their shield of orthodoxy.[39]

37. Ibid., 304.

38. Ironically, this fine was the basis for throwing out the conviction on a technicality. Scopes's legal team unsuccessfully appealed to the Tennessee Supreme Court on a range of issues broadly related to freedom of speech and religion, but the Court ruled the fine should have been determined by the jury rather than the judge.

39. "In the eyes of many southern Protestants, this cataclysmic court decision proved that modernist pedagogy prevalent in the North had pierced the shield of theological orthodoxy that once protected their society. With fears of secularization rapidly mounting and faith in state schools diminishing, southern evangelicals began shoring up their church colleges and looking to vocational schools as an necessary alternative. One response to Scopes came in the form of the independent Bible school. A groundbreaking evangelist from Alabama set an example for this approach when, in 1927, he started Bob Jones College. Bob Jones's lofty ambition was to combat 'all atheistic, agnostic, pagan . . . adulterations of the Gospel' through traditional Bible teaching and create the 'greatest interdenominational, orthodox education center in the world.'" Dochuk, *From Bible Belt to Sunbelt*, 53.

The Rise of the Alternatives (to the Integrated Government School)

A seventh grader using Bob Jones University Press curricula would read, "Bible-believing Christians cannot accept any evolutionary interpretation. Dinosaurs and humans were definitely on the earth at the same time and may have even lived side by side within the past few thousand years."[40] On the topic of dragons, the child would read "is it possible that a fire-breathing animal really existed? Today some scientists are saying yes."[41] In eleventh grade the student would read, "A few slave holders were undeniably cruel . . . The majority of slave holders treated their slaves well."[42] A twelfth grader studying American government according to Abeka would read, "Ignoring 3,500 years of Judeo-Christian civilization, religion, morality, and law, the Burger Court held that an unborn child was not a living person but rather the 'property' of the mother (much like slaves were considered property in the 1857 case of *Dred Scott v. Sandford*)."[43] If studying economics according to Abeka, she'd learn, "Global environmentalists have said and written enough to leave no doubt that their goal is to destroy the prosperous economies of the world's richest nations."[44] As mentioned above, BJU Press, ACE, and Abeka produce the lion's share of curricula for private Christian and home schools. Their counter-histories are audacious yet mainstream. Remember that four Americans in ten reject evolution altogether. As we also saw, only four in ten Americans acknowledge slavery was the primary cause of the Civil War (slightly less than half believe the cause was states' rights). Of course the overlap is not absolute, but I'd expect the Venn diagram would be fairly close to a single circle. Rejection of widely-accepted evidence is integral to the white evangelical's sense of embattlement.

They see a fight everywhere. To give ground on one point is to signal to the enemy—everyone else—that more ground will give way. In the mid-twentieth century, the cause of religious freedom became a metonym. Religious freedom seemed innocuous, but as a metonym it substituted for more embarrassing impulses. Between the 1940s and 1960s, education became a battleground of interconnected fronts: segregation, capitalism, evolution,

40. BJU Press, *Life Science,* 134.

41. Ibid., 133.

42. BJU Press, *United States History for Christian Schools,* 219.

43. Bowen and Ashbaugh, *American Government in Christian Perspective,* 19.

44. Kirk, *Economics,* 253.

and sex education.[45] Historian Darren Dochuk suggested the anxiety tapped into the belief that people rationally choose salvation, thus, "Christian parents shuddered at the prospect of communists brainwashing their children before they were able to make decisions for Christ."[46] Even UNESCO was criticized as a Leftist ploy, and officials in Los Angeles came under such pressure that they banned its educational material. In California, Proposition 3 (1952) delivered tax-exempt status to religiously affiliated schools. In 1958 the ACLU-sponsored Proposition 16 (aiming to revoke tax-exempt status) failed to match the support mustered by the coalition Protestants United Against Taxing Schools. The effort was lead by the education activist and pastor Bob Wells and Rolf McPherson, the latter being the son of leading anti-evolutionist and Angelus Temple megachurch pastor Aimee Semple McPherson. The National Association of Christian Schools (NACS) was founded by the National Association of Evangelicals in 1947 and served 228 schools by 1965. In the headlines of the NACS magazine *Christian Teacher*, its director Mark Fakkema saw a "modern revolutionary war" in the classroom to "combat subversive tendencies."[47]

As early activists in the burgeoning Christian education movement, Wells and Fakkema lead the way in rhetorical maneuvering. In Orange County, Wells's Christian school Heritage High advertised:

> [Public] schools no longer WANT to turn out INDIVIDUALS. Instead, they seem intent on molding children into socialist "Group-concept" patterns [and] a "peaches and cream" world in which everyone passes and no one fails. . . . A "never-never land" in which the bright students are held back, so that slower students won't be embarrassed, feel discouraged or "left-behind."[48]

Fakkema delivered similar sentiments:

> The battle of this generation is not against child indoctrination. All real education of children implies indoctrination of some sort. This all-important question is: who shall indoctrinate—the parents or the subversively slanted education of "planners"? This

---

45. Dochuk explains the rise of metonymic causes standing in for others, writing, "The fear of losing white racial privilege was certainly one critical concern for southern evangelicals, but in their rhetoric, at least, it was trumped by a fear of losing religious freedom." Dochuk, *From Bible Belt to Sunbelt*, 104.

46. Ibid., 202.

47. Ibid., 204–5.

48. Wells, as quoted in ibid., 206.

is the battle at the educational front today. The parent-controlled school system clearly occupies the Scriptural position.[49]

By the 1960s, Tim LaHaye (later of *Left Behind* fame) began his activism against Darwinism in the classroom in southern California. He linked it to any number of interchangeable evils and warned, "destructive systems such as communism, fascism, racism, and animalistic amorality have been conceived and nurtured in an educational milieu emphasizing the evolutionary doctrines of struggle and survival."[50] Notice the conflation of Far Right and Left positions; many conservatives today still believe fascism is a left-wing ideology. In that same decade, Wells led the fight against sex education, especially material on gay and lesbian relationships. Anything beyond the scope of Protestant family values and matrimony was taboo. Wells delivered sermons with titles such as "Is Sex Training Sin Training?" while his church's annual evoked education as a metonym for many other issues:

> WE BELIEVE: In the Book, the Blood, and the Blessed Hope; In a strong Bible teaching-Bible preaching emphasis; That soul-winning evangelism and training in discipleship are the primary responsibilities of the church; In providing for the total and balanced education of our children as a vital part of the church program; In basic, old-fashioned Americanism and free enterprise system; In an uncompromising stand against Modernism, Socialism, Communism and every form of "One Worldism"![51]

Soon after, Anaheim reporter John Steinbacher wrote *The Child Seducers*, a book claiming sex education was a back door by which communists would drive students away from patriotism. The context was the Red Scare and *Brown v. Board*, but the rhetoric was about protecting the child. The child might learn they were an ape, or prone to sexual desire, or not naturally a capitalist! The figure of the child, whose innocence was robbed by progressivism run amuck, oscillated across multiple interest groups such that, by the time of *Roe v. Wade* (1973), the figure of the child served as the organizing cause of a conservative-theocratic coalition. The protection of the child was the metonymic pretext for alternative models for resegregation.

49. Fakkema, as quoted in ibid., 205.
50. LaHaye, as quoted in ibid., 301.
51. Wells, as quoted in ibid., 167.

The Private School and Abortion

Southern private school enrollment surged as lawsuits filed in the 1940s began concluding with the desegregation of graduate and professional schools. The graduate level alone triggered the first wave of panic. As we saw, between 1950 and 1965 southern private school enrollment soared while southern legislatures enacted hundreds of pieces of legislation to postpone integration. The overwhelming whiteness led to a legal battle over the new term "segregation academy."[52] The story of the Religious Right is misunderstood as a battle against reproductive choice bringing religious conservatives into alliance with neoliberals.

As religion historian Randall Balmer has shown, the foundations of the Religious Right in opposition to abortion is purely a myth. Heritage Foundation co-founder Paul Weyrich once admitted the idea to take up abortion actually came late in the seventies when Religious Right activists needed a cause with more long-term viability than segregation and tax credits. Weyrich said abortion was suggested by an unknown voice on some conference call in an unknown year. It was a flippant gimmick fueled by careless misogyny, not concern for the fetus.[53] The abortion myth covered for segregationist desire,

52 According to the Southern Education Foundation, "What was once the South's 11 percent share of the nation's private school enrollment had reached 24 percent in 1980. The eleven Southern states of the old Confederacy enrolled between 675,000 and 750,000 white students in the early 1980s, and it is estimated that 65 to 75 percent of these students attended schools in which 90 percent or more of the student body was white." Suitts, "Race and Ethnicity in a New Era of Public Funding of Private Schools."

53. I wish to credit Randall Balmer for providing insight into the role of private school tax exemptions (rather than abortion) in the rise of the Religious Right. In his book, Balmer discusses the "abortion myth" of foundation by telling of a conference he attended in 1990 with the old leaders of the Religious Right. In one session Paul Weyrich reminded the attendees that the Christian leaders came together not over *Roe* but over the tax exemption battle with Bob Jones University. Surprised and yet finding the story intuitively true, Balmer followed up with Weyrich and various other early Religious Right leaders, all of which eventually confirmed Weyrich's claim. Weyrich reported that the turn to abortion actually began during a conference call searching for new causes to rally around, and an unidentified voice on the conference call suggested abortion (which to that point had been considered too controversial with so many Christian conservatives and Republicans taking pro-choice stances). Weyrich had been attempting and failing to organize right-wing activism around supporting prayer in schools, opposing the Equal Rights Amendment, and opposing abortion for years, and Balmer cites Weyrich as defeatedly conceding, "I was trying to get those people interested in those issues and I utterly failed . . . What changed their mind was Jimmy Carter's intervention against the Christian schools, trying to deny them tax-exempt status on the basis of so-called de facto segregation." Note that this tax exemption issue actually began under Nixon, just as

which means that—counterintuitive though it may seem—the discussion of abortion belongs here in a chapter on education more than it belongs in my chapter on sexuality and gender. The master signifier "pro-life" was clearly a metonym, just as "religious freedom" was a metonym, for segregation. We see this in the battle of tax exemptions.

Bob Jones University had been a stalwart of Christian conservatism for a half-century by the time it came under fire as a segregated university, which threatened its tax-exempt status. A series of events linked the integration of public schools to legal status of Christian universities. After *Brown v. Board*, states were given leniency in their integration timelines. As Mississippi integrated in 1969–1970 after the end of the dual system,[54] a group of parents in Holmes County watched as white students fled the public schools to three new private academies. Within two years of integration, zero white students remained in the county's schools. The group of parents sued to deny three of these K–12 schools tax-exempt status, arguing segregated academies weren't charitable. The resulting case *Green v. Connally*[55] continued a domino effect running from *Brown v. Board* to the Reaganite Religious Right.

In 1971, the Supreme Court affirmed a district court's recent decision on *Green v. Connally* and said the Internal Revenue code shouldn't lend charitable status to segregated private schools. The Court was also upholding a position the IRS already announced in a two-page ruling that launched conservatives into revolt.[56] The IRS sent its first inquiry to Bob Jones University in 1970, at which point the school denied entry to African

---

the election of Reagan did not result in overturning *Roe*. The actual causes of problems and the results of power didn't seem to matter even for the first leaders of the Religious Right, for the only real desire all along was power. For more reading, see chapter 1 of Balmer, *Thy Kingdom Come*. Or see a brief version of this argument online in Balmer, "The Real Origins of the Religious Right."

54. One way states resisted integration was to allow school choice so that black students could theoretically transfer to white schools, though in practice the pervasive white supremacist terror kept schools segregated. In 1969, the Supreme Court ordered the termination of the dual school system.

55. The case went by several names between its initial filing and the final Supreme Court affirmation. For the sake of clarity, I use the most familiar name *Green v. Connally*, which was settled by the U.S. District Court for the District of Columbia in *Green v. Connally*, 330 F. Supp. 1150.

56. The two-page IRS ruling triggering the great revolt of the Christian Right began with this guidance: "A private school that does not have a racially nondiscriminatory policy as to students does not qualify for exemption." Rev. Rul. 71-447, 1971-2 C.B. 230.

Americans. The changing legal landscape forced the university through a series of stalling tactics, such as admitting a black employee to a short-lived stint as a part-time student. It experimented with admitting black students who were married and enforced rules against interracial dating until the year 2000. The university lost its tax exemption in January 1976. The moment was a flashpoint for conservative Christians, but segregation was no longer a viable long-term cause. Another issue was needed.

In the rise of the Religious Right, *Green v. Connally* was the motive while *Roe v. Wade* was the cover. In the 1972 and 1976 elections, Democrats were slightly more pro-life than Republicans, a fact which ceased to be true in all elections but one after 1980.[57] Early Christian opposition to abortion was Catholic, not Protestant. Even the ultra-conservative Southern Baptist Convention (SBC) adopted a resolution in 1971 supporting abortion access in some cases.[58] Just after the *Roe* decision, Texas pastor and former SBC president W. A. Criswell told *Christianity Today* it wasn't up to him: "I have always felt that it was only after a child was born and had a life separate from its mother that it became an individual person, and it has always, therefore, seemed to me that what is best for the mother and for the future should be allowed."[59] It would be a mistake to say, as many too simply claim, that Baptists were pro-choice and then turned pro-life, but there was a significant ideological shift at the decade's end.[60] The SBC's shift mirrored the broader conservative about-face on church-state separation over the course of a few

57. The exception was 1988. See Carmines and Woods, "The Role of Party Activists in the Evolution of the Abortion Issue," 366.

58. The resolution called for "high view of the sanctity of human life, including fetal life" while remaining supportive of abortion in cases of fetal abnormalities, assault, or incest. The resolution clearly resists taking a hard line either way, and while it does not treat abortion as an issue without moral import, neither does it frame the fetus as a full human. See Southern Baptist Convention, "Resolution on Abortion."

59. Criswell, as quoted in *Christianity Today*, "Abortion Decision," 43.

60. I want to be very clear on this point, because the data we have even on SBC views on abortion is incomplete at best. The shift in resolutions is easy to measure, and survey data picks up in the 1980s, but the views of the average layperson are difficult to measure with incomplete data. Moreover, I'm using the SBC as a particular example primarily because they most closely reflect the mode white evangelicalism took in the 1980s. The type of white evangelicalism I'm exploring in this book did not quite exist in its contemporary political form yet in the 1970s, so I use the SBC as a proxy. And just as surely as there was a dramatic shift against support for abortion among the budding Religious Right, there was surely also a large segment of Baptists who already opposed the resolutions their denomination offered in support. Let us not make the mistake of overstating our case.

interesting years. Baptists are particularly interesting here as a group that traditionally supported the separation of church and state.

The Baptist Joint Committee for Public Affairs supported the Supreme Court's ruling against prayer time in schools in *McCollum v. Board
of Education* (1948).[61] The SBC passed resolutions against public funds for
religious schools over and over again between the end of World War II and
Roe. It fully supported the establishment clause until something changed.
The fundamentalist wing grabbed power in the late seventies. It's actually
due to the fundamentalist takeover and purge of moderates that we have
the data to document the shift, especially after Richard Land took charge of
the Christian Life Commission (CLC, now the Ethics and Religious Liberty
Commission) in 1988. The CLC began using questionnaires on the topics
of public funding for religious schools, an amendment for school prayer,
and abortion. There was a dramatic increase in support for tax credits for
religious schools during the 1980s. The SBC's six resolutions offering qualified support for at least some abortion rights stretched from 1971 to 1979,
at which point they stopped entirely.[62] There is so much history we could
explore for further context in this decade, but one way to think of it is an
opposition between two camps. One believed the conservative church was
best served by a strict separation of church and state, while theocrats who
won the fight believed theological interests were best served by rooting
those interests in the law.[63]

Opinions on abortion were fairly quiet between 1973 and 1978 and
shifted dramatically in the decade's final two years. The SBC elected its first
adamantly anti-choice president, Adrian Rogers, in 1979 and adopted an
anti-choice resolution the following year. In concert with Francis Schaeffer, whose warnings of "secular humanism" would soon gain wide audience, the Heritage Foundation co-founder Paul Weyrich helped galvanize

61. James Wood, Jr. (director of the Baptist Join Committee for Public Affairs, 1972–
80) even used the first amendment to argue in favor of abortion rights. He argued the
government should not get into the business of legislating religious views. He even testi-
fied against the Hyde Amendment in court. It's safe to say that Richard Land's activism
was a direct contest to Wood's concept of the church-state relationship.

62. For much of the analysis in this paragraph, I am indebted to Lewis, "Abortion
Politics and the Decline of the Separation of Church and State."

63. When Richard Land took over his position, he argued that legislating against
abortion was not that same as legislating in favor of a particular religion. Instead, he argued the law often corresponds to the same ethical ideals promoted by religion precisely
because law is rooted in the same moral tradition as its people's faith. This was a political
theology—law or theology, there was no difference.

a Protestant coalition around abortion. Many early evangelical activists joined the cause. Tim LaHaye launched Californians for Biblical Morality. Robert Grant founded American Christian Cause, which published "moral report cards" spread in churches prior to elections. College ministry Campus Crusade for Christ founder Bill Bright joined forces with the Heritage Foundation. Along with Schaeffer, the future Surgeon General C. Everett Koop produced the anti-choice film series *Whatever Happened to the Human Race?* Liberty University founder Jerry Falwell published the newspaper *Moral Majority Report.*[64] Falwell's Moral Majority was the base from which the anti-choice Religious Right grew, but in 1978 his focus was the child in the school rather than the womb. Christians, he warned, must be politically aware of government forces which "affect the vitality and very existence of our churches and Christian schools."[65] Nevertheless, this was the same year in which Falwell proclaimed his opposition to reproductive choice. His coalition vehemently opposed the Equal Rights Amendment as well, since Falwell believed equality between men and women would destroy the traditional family.

The pro-life moniker worked. In 1978, an Iowa incumbent Democratic Senator who was overwhelmingly projected to win reelection lost to a Republican running as pro-life. Two years later, the Moral Majority proved successful at defeating Carter and installing Reagan on the same issue. The Johnson Amendment was nearly three decades old by this point, but this rule ostensibly prohibiting non-profits from endorsing candidates couldn't keep up. The Right chose to forget how tax exemptions were revoked under Nixon, a Republican. By the time Pat Robertson and Ralph Reed launched the Christian Coalition in 1989, everyone took for granted they had always felt great concern for the fetus. Evangelicals shrouded themselves in pro-life rhetoric, and the Christian Right was born—white evangelicalism was born. It was born shrouded in the abortion myth as the white child in the school was rhetorically eclipsed by the child in the womb.

Bob Jones University's tax exemption case reached the Supreme Court during the Reagan administration. With only one dissenter, the Supreme Court finally settled the matter and ruled against the school in May 1983. Segregation was no longer an option for a tax-exempt school. In a perverse twist, the sole dissenter, William Rehnquist, was rewarded when Reagan

64. See Dochuk, *From Bible Belt to Sunbelt*, 384–85, and Balmer, "The Real Origins of the Religious Right."

65. Dochuk, *From Bible Belt to Sunbelt*, 385.

promoted him to Chief Justice. However, damage was done and the threat was clear enough to conservatives. Today, white students overrepresent in private school enrollment in forty-three states. Researchers Sean Reardon and John Yun found "the strongest predictor of white private enrollment is the proportion of black students in the area."[66] In the domain of education, white flight and alternative knowledge remain inseparable.

The Homeschool

In the documentary *Jesus Camp* (2006), a scene depicting a Missouri home-schooling family opens with students watching a video declaring, "Time of Creation—Garden of Eden: approximately six thousand years ago." The children watch as the narrator asks, "Was it an explosion? Did we come from a glob of goo? . . . Is this scientific, or is it just based on a belief?" One child is beckoned over to the kitchen table by his mother who displays a sample lesson. They discuss global warming and evolution. The mother probes her son's capabilities for dismantling science. The mother asks, "What if you had to go to a school where the teacher said 'Creationism is *stupid*, and you're stupid if you believe in it!'?" She takes pleasure in her son's answers, which are dismissive and trite. The screen's caption reads, "75% of homeschooled kids in the United States are Evangelical Christians."

"God didn't say 'Have children and give my kids to someone else for eight hours a day," the mother explains. "And if I can homeschool them as well as the school can public school them, why would I send them somewhere else for eight hours a day?" She speaks while preparing a meal in the kitchen, showing how her motherly duties and work as an educator blend together. She takes for granted she's qualified to teach. She explains that the United States was founded on "Judeo-Christian values," a common term (emerging prominently during World War II-era anti-Semitism) which fantasizes semi-pluralism with at least one other faith. She claims the nation shifted at a precise moment: "We know when things started changing, you know, prayer got taken out of school, and, um, uh, the schools started falling apart. And now the rest of us are going 'Wait a minute! Where is my country?'" She says there are two kinds of people, those who love Jesus and those who do not. The mother was repeating a theme of Jerry Falwell, who in 1980 wrote, "I believe that the decay in our public school system suffered

66. Suitts, "Race and Ethnicity in a New Era of Public Funding of Private Schools," 36.

an enormous acceleration when prayer and Bible reading were taken out of the classroom by our U.S. Supreme Court."[67]

The second type of alternative educational arrangement is the homeschool. More white students are homeschooled than black and Latinx students combined.[68] The Department of Education estimates there are fifty-seven million students in public elementary and secondary schools, and more than 3 percent of all students are homeschooled.[69] The history of the phenomenon is, in some respects, as old as education itself. But as a political phenomenon in the United States, the explosion of the homeschool as a conservative, Christian reaction to fears of segregation and creeping secularism is a distinct phenomenon with a cottage industry of associations, curricula, and legal battles.

In 1904, an Indiana Appellate Court ruled that a homeschool served as a private school under its definition of a school as "a place where instruction is imparted to the young."[70] An even more important ruling was handed down when the New Jersey Superior Court decided in 1967 that homeschooling met the requirements for compulsory education and that the parent teacher need "need not be certified by the State of New Jersey to so teach."[71] The Supreme Court's ruling in *Wisconsin v. Yoder* (1972) was the most pivotal for the homeschool's legal basis. The case asked whether Amish families must educate children until age sixteen, as mandated by Wisconsin law, or if education could cease after eighth grade. The Court held that the state's interest in education must be balanced against the First Amendment's free exercise clause. The decision handed future culture warriors a religious loophole to compulsory education: "Respondents have amply supported their claim that enforcement of the compulsory formal education requirement after the eighth grade would gravely endanger if not destroy the free exercise of their religious beliefs."[72]

The homeschool trend surged with legal footing while the private school fought for tax exemptions. In 1961, Bill Gothard began the groundwork

---

67. Falwell, *Listen, America!*, 205.

68. Suitts, "Race and Ethnicity in a New Era of Public Funding of Private Schools," 67.

69. See National Center for Education Statistics, "Back to School Statistics," and National Center for Education Statistics, "National Household Education Surveys Program of 2016," 475.

70. *State v. Peterman*, 32 Ind. App. 665, 70 N.E. 550 (1904).

71. *State v. Massa*, 95 N.J. Super. 382, 231 A. 2d 252 (1967).

72. *Wisconsin v. Yoder*, 406 U.S. 205 (1972).

for the homeschooling organizations (Institute in Basic Life Principles and Advanced Training Institute), which made him a leader in the movement. Abeka Books was founded in 1972, followed by Bob Jones University Press a year later. In 1977, Nancy Campbell began the Quiverfull magazine *Above Rubies*, which was supportive of homeschooling. Educator John Holt wrote a series of books arguing that forced learning was detrimental to the child's natural curiosity. Holt drew a wide following with a mixed bag of mildly insightful and outrageously ridiculous ideas. He became the figurehead of the "unschooling" sector of homeschooling. Holt likened public education to compulsion or slavery, and the solution was an "underground railroad" of the homeschool. He launched the first homeschooling newsletter *Growth Without Schooling* and networked with parents across the nation. Along with homeschool advocates Bob and Linda Session, Holt's appearance in 1979 on *The Phil Donahue Show* gave him the national spotlight. The first sex scandal within Gothard's organization came to light around that same time. The legal basis, publications, scandals, theory, and national platform were established by the end of the decade. *Time* ran a story on the homeschool in 1978. Its opening description of Holt reads like an apocalyptic preacher ready to abandon the old world:

> Educational Theorist John Holt, author of *Why Children Fail,* used to tour the lecture circuit trying to persuade elementary and secondary schools to ease rigid rules and cut red tape. No longer. Despairing of reform within the nation's educational establishment, Holt has now decided to proselytize among parents, urging them to keep their children out of school and teach them at home.[73]

The Homeschool Legal Defense Association (HSLDA) formed in 1983, the same year the Supreme Court ruled against Bob Jones University for segregating its admission. By the middle of the decade, an estimated 50,000 students were homeschooled in the United States. The conferences ballooned, and the networks took shape. In the nineties and early aughts, a law school for homeschoolers, sports networks, and various homeschooling alliances grew. HSLDA founder Michael Farris also launched Patrick Henry College in 2000. The college was an hour's drive from Washington, DC and courted homeschool parents who dreamed of sending their sons and daughters to fight secularism at the heart of the nation. The late advent of homeschool networks specific to black or Muslim families underscored the white Christian default. The movement grew as the years of scandal

73. *Time*, "Education."

approached. Ever since founding the Advanced Training Institute to publish homeschool curricula (called "Wisdom Booklets"), Bill Gothard was perhaps the most preeminent figurehead of Christian homeschoolers. He was awarded a lifetime achievement award by the HSLDA in 2010 in recognition of his service. In 2014 he resigned from the Institute for Basic Life Principles in the wake of investigations into sexual misconduct. The next year, sexual scandal also engulfed the Duggars, a reality TV family with so many kids (and counting) which by sheer coincidence used Gothard's curricula. Suddenly a movement that seemed odd for cultural and educational reasons was spotlighted again.

A reckoning was on the way. In 2013, a group calling itself Homeschoolers Anonymous—later incorporated as the nonprofit Homeschool Alumni Reaching Out (HARO)—formed "to bring awareness to, and healing from, different forms of abuse in extreme homeschooling subcultures."[74] I should note my indebtedness to its founder R. L. Stoller for much of the history presented here.[75] Having been homeschooled from kindergarten through high school, Stoller went on to higher education and holds a master's degree. As for his motivation for founding the group, Stoller perceived the common features and stresses of homeschool alumni: "I think, for a lot of us, we are afraid to say what we feel, to say we have changed. A lot of us perceived the message of our world as 'shut up, get in line, and prepare to take back the culture.'"[76] The group perceives itself as a space for conversation rather than an attack. Stoller explained the goals as such:

> This isn't anti-homeschool in any way. At the end of the day, this isn't even about conservative politics or Christianity. It is more about anywhere and everywhere that communities and adults use religious or political ideology to deny children their humanity and freedom to be for the sake of advancing that ideology. That's a cult mentality. And wherever that mentality exists, you create emotional, mental, physical, and even sexual abuse and trauma for children. We want to be a strong voice in opposition to that mentality through our life stories, through education and information.[77]

74. Ducote, "For the Media."

75. See Stoller, "The History of Homeschooling, 1904–Present."

76. Stoller, as quoted in Ducote, "For the Media."

77. Ibid.

The homeschool, like the private school, is about white flight. Its peculiar feature of close, parental monitoring stands out as the obvious selling point. More so than the private school, the homeschool is not just a mostly white space but a socially, sexually, informationally, and politically controlled space. The focal point is the figure of the child, especially the young girl, who must not be corrupted by the creeping secularism of the public school. She shall be protected from free inquiry, sciences, feminism, a non-praying school environment, and from adolescent sexual exploration. It's a regime of power protecting the child from the fantasized corruption of the (integrated) school.

From the government school to the rise of alternative educational models, fantasies intertwined with concrete manifestations of anti-educational regimes seeking racial and hetero-patriarchal hegemony. My descriptions would feel foreign and offensive to those involved, and, to be sure, I would not have considered myself anti-education or anti-black while attending the private school of my youth. The lack of more than one or two persons of color in any class at my school did not raise the question of race for me as a child, and neither did I find concerning my school's perpetual reaction against standard history and science. As a child, I simply believed what the adults told me: I should take pride in my education's supposed superiority, because the public school provided a substandard education, fostered crime, and taught a political agenda. Theocratic and conservative agendas in my own education didn't cross my young mind. My textbooks took an imaginative view of history that seamlessly integrated the Bible with history. So before concluding with the state of education and anti-education today, let us take a look at a more vivid experience integrating whiteness, theocracy, and alternative science.

A Pilgrimage for Fantasy

One site brings together these cultural, hegemonic trends in a vivid display of political desire, and it's unfortunate that its revanchist politics are lost for all the focus on ridiculous dinosaur exhibits. Ken Ham is one of the leading proponents of creationism in the world today. Born in 1951 in Australia, Ham's career began as high school science teacher until 1975. In his telling of the story, he was shocked to see students learning the Bible was untrue according to textbooks teaching evolution. He lasted as a teacher for four years, and in that period he began lecturing on creationism at churches.

After resigning his position, he launched creationism-oriented educational resources which eventually resulted in the Creation Science Foundation. A few years after relocating to the United States in 1987, he decided the organization needed a new name: Answers in Genesis (AiG). In 2007, he completed his dream of opening the Creation Museum.

The Creation Museum presents the Earth as roughly 6,000 years old, a number derived from adding the lifespans described in the Hebrew Bible. The museum famously depicts interaction between human beings and dinosaurs. "We're taking the dinosaurs back," Ham boldly declared. "They're used to teach people that there's no God, and they're used to brainwash people. Evolutionists get very upset when we use dinosaurs. That's their star."[78] The museum rejects not only evolution and the Big Bang but "old Earth creationism" as well. AiG claimed more than 400,000 people visited in the first year.

The museum is organized as an immersive procession. The beginning scene displays paleontologists uncovering fossils and giving alternate explanations, asking whether this dinosaur died in a local flood or the Genesis flood. Next, visitors are treated to a type of "choose your own adventure" experience in which one path presents mainstream science and another presents the Bible. Mannequins of Hebrew prophets watch over the visitor as she reads placards warning embattlement but reassuring her "God's Word has TRIUMPHED against every Attack." After this point, the visitor enters a room depicting the results of elevating that human reason with newspaper clippings telling of rampant euthanasia and same-sex marriage. A graveyard contains tombstones reading "God is dead." Graffiti fills the hallways while the visitor learns that rejecting God's word leads to same-sex marriage and abortion. A video exhibit portrays Adam and Eve as well as Mary and the crucifixion of her son. Awkwardly, AiG later discovered that an actor portraying Adam in an early video also ran a gay pornographic website, which didn't sit well with the heterosexist ministry. The famous dinosaur exhibits arrive in two parts. After a brief dinosaur hall, the visitor enters a room linking drug use, the atomic bomb, and child malnutrition to the rejection of Scripture. Finally the visitor enters the last dinosaur exhibit, but note that dinosaurs, shown living side-by-side with humans, come only after a lengthy immersion into pseudo-science, alternative history, and emotive, political embattlement.

78. Powers, "Adam, Eve and T. Rex."

More recently, Ham built a full-scale replica of Noah's Ark. The 2016 opening of Ark Encounter replicates the apologetic theme of the Creation Museum as well as the aesthetic of mannequins and placards endeavoring to convince the visitor not only that a 510-foot wooden ark could float but that at least two of every kind of animal could join on board. The exhibit was mocked for its various hypocrisies, most notably the scandal over taxpayer subsidies.[79] And while the ark in Genesis was built by Noah and three sons, the Ark Encounter was constructed by more than a thousand laborers. It's as if the construction itself served as an unconscious testimony to implausibility. AiG claimed a million visitors in the Ark Encounter's first year.

Biblical literalist fantasies aim for affects. They need not operate at the level of fact or even plausibility. A vision is cast, and the extent to which the projects prove lucrative depends on a receptive public. Given the poverty of domestic options for American evangelicals wanting a spiritual pilgrimage, these exhibits serve a hybrid vacation-pilgrimage role. The family can enjoy a good time while indoctrinating the next generation. They'll be served by 900 park workers, each of whom must sign a statement of faith rejecting evolution and any form of sexual immorality (defined as "adultery, fornication, homosexuality, lesbianism, bisexual conduct, bestiality, incest, pornography, or any attempt to change one's gender . . .").[80] The vision is not just an apologetic but an explicit criticism of liberalism, secularism, sexuality, and egalitarianism, to say nothing of its out-of-hand rejection of academic biblical studies. Whether it's linking secularism with teen drug use and abortion or with the flood and the drowning of the unfaithful, the pilgrimage site casts a vision of God's ultimate and unavoidable violence against all those who are not among the tribe.

The tactile experience of a pilgrimage vivifies perceptions of realness. It reinforces the possibility of believing the experts are wrong, that counter-arguments have been intentionally suppressed as part of an ungodly agenda to deceive. The function is not to produce a convinced subject (armed with apologetic arguments) but instead to wear down the subject's desire to feel convinced of anything. In other words, a creationist need not believe that she is right—all that's needed is to believe that nobody knows for sure. Plato was fascinated with this dynamic between knowledge and opinion. Knowledge was the discernible truth, while opinion was unsupported belief. For

79. Nearly two-thirds of the $100 million price tag was carried through municipal bonds.

80. Answers in Genesis, "Statement of Faith."

those with no respect for expertise—indeed, for those who see expertise as nothing more than secular dogma—there is *only* opinion.

Education is a battleground, and its purpose is contested as much as its content and form. The most important job in society, the teacher, is poorly compensated and overworked all while being demonized in the political realm.[81] We teachers regularly hear that we should "just do our job," as if the nature of the job or the goal of education is commonly accepted. *Just focus on teaching and leave the politics out of it*, so the reactionaries say. However, politics is nothing other than ethics and desire writ large. The idea that one could teach philosophy, religion, or ethics without connecting political implications is absurd, but this bland talking point also reiterates the contested purpose of education. For many, education's purpose is ideological reproduction. For the revanchist, the unconscious purpose is the active erasure of critical thought while the world is burning.

81. Elementary and secondary public schools are funded largely through property taxes, which mean the schools in lower-income neighborhoods—typically neighborhoods of color—do not receive the same resources of a wealthier or whiter community. This is the form of the racist history bearing fruit in the present, which the powers that be imagine will be fixed with standardized testing and punitive measures for struggling educators. The form of the metric invades the post-secondary education as well, and universities increasingly face pressure to codify achievements in quantitative data. The profession of the university professor is disappearing altogether; whereas three quarters of professors were tenured or full-time/tenure-track in the 1970s, less than a quarter are today. The vast majority of professors are affiliate adjuncts who must teach at least twice as much to make half the pay of the full-time professor; the average adjunct salary is approximately $20,000 without benefits, a sum only possible by stitching together multiple positions at local schools. The form of education then is one of impossibility; it is not possible for teachers to care for students as well as they could have with the support enjoyed only decades prior. State funding support continues to plummet, departments are cut, programs are eliminated, and alternative educational models with little foresight steal the spotlight. This will not end well.

3

Against Sexuality

Sadomasochism in Purity Culture

"The only prohibition on sex in the Scripture relates to extramarital or premarital activity. Without question, the Bible is
abundantly clear on that subject, condemning all such conduct.
God is the creator of sex."
—TIM AND BEVERLY LAHAYE

"The most mediocre of males feels himself a demigod
as compared with women."
—SIMONE DE BEAUVOIR

How (Not) to Enjoy

In December 1994, the United Nations held a conference which lead directly to the dismissal of United States Surgeon General Jocelyn Elders.
She'd already drawn conservative ire while advocating for contraceptive
distribution in schools. The key moment arrived when she was asked about
ways to prevent the spread of AIDS, the conference's topic. After insisting
sex education should be taught early, she circled back to tell her audience,
"As per your specific question in regard to masturbation, I think that is
something that is a part of human sexuality and it's a part of something that
perhaps should be taught. But we've not even taught our children the very
basics."[1] Though she had worked with Bill Clinton since her time as director of the Arkansas Department of Health, and though the first African
American Surgeon General commanded strong support from women's

---

1. Jehl, "Surgeon General Forced to Resign by White House."

health and gay rights groups, the White House bent to conservative pressure and pushed her out the following week.

We could question whether responding to AIDS with masturbation was a real solution, but conservative ferocity toward Elders had nothing to do with finding the proper solution to the plague. The Reagan administration's indifference to the epidemic and consequent death toll made that obvious. What drew the ire was the optics of an official (a black woman, no less) naming what society would prefer to repress with regard to the adolescent's sexuality. She interrupted a fantasy. Let's begin this chapter on sexuality with two other odd ways to ignore or displace reality.

The psychoanalytic revolution emerged from studies on hysteria, showing its symptoms to be a return in the body of conflict in the psyche. It was a novel idea. Hysteria meant something dramatically different for centuries. The word *hysteria* comes from the Greek for uterus. Hippocratic texts described it and guessed at a wide variety of cures from pregnancy to herbal remedies.[2] In the medieval period it was conflated with demonic possession or mystical rapture. By the late nineteenth century, hysteria designated a cluster of symptoms: anxiety and nervousness, insomnia, depression, and the like. It was diagnosed in women expressing heightened or absent sexual desire. It was everything and nothing in particular, but it was a woman's diagnosis. Patriarchy took for granted that whatever anxiety or depression men exhibited or shoved down must be different in kind from woman's hysteria.

In various times and locations over the centuries, hysteria was attributed to a "suffocation of the womb" or a "wandering womb." Yes, the hypothesis suggested the womb retreated upward against the internal organs and put pressure on the heart, which in turn led to any number of abnormal symptoms in the female patient.[3] Woman's desire was relegated to an after-

2. "For the Hippocratic writers, however, the texts that have been used in the construction of hysteria described something resulting from a firmly organic cause, the movement of the womb . . . The Hippocratic texts suggest that movement of the womb is caused by menstrual suppression, exhaustion, insufficient food, sexual abstinence, and dryness or lightness of the womb, and that it can be cured by marriage and/or pregnancy, scent therapy, irritant pessaries, and various herbal concoctions administered by mouth, by nose, or direct to the vulva." Gilman et al., *Hysteria Beyond Freud*, 14.

3. There is, of course, the theory famously presented by historian Rachel Maines that certain doctors who treated "hysterical paroxysm" (in cold, clinical terms, it was not even acknowledged as orgasm) invented electric vibrators to resolve hysteria as a symptom of sexual dissatisfaction and the wandering womb. Since I am not in a position to have an opinion on the merits of Maines or those contesting her research, I can only

thought. Her experience was framed in man's terms, and her body was a problem to be medically solved.

Let's read this level of ridiculous ignorance alongside a type of displaced or redirected sexual drive. The internet was practically built for pornography, and by the early aughts evangelicals were catching up with a response of their own. Companies like Covenant Eyes and X3 Watch wrote so-called accountability software, the idea being that a bit of shame might chasten the impulses indulged by all. Since 2002, X3Watch.com has advertised itself as a three-step anti-pornography platform. First one signs up with an accountability partner, then the partner receives an email containing all browsing activity across all connected devices, and finally there's a conversation. Presumably, the conversation is shame-based when viewing habits are sinful. The site's banner includes a trim man in a swimsuit who is jumping jubilantly next to text reading "Live a porn free life with the power of internet accountability." The company suggests its mainstream appeal with an "as featured by" section including the New York Times, MTV, and TED Talks. It advertises its success with this statistic: "87% of our users feel confident about quitting porn after just one month!" Users can sign up for individual plans or, for only 50 percent more, sign up their whole family together.

What's going on here? First, obviously pornography stands in for masturbation. The fantasy of abstinence is augmented by the technological gaze of shame. As far as feats of repression go, it's a remarkable achievement when an anti-masturbation message finds a receptive audience among adolescent and college ministries. The demand might even persist in the adult who enjoys self-imposed rules. Secondly, the abstinence itself is a mode of (substituted) sexual enjoyment. The subject sublimates their desires and feels a narcissistic reward at the level of ego, because they are following the superego's (God's) demand to behave. Narcissism balances out the dissatisfaction of the id.

Finally, and most importantly, a fantasy that disavows or redirects sexuality is revealing a very specific idea about choice. These fantasies assume lust is containable. It's a free choice to be indulged or dissolved. The fantasy of complete, free will or choice in sexuality undergirds a vast array of self-imposed injunctions we see in conservative Christian views on sexuality. These seemingly anti-sex fantasies drive a peculiar type of sadomasochism in purity culture.

recommend that the reader see Maines, *The Technology of Orgasm,* as well as Saul, "On Treating Things as People."

True Love Waits (and Reality)

Almost a conservative answer to Alex Comfort's *The Joy of Sex* (1972), Tim and Beverly LaHaye's bestseller *The Act of Marriage* (1976) brought a message of sexual license within the boundaries of matrimony. It displayed early iterations of so many themes destined to become standard heteropatriarchal teachings in white evangelicalism. Early in the book, LaHaye described his first "sex counseling experience" in which a man arrived despondent over a secret conflict. Eventually he blurted out, "How long do you think I should go along with married celibacy?"[4] The man's wife believed sex was only for procreation, LaHaye complained. The message was clear: the woman was at fault and had a damaged view of sexuality. In the next story, another woman described her husband's affair after twenty years and four children. LaHaye knew how to distribute blame again, writing, "While his decision to leave his family cannot be condoned in a Christian, I am confident, knowing the youthful character of the man and his commitment to Christ, that it would not have happened if his wife had not been afflicted with an unbiblical mental attitude toward married lovemaking."[5]

The most troubling and revealing thing about this book's message and the culture to which it speaks is its concept of consent. It's something that either doesn't exist or is permanently bestowed. If her God-given role is to submit, or to give in to male desire, then consent is essentially something that cannot be meaningfully revoked after wedding vows are exchanged. There is no spectrum or nuance or layers of power; there is only varying male and female levels of sexual desire. That is what is truly on display. Throughout the book, the LaHayes took for granted that men are more sexual than women, that aggression is natural,[6] that if a woman understood male sexuality she wouldn't dress inappropriately, that he desires sex while she desires emotional connection, and that the woman should choose to be sexually available to the husband. The selling point of the book—everything

4. LaHaye and LaHaye, *The Act of Marriage*, 22.

5. Ibid., 23.

6. Just as concerning, the male is portrayed as the "aggressor" in a way that sees aggression just as natural as providence and leadership. The LaHayes wrote, "It is usually agreed that the male in all species of living creatures has the stronger sex drive, and Homo sapiens is no exception. That does not suggest that women lack a strong sex drive, but . . . hers is sporadic whereas his is almost continual. God designed man to be the aggressor, provider, and leader of this family. Somehow that is tied to his sex drive. The woman who resents her husband's sex drive while enjoying his aggressive leadership had better face the fact that she cannot have one without the other." Ibid., 34.

is permitted (within marriage)—was a command to enjoy, albeit with a critical look toward the woman who does not enjoy.[7] LaHaye's criticisms of men appear to prop up his own virility and know-how. Of men who don't satisfy their partners, he says, "Such men were (and some still are) sexual illiterates, totally failing to comprehend a woman's emotional and physical needs."[8] The book's short, declarative sentences about human sexuality are not at all inquisitive, and neither does it recognize the heteropatriarchal assumptions orbiting around man, never the woman. Just as men either do or don't know how to have sex as well as LaHaye, and just as women either give in to sex or else resist their God-given duty, everyone is either righteous or sinful. Women are submissive or rebellious, and men are good guys or bad guys. It's not a book asking questions.

How does sexuality become a threat to a faith or culture? Several fantasies extend to justify sex-negative thinking. Haven't we heard them all? The Bible condemns sex outside of marriage. Marriage only exists between opposite-sex partners. Sex outside of marriage does not express love and trains for divorce. Sexuality is a choice—surely repression doesn't return as something else. The adolescent isn't (or shouldn't be) sexual. Women are not sexually driven like men. Men deserve to have opinions on what women should do with their bodies. The list goes on. These fantasies support repression of the self and the oppression of the other. I'm tempted to truncate my claim to this: if you want to understand why parents torture their LGBT children with conversion therapy, it helps somewhat to understand how college students join ministries celebrating intense self-repression, demanding abstinence not only from sex but even from masturbation. There's a specific species of narcissistic satisfaction involved, not to mention the hypocrisies that serve to relieve repression and induce shame as a control mechanism.

The abstinence pledge is a shame-control mechanism. It shows how the Lacanian theory of superego works: prohibition generates desire. There was a difference between Freud and Lacan in how they thought about the pleasure principle, which demands we take every opportunity to enjoy, and the reality principle, which accepts the reality that we can't chase enjoyment all the time. Rather than the Freudian superego that imposes a limit

7. Reading it reminds me of Lacan's suggestion, "On what, in short, is the Freudian discovery based—if not on this fundamental realisation that the symptoms of the neurosis reveal an indirect form of sexual satisfaction." Lacan, *Freud's Papers on Technique*, 118.

8. LaHaye and LaHaye, *Act of Marriage*, 48.

and invokes the reality principle against counterproductive behavior, the Lacanian superego invites the subject to enjoy precisely because enjoyment is taboo. In Lacan's thinking, the superego condemns us for *not* enjoying. Isn't that precisely LaHaye's message for women?

I'm reminded of a moment some years ago on the rhetoric of shame-control mechanisms. I spent some time with a community in Devon, a small village on the coast of England. One of my friends must have joked about Christian abstinence teachings, because the conversation spiraled into various ways we'd heard sex outside of marriage described in our youth. One recalled her ministers saying sex with multiple partners was like letting multiple people take bites out of a bar of chocolate. It tarnished the experience for everyone else and spread germs. I recall thinking this was the difference between English culture and my American culture. We had no elegant chocolate metaphor—for Americans, it was a cup passed around the room for people to spit in. Even the nature of the crude, gender-specific example was tuned to shame girls, not boys, as the focal point of abstinence.

In American evangelical culture, the 1990s were overrun with abstinence campaigns. True Love Waits was the most well known. It was organized by the Southern Baptist Convention in 1993 and promoted through concerts, literature, and various rallies targeting adolescents. Participants often wore purity rings, a symbol of one's pre-betrothal to a future spouse. Nashville youth minister Richard Ross claimed the idea for True Love Waits dawned on him when two teenaged girls confided, "We're the only virgins left in our school." The organization's pledge read:

> Believing that true love waits, I make a commitment to God, myself, my family, my friends, my future mate, and my future children to a lifetime of purity including sexual abstinence from this day until the day I enter a biblical marriage relationship."

More than two million adolescents took the pledge in the first couple of years.[9] Not surprisingly, the promise didn't work insofar as the goal was stopping extramarital sex, but it had massive effects on emotional health and maturation. The group used the language of virginity as well as what it called secondary virginity, the latter bestowing a sense of forgiveness within the rubric of shame. True Love Waits bolstered repressive sexual mores with marketing glamor. Popular Christian musicians were recruited to spread the word, and, for one example of the spectacle, a 1996 rally filling

---

9. See Brückner and Bearman, "After the Promise."

Atlanta's Georgia Dome ended with 340,000 pledge cards (many mailed in) strung up over the crowd. The message was clear: chastity is good, and you are not alone.[10] Several groups with similar messages proliferated around the same time as part of what Elizabeth Abbott called a youth chastity movement of power virgins:

> Celibacy is at the heart of True Love Waits, a positive, confident, reassuring celibacy. It validates and shores up those tough people who remain chaste, but also embraces legions of remorseful non-virgins it designates "secondary virgins." Students who have failed sexually can be invited to seek God's forgiveness and make a True Love Waits pledge "from this day forward." Ergo, instant redemption, and though even True Love Waits cannot repair broken hymens, it does comfort the contrite and pardon the penitent.[11]

Even the movement's T-shirts, purity rings, and events were marked with slogans marketing celibacy as a hot new trend. Examples of these slogans range from simple regret ("I miss my virginity") to ridiculous ("Stop your urgin', be a virgin"). The slogans all worked through a combination of pride and shame. A 2013 study showed 12 percent of American female and 7 percent of male respondents under age 25 had taken an abstinence pledge.[12]

Numerous studies indicated relationships between such pledges and riskier sexual behavior, including but not limited to lack of protection against disease and pregnancy. Pledgers were slightly less likely to have sexual intercourse as soon, but they were even more likely to engage in oral sex. Sociologists Hannah Brückner and Peter Bearman analyzed data from nearly 12,000 adolescents and found while pledges delay sex, 88 percent of pledgers and 99 percent of non-pledgers eventually had sex outside of marriage. Pledgers were more likely to engage in oral or anal sex without vaginal sex, and pledgers were more likely to forgo use of condoms.[13] What a study cannot so easily measure is the overwhelming sense of shame attached to the nearly universal transgression of the taboo.

Shame was part of the illicit fantasy. Purity culture saw premarital sex as cheating on one's future husband or wife. One book published in this period captured this fantasy by recasting dating as a type of courtship. It

10. For further reading, I highly recommend Abbott, *The History of Celibacy.*

11. Ibid., 396.

12. Paik, Sanchagrin, and Heimer, "Broken Promises," 547.

13. See Brückner and Bearman, "After the Promise," and Bearman and Brüchner, "Promising the Future."

harkened to traditionally heteropatriarchal ideals of control and parental consent (rather than consent of the partners involved). Merely twenty-one years old at the time, Joshua Harris claimed his only sexual experiences were with pornography when he published *I Kissed Dating Goodbye* (1997). The book sold 1.2 million copies and served as a primer for teenage courtship. It opened with a wedding between characters named David and Anna. Just as the vows were read a woman in the congregation stood to take David's hand. More women followed until six stood alongside him. The groom confessed these were girls from his past: "I've given part of my heart to each of them . . . Everything that's left is yours."[14]

The scene turned out to be a dream described in a letter. The writer told of her shame imagining the number of men who could line up next to her at the altar. Do we not have a type of Freudian dream here?[15] Anna's angst projected into the dream state, and perhaps there's a wish attached as well. Perhaps her indoctrination into this culture told her she must torment herself and generate shame, or perhaps she secretly hoped her future husband would sin in equal proportion such that the transgressions might be zeroed out by comparison. Clearly her angst drew from messages suggesting her value dropped. Harris's allegory aimed to instill anxiety over a wedding day clouded with affairs from teenage years.

Harris's own interpretation of this dream underscores how one is never backed far enough away from the ambiguous line of transgression. The heart is inclined to evil all the time, so to speak. "Giving away part of your heart" is a euphemism for sex, but the phrase extends to almost any transgression. In fact, Harris followed Anna's story by describing an adolescent relationship in which he did not have sex and yet felt was heading in a "dangerous direction," which was dishonoring to God: "We were violating each other's purity, and our spiritual lives were stagnant as a result."[16] The freewill actor must toil and root out her sexuality. At least, this is the fantasy. Since the numbers show it all to be a fiction, what role does a fantasy play if nobody lives up to it?

After a decade of True Love Waits, the National Institutes of Health published an unrelated survey of premarital sex trends from over the prior five decades. The results starkly contradicted the myth of waiting

---

14. Harris, *I Kissed Dating Goodbye*, 14.

15. The name Anna is surely ironic for the Freudian, since the talking cure was found through another Anna's symptom.

16. Harris, *I Kissed Dating Goodbye*, 17.

for marriage: 95 percent of respondents had had extramarital sex by age forty-four.[17] The numbers had changed some but not much over time, and the rising age of first marriage accounted for much of the difference. The survey matched many others finding percentages in the mid-eighties for those who have sex before a first marriage, but the NIH study went above and beyond the normal phrasing to inquire up to age forty-four. Seventy percent of women and 65 percent of men had sex by age nineteen. The minority who initially abstained until marriage would usually change their mind later, and 97 percent of those who had ever had sex by age forty-four had done so outside of marriage. Additionally, the study only defined extra-marital sex as "either having had vaginal intercourse before first marrying or ever having had intercourse and never having married," which suggests the numbers would be higher if non-heterosexual sex or a larger range of sexual behaviors were measured. In short, virtually nobody lives up to the purity ideal, but it nevertheless persists as an operative fantasy.[18]

Between a quarter and a third of Americans believe sex outside of marriage is wrong in some or all instances, a view which has dropped dramatically since the sexual revolution even if our actual behavior hasn't changed nearly so much. Fewer than half of Americans see pornography as morally acceptable,[19] though viewing habits suggest otherwise. There's a clear disconnect between the ideal and the reality, but accusations of hypocrisy go nowhere. What's interesting is that certain fantasies nevertheless persist. The fantasy sustains desire for the object of desire, and, perversely, the fantasy itself can become the object of desire.

17. "Data from the 2002 survey indicate that by age 20, 77% of respondents had had sex, 75% had had premarital sex, and 12% had married; by age 44, 95% of respondents (94% of women, 96% of men, and 97% of those who had ever had sex) had had premarital sex. Even among those who abstained until at least age 20, 81% had had premarital sex by age 44. Among cohorts of women turning 15 between 1964 and 1993, at least 91% had had premarital sex by age 30. Among those turning 15 between 1954 and 1963, 82% had had premarital sex by age 30, and 88% had done so by age 44." Finer, "Trends in Premarital Sex in the United States, 1954–2003."

18. "In addition, public opinion polls over the last 20 years have consistently shown that about 35% of adults say premarital sex is always or almost always wrong. (Unpublished tabulations of data from the General Social Survey, 1982–2004.) In the same vein, there is a common popular perception that most or all of those who came of age before the 'sexual revolution' of the 1960s and 1970s waited until they married to have sex, and that it is necessary to revert to the behaviors of that earlier time in order to eliminate the problems of unintended pregnancy and sexually transmitted diseases. However, research has questioned whether such a chaste period ever existed." Ibid.

19. Dugan, "More Americans Say Pornography Is Morally Acceptable."

Disciplinary Regimes of Purity

Purity culture remodels and amplifies archaic ideals. It wants control of woman's sexuality, and to accomplish its mission effectively it must convince the woman that patriarchal desire is good for her and something she desires (just as it must convince the man that patriarchal control is God's desire, not man's abusive desire). The Bible is the first weapon in the arsenal. Though one will search in vain for a biblical passage plainly condemning sex outside of marriage, there were clearly various taboos at work in the Scriptures to regulate the production of heirs in the Hebrew Bible, to distance Christian communities from so-called pagan practices in the New Testament, to control women's sexuality in all patriarchal traditions, and so on. In many respects, purity culture is nothing new at all. The woman's virginity plays a disproportionate role to the man's across so many cultures, and various social and economic implications were tied to the virgin status.

The suspicion of sexuality in Rome was a far cry from its celebration in Greek culture. The chaste Greek goddesses Hestia, Athena, and Artemis (worshiped by Romans as Vesta, Minerva, and Diana) were the exception. Women were sometimes considered the more lustful sex, which is the underlying joke of Aristophanes's comedy *Lysistrata*. In the story, the women of Athens and Sparta, tiring of a war stretching decades, made a pact under the leadership of the Athenian Lysistrata to withhold sex from their husbands until they sue for peace. The sexual strike persisted for six awful days until the men and women alike couldn't bear it and brought war to a close. According to the interpretation of historian Elizabeth Abbott, the reason it's a comedy is simple. The Greek imagination would have found it hilarious to think of women or men controlling urges for nearly a week.

The situation changed by the time of Plato, at least partly due to the influence of the cult of Pythagoras and its valorization of chastity. Plato opened *The Republic* with an odd conversation between Socrates and Cephalus on their preference, in their old age, for good conversation rather than sex. Rather than simply being a crude reference to licentious youth, Plato was signaling his belief that the proper man could and should control his animal impulses. Early Christianity took a similar position, if for different reasons. We have ample record of sexual skepticism or phobia in the early church. Paul and Jesus both spoke against carnal lust, and the Patristic theologians (so many celibate men) valorized virginity. Several early Christian cults prohibited marriage or enforced celibacy within marriage, but the more practical view of St. Augustine (354–430 CE) probably represents a more dominant perspective.

In *The City of God*, Augustine wrote as a pastor after the sack of Rome. The brutality visited upon a population by an invading army led Augustine to argue that rape does not rob a woman of her virtue, for her spirit did not consent.[20] In *On the Literal Meaning of Genesis*, he speculated that sex was a necessary evil after the fall of man inasmuch as it provided a solution to the new problem of decay and death.[21] In *Against Julius*, Augustine said that without marriage we'd engage in indiscriminate sex "in the manner of dogs." He argued that sex, even in marriage, should be handled in moderation rather than freely, for it was ever contaminated by sin. Lust had one redeeming virtue, childbirth, making it less than wholly evil.[22] Even so, early Christian veneration of virgins and celibates (especially as veneration of Mary grew more popular) cemented a negative view of sexuality. Women were especially suspect as the weaker sex luring men to sin. So it is not true to say purity culture is anything distinctly new.

What's new are the particular rituals, given reasons, authorities, and disciplinary regimes intensifying and de-historicizing traditional sources of purity taboos.[23] No longer must the woman remain a virgin in order to ensure her children were indeed sired by the husband raising them; she must now remain a virgin because God says so. No longer must she remain a virgin to earn her father a good bride price; she must now remain a virgin so her father will not feel shamed for his lack of parental control. Whereas purity ideals were once about property (or heirs) and covered with divine demand, the contemporary situation drops concerns with property altogether and intensifies divine demand as an end in itself.

The concept of marriage changes dramatically enough across time that a clear anti-extramarital sex taboo would be practically useless in relation to contemporary iterations of marriage. While it's not clear to me when exactly extramarital sex became such a taboo for United States Christians, we can see an explosion of literature using the terms "premarital sex," "extramarital sex," and "sex outside of marriage" during the 1970s through

---

20. Augustine, *City of God*, bk. 1, chs. 16–18.

21. Augustine, *On the Literal Meaning of Genesis*, bk. XI.

22. Augustine, *Against Julius*, bk. III, ch. 7.

23. I highly recommend Abbott, *The History of Celibacy*, to which I'm indebted for the material above.

1990s.[24] These terms begin appearing in the 1920s and skyrocket in popularity during the seventies. The first two terms taper off by the turn of the millennium in a way that "sex outside of marriage" does not, perhaps suggesting the latter term is less morally loaded.

Purity culture is a loose term denoting disciplinary regimes infusing parental control over the adolescent's sexual experience, which is why courting is preferred over and against dating. The daddy-daughter date or dance underscores the parent's role. Young girls in the midst of adolescent development go on dates so that the father can model how any prospective boy should treat her. Much less common are mommy-son dates, and daddy-son dates never exist. Obviously heterosexist to begin with, many adherents believe an LGBT child is evidence of failed parenting. It's not just about prohibiting sex outside of marriage. It's a sophisticated, interconnected regime of discipline. Since participants are always failing to live up to impossible demands, they must unconsciously depend on the stress or angst inculcated by the disciplinary regime. There are clearly multiple lines of cultural, ideological, and racial purity built into the trap as well. Not only must one not have sex but instead, in the Foucauldian sense of panopticon, one must police one's own innermost thoughts. Little to no consideration is given to the ramifications of actually following all these injunctions. The parent or minister rarely has personal experience following the demands they place upon the child. This is the fantasy: one can repress without that repression returning in surprising, detrimental ways.

Force always aims at transforming into automated discipline. In *The History of Sexuality*, the philosopher Michel Foucault framed disciplinary power as a process beginning with multiple relations of force. The relations undergo a series of transformations and reify support for those transformations. Finally, power relations adopt new strategies or avenues for amplifying control.[25] It's at this final point that automated self-discipline appears a free choice (abstinence by choice). Foucault names four results emerging from these power relations: (1) framing woman's symptom as hysteria, (2) controlling the sexuality of children, (3) classifying and authorizing "normal" sexual behaviors and delegitimizing alternative sexualities as perversions, and (4) disciplining populations through this schema of regulated

---

24. This claim is a result of running an Ngram on these terms. The tool has its limits but demonstrates when these terms begin trending in the literature.

25. See part IV of Foucault, *The History of Sexuality.*

sexuality.[26] Do not each of these appear in purity culture? Foucault targeted nineteenth-century Victorian mores, but the four lessons line up tragically well with today's conservative.

First, while the onus is ostensibly on all to resist sexuality, any woman raised in this culture will surely concur that she felt the disproportionate burden of celibacy. She is told she does not desire sex like the male, but instead she might succumb to emotional fantasies rather than carnal lust. She might be told women trade sex for love whereas men trade love for access to sex. We could draw any number of extremely concerning conclusions about this transactional view. The woman's desire is dismissed as hysterical in the classical, outdated sense—the woman is at once non-sexual and too sexual, too emotional and too cold. She is both naive and knave, just as Eve was duped by the serpent yet still able to trick Adam.

Second, children's sexuality is configured via discursive labels, often the good boy and the bad boy but always the good girl and the bad girl (or more offensive terms). There's no spectrum of morality just as there's no spectrum of consent in this worldview; instead there's only a line policed by the parent, the minster, or the deity. If one girl has sex, she influences others and must be cast as a threat; she will be labeled, shunned, mocked, and so on. Likewise, turning adolescent sexuality into a pathology means even the most common, early sexual experiences are a threat. The prohibition against masturbation is a microcosm of ingrained power purity culture projects upon subjects who must regulate their own sexuality even if nobody is watching (except for God, who sees all shame). The regulation of children's sexuality does produce limited measurable effects. After all, evidence suggests the abstinence pledge delays the first sexual experience by only a few months. The long-term effect of closely associating sexuality and shame proves more difficult to measure.

The third and fourth results Foucault explored are less confined to contemporary purity culture. Even in mainline Protestantism, it's uncommon for a leader to encourage or clearly condone sex outside of marriage. The taboo operates with different intensities between conservative and

---

26. "Hence the domain we must analyze in the different studies that will follow the present volume is that deployment of sexuality: its formation on the basis of the Christian notion of the flesh, and its development through the four great strategies that were deployed in the nineteenth century: the sexualization of children, the hysterization of women, the specification of the perverted, and the regulation of populations—all strategies that went by way of a family which must be viewed, not as a powerful agency of prohibition, but as a major factor of sexualization." Foucault, *The History of Sexuality*, 114.

liberal faiths, but sexual taboos exist in each. Even though the monogamy ideal is a bit of a farce—rates of divorce and extramarital sex are roughly equal in purity culture and broader culture—it is the cultural fixation (purity) substituting for a more instinctive fixation (sex). Once the substitute fixation activates, contrary impulses must be repressed.[27] Of course, the repressed is the true seat of power. It's no exaggeration to suggest the evangelical's campaign against marriage equality or against a sexually permissive culture is directly linked to the repression of sexuality not only prior to marriage but also within. Once marriage fails to be a hedonistic Eden, whoever wasn't duped must be hated or pathologized. This is precisely why we see so many conservatives claiming that Christians have the best or the most sex. The anxious need to make that claim is a symptom speaking an inverted truth.

Finally, if everything is permissible in heterosexual marriage, all sex beyond that boundary must be perverse. The pathologization of LGBT individuals stands out as the clearest example. The fantasy of what a gay person even is has shifted as evangelicals incrementally gave up on labeling an orientation itself as pathological. Instead of saying it is a sin to be gay, they now prefer to label the relationship or its "practice" as sin. They compartmentalize sexuality as a non-essential aspect of a person, or they assume people do not inevitably have sex. The believer will ensure you she is no bigot, for she is only repeating God's word—you can blame God, if you like.

Foucault credits the recognition of sexual orientation to Carl Westphal's description of "contrary sexual sensations" in 1870. Medical literature followed suit and labeled the gay person an "invert." It wasn't until 1946 that the Revised Standard Version became the first English Bible to use the term *homosexual*. There are, of course, only six "clobber passages" in the Hebrew Bible and New Testament that now appear as anti-gay. It should be obvious that the Greek words sometimes translated as *homosexual* (*arsenokoitai* and *malakoi*) couldn't possibly mean the same thing as an orientation that wouldn't be described (in our modern sense) for

27. This is Freud's lesson with the *fort-da* game, wherein his infant grandson played a game to distract himself while his mother was away. The mother was an idealized fixation which the infant associated with the satisfaction of drives (for nourishment, security, etc.). When the idealized fixation was absent, the infant could either (1) express anxiety over her absence or (2) generate a substitute, which is not quite a replacement. The mother's absence was repressed, and the repressed returned as the distracting game played by the infant. Likewise, my claim is that purity ideals operate as substitute fixations covering over dissatisfied drives. See Freud, *The Ego and the Id*.

nearly two millennia. Nevertheless, this isn't obvious to those who unconsciously wish for the Bible to shut down debate or justify their condemnation. The concept of orientation legitimated what had previously been seen as the occasional deviation by an individual who was otherwise (for lack of better words) straight by default. Clearly though, the new term *homosexual* was equally suited for abusive misuse by shameless narcissists who take great joy in exclusion.

A century and a half on from the discovery of sexual orientations, it's still troublingly common for parents to abuse their children with gay conversion therapy. The practice proliferated over the course of the twentieth century, and it's progressed from a clinical setting to torturous retreats or camps to which children are sent. For most of the twentieth century, conversion therapy was the purview of the reactionary psychologist in the clinic. Conversion therapy took a turn between the seventies and early aughts. The National Association for Research and Therapy of Homosexuality (NARTH) was founded in 1992. One of its founders claimed he'd cured roughly a third of his thousand gay patients, and he attributed their orientation to an absent father or overbearing mother. Another NARTH cofounder told the *New York Times* he didn't believe anyone was actually gay, but instead, "I believe that all people are heterosexual but that some have a homosexual problem, and some of these people attempt to resolve their conflict by adopting a sociopolitical label called 'gay.'"[28] Prior to NARTH, Exodus International (founded 1976, closed 2013) worked for years to blend evangelical theology with anti-gay pseudo-science. The youth camps portrayed themselves as an improvement on the old methods of reparative therapy, which often meant electrocution or lobotomies. Known colloquially as "pray away the gay" ministries, in reality these organizations often resolved to physical torture in addition to psychological. One such organization which hosts retreats for men, Journey into Manhood (founded 2000, now rebranded as Brothers Road), includes a testimonial from its founder, Rich Wyler. He wrote of entering "reparative therapy" in 1997 and attributed his orientation to "a lifetime of perceived rejection from men." Consistent with the emerging stereotypes of bullying or poor parenting as the cause, Wyler insisted, "the anger spilled out of me: anger at my father for being emotionally checked out of my life; rage at Mike the Bully for his constant ridicule of me in high school; rage at my mother for shaming me

28. Eckholm, "'Ex-Gay' Men Fight Back Against View That Homosexuality Can't Be Changed."

over my maleness; hurt that I had been carrying around inside of me my whole life, where it could continue to attack me from within."[29] Recent laws in several states ban the practice, and physicians and psychologists have been vocal about its detrimental effects.

Even so, conversion therapy is currently legal in thirty-six states. The UCLA Williams Institute estimates 698,000 LGBT adults in the United States have suffered conversion therapy. Some 350,000 went through this process as an adolescent.[30] This is how pathologization networks with fantasy. Multiple fantasies interconnect to support abuse: sexual orientation can and should be altered, the post-1946 Bible does not approve, and God's desire outweighs the child's mental and physical health. As sexual orientation and gender identity ever so slowly gained more mainstream acceptance, any opportunity for heteropatriarchy became the conservative's line in the sand. Recall the conflation of gay men and Communism in the McCarthy hearings. Recall the Stonewall Riots, which occurred within the timeframe of the sexual revolution and consequent conservative panic in the sixties. Recall reaction against reproductive rights at the end of the seventies. Recall the cruel indifference to a deadly epidemic during the Reagan administration, against which groups like ACT UP literally fought for their lives in the eighties. Among the Christian Right, there was no effort to understand but only to oppose. Turning a child into a pathology to be treated required parents who already and unwittingly submitted their own sexual desire to disciplinary regimes. It was easier to torment their child than to question their own baggage.

Sadism and masochism work in tragic tandem. Doesn't the policing of one's innermost private thoughts and experiences work along the lines of Foucault's lesson on panopticon? The panopticon devised by Jeremy Bentham was a prison organized as a circular ring of cells stacked atop each other. A guard tower stood at the center. Each cell had a window facing the outside world, from which light entered to fully illuminate the cell, and another barred window facing the guard tower. The prisoner would see neither his right nor left neighbor but only the guard. Venetian blinds on the guard tower would prevent the prisoner from knowing at any moment whether he would be watched next. The whole apparatus rendered power visible but unverifiable; the prisoner could see the guard tower but never

29. Wyler, "A Change of Heart."

30. The Williams Institute, "More than 20,000 LGBT Teens in the US Will Be Subjected to Conversion Therapy."

know whether he was under surveillance. "[The prisoner] is seen, but he does not see; he is the object of information, never a subject in communication," Foucault writes, because "invisibility is a guarantee of order."[31] The design makes escape more difficult, but what's more interesting is that it creates a prisoner who no longer even tries to escape. Panopticon aims "to induce in the inmate a state of conscious and permanent visibility that assures the automatic functioning of power."[32] Panopticon is not only for prisoners, Foucault is careful to note—it is for the madman, the worker, the patient, and the schoolboy.[33]

The software monitoring pornographic viewing habits is panopticon. The user is seen but never sees. He can't know whether his transgression will be caught. He is the early prisoner in the panopticon who hasn't yet given up. The later stage of panoptico, wherein the subject self-represses, is the ultimate aim of purity culture. However, since sexuality is never contained and repression always returns, there is no perfect subject who perfectly accords him or herself to the taboos. There are always transgressions that produce shame. Shame is the affective and effective technology of the purity panopticon.

Shame is not quite guilt. To the psychoanalyst, guilt is a debt to the Other. If feeling guilt, I believe I've transgressed. If feeling shame, I fear I can't be redeemed. The catch is that guilt is guaranteed in conservative Christianity. All are guilty before God, all forgiven by God. Or, all are already guilty and the chosen are already forgiven. Recall from the first chapter our lesson from Joan Copjec, who said, "In shame, unlike guilt, one experiences one's visibility, but there is no external Other who sees, since shame is proof that the Other does not exist."[34] Shame doesn't seek to redeem itself. We prefer guilt to shame, since guilt at least tells us where we stand.

---

31. Foucault, *Discipline and Punish*, 200.

32. Ibid., 201.

33. Even if his ideal prison was never built, Bentham's true target was always the pauper. If the prison could be turned into a convict-run factory, then why not turn out the poor for the same purpose. The result was the Industry-House. One schematic planed five stories divided into twelve sections. Hundreds of industry houses were proposed, and Bentham saw them as a repository for the out-of-work poor, the seasonally unemployed, those cast out of work due to machinery, and so on. Whether we are talking about the prison, the Industry-House, or sexuality, panopticon makes a perfectly repressive situation of each. For more on Bentham's use of panopticon in industry, see chapter 9 of Polanyi, *The Great Transformation*.

34. Copjec, *Imagine There's No Woman*, 127.

Performativity in the Myth of the Eternal Feminine and the Full Quiver

Rather than being something one is born into, gender is a role we perform. "[G]ender is always a doing, though not a doing by a subject who might be said to preexist the deed."[35] This was Judith Butler's lesson. Gender is a masquerade in which woman is expected to play a part for man's desire at the cost of her own.[36]

> In other words, acts, gestures, and desire produce the effect of an internal core or substance but produce this *on the surface* of the body, through the play of signifying absences that suggest, but never reveal, the organizing principle of identity as a cause. Such acts, gestures, enactments, generally construed, are *performative* in the sense that the essence or identity that they otherwise purport to express are *fabrications* manufactured and sustained through corporeal signs and other discursive means. That the gendered body is performative suggests that it has no ontological status apart from the various acts which constitute its reality. This also suggests that if that reality is fabricated as an interior essence, that very interiority is an effect and function of a decidedly public and social discourse, the public regulation of fantasy through the surface politics of the body, the gender border control that differentiates inner from outer, and so institutes the "integrity" of the subject.[37]

Butler traced her concept of performativity to how we become subjects before the law. The force of law requires us to act in certain ways, defer or submit to authority, and so on. Performance before law, like performance of gender, is not innate but rather a ritual.[38] Sexuality is one of many performative aspects

35. Butler, *Gender Trouble*, 34.

36. Ibid., 64.

37. Ibid., 185.

38. While reflecting on her innovative notion of gender performativity in her new preface, Butler explained the origin of the idea. "I originally took my clue on how to read the performativity of gender from Jacques Derrida's reading of Kafka's 'Before the Law.' There the one who waits for the law, sits before the door of the law, attributes a certain force to the law for which one waits. The anticipation of an authoritative disclosure of meaning is the means by which that authority is attributed and installed: the anticipation conjures its object. I wondered whether we do not labor under a similar expectation concerning gender, that it operates as an interior essence that might be disclosed, an expectation that ends up producing the very phenomenon that it anticipates. In the first instance, then, the performativity of gender revolves around this metalepsis, the way in which the anticipation of a gendered essence produces that which it posits as outside

of gender, so exploring a disposition "against sexuality" requires us to also think about how heteropatriarchy inscribes its demands in sexual or gender roles alike. What counts as a good or bad performance is constantly shifting and mutating in new directions. The expected performance of gender at any moment is an orthodoxy, and a deviation is a heresy. Heresies of today might be orthodoxies tomorrow and vice versa.

When members of one group ask for equality, another group de-historicizes the conflict and retroactively proclaims the plea for equality as a type of special treatment. It seems the refusal to listen is a defense deployed by one who fears he'll discover his sins. When structural patriarchy rises to the level of conscious misogyny, various slurs erupt from the heterosexist who feels a woman isn't performing gender properly. Of course, the libidinal charge against equality rises in equal proportion to the insecurity triggered among men swimming in repressed feelings of inadequacy. Recently, the "involuntarily celibate" or "incel" is the pathetic example of how this mixture of fantasy and sexual insecurity or inadequacy turns into aggression. He feels rage at himself, then displaces the rage, and finally vocalizes a crude version of: you aren't performing your gender the way I demand. It's worth looking at one of the best, early explanations of this pattern.

She wrote several decades before the evangelicals we've covered, yet clearly she was still a century or two ahead of them in thought. In *The Second Sex* (1949), Simone de Beauvoir named the fantasy right away: the *eternal feminine*.[39] The misogynist's notion that woman was always a certain way (up until the pesky feminist liberation) worked precisely the same way as the

---

itself. Secondly, performativity is not a singular act, but a repetition and a ritual, which achieves its effects through its naturalization in the context of a body, understood, in part, as a culturally sustained temporal duration." Ibid., xv.

39. See Beauvoir, *The Second Sex*, xxix. Beauvoir explains her use of the term at length in her chapter "Myth and Reality," where she tells us: "There are different kinds of myths. This one, the myth of woman, sublimating an immutable aspect of the human condition—namely, the 'division' of humanity into two classes of individuals—is a static myth. It projects into the realm of Platonic ideas a reality that is directly experienced or is conceptualized on a basis of experience; in place of fact, value, significance, knowledge, empirical law, it substitutes a transcendental Idea, timeless, unchangeable, necessary. This idea is indisputable because it is beyond the given: it is endowed with absolute truth. Thus, as against the dispersed, contingent, and multiple existences of actual women, mythical thought opposes Eternal Feminine, unique and changeless. If the definition provided for this concept is contradicted by the behavior of flesh-and-blood women, it is the latter who are wrong: we are told not that Femininity is a false entity, but that the women concerned are not Feminine." Ibid., 253.

racist's notion of a "black soul" or "Jewish character."[40] The label projected and essentialized in the object-person something that only existed in the feelings of the bigot. Just as the anti-Semite tells us there is simply a way that Jewish people are, or just as the white person suggests society is fair to all those who work hard, the misogynist tells us women have a traditional manner of speech, a modest form of dress, a role in the home, a less-sexual desire, or a happiness in submission. While it's less and less common for racial bigotry to justify itself with appeals to so-called race science today, woman is still assailed by appeals to biology. Beauvoir laments that women:

> . . . have no past, no history, no religion of their own; and they have no such solidarity of work and interest as that of the proletariate . . . They live dispersed among the males, attached through residence, housework, economic condition, and social standing to certain men—fathers or husbands—more firmly than they are to other women. If they belong to the bourgeoisie, they feel solidarity with men of that class, not with proletarian women; if they are white, their allegiance is to white men, not to [black] women.[41]

She tells a story of a male writer who ignored her, saying, "You think thus and so because you are a woman." Beauvoir wanted to live in a world where it was socially acceptable to reply with the truth: "And you think the contrary because you are a man."[42] The same theme appeared when a man insisted every woman entering medicine or law robbed a man of a job. She retorted, "the most mediocre of males feels himself a demigod as compared with women."[43] Comedian Hannah Gadsby brilliantly described the misogynist as hating that which they desire.[44] This is precisely how fetishism works. It's the lesson Beauvoir explored when claiming (in a Hegelian sense) man sees himself as the default Subject, Self, or Absolute, while woman is the Other.[45] She recalled the old Aristotelian thinking of

40. Ibid., xxix.

41. Ibid., xxv.

42. Ibid., xxi.

43. Ibid., xxx.

44. "Is misogyny a mental illness? Yeah. Yeah, it is! Especially if you're a heterosexual man. Because if you hate what you desire, do you know what that is? Fucking tense! Sort your shit out." Gadsby, *Nanette*.

45. Throughout her life, woman was the Other and man is the Subject. Just as villagers see the newcomer as an outsider, so men see the woman as the Other. But Beauvoir's most prescient observation for today might be her distinction between abstract and existing equalities. As she writes, "For him she is sex—absolute sex, no less. She is

Thomas Aquinas in which woman wasn't her own gender but instead incidental or "imperfect man."[46] Rather than being unique, the female was a lack of qualities. In the old view, woman didn't even contribute to the traits of her offspring; the man planted the seed, and the womb incubated. Men want egalitarianism in the abstract, but the moment inequalities are named any number of excuses—religious, philosophical, scientific, etc.—rise against actual equality.[47] When equality doesn't feel like a threat, even the misogynist is on board. When his position is threatened, he will reveal himself and start off by saying "Actually . . ."[48]

"One is not born, but rather becomes, a woman."[49] This famous line from Beauvoir about the indoctrination of the young girl drove so many consequent observations. We could turn to Mary Daly's observation "if God is male, the male is God,"[50] or Judith Butler's "If one 'is' a woman, that is surely not all one is."[51] If she's becoming woman within the patriarchal field, she's learning the desires of patriarchy. Is this not Beauvoir's implication when she says that the goal should not be happiness but liberation? Let's examine the *eternal feminine* intertwined with complementarian and Quiverfull thought, which display the way white evangelicalism feels gender should be performed.

---

defined and differentiated with reference to man and not he with reference to her; she is the incidental, the inessential as opposed to the essential. He is the Subject, he is the Absolute—she is the Other." Beauvoir, *The Second Sex*, xxii.

46. Ibid.

47. "In proving woman's inferiority, the antifeminists then began to draw not only upon religion, philosophy, and theology, as before, but also upon science—biology, experimental psychology, etc. At most they were willing to grant 'equality in difference' to the *other* sex." Ibid., xxix.

48. "When he is in a co-operative and benevolent relation with woman, his theme is the principle of abstract equality, and he does not base his attitude upon such inequality as may exist. But when he is in conflict with her, the situation is reversed: his theme will be the existing inequality, and he will even take it as justification for denying abstract equality." Ibid., xxxii.

49. Ibid., 267.

50. See chapter 1 of Daly, *Beyond God the Father*.

51. "If one 'is' a woman, that is surely not all one is; the term fails to be exhaustive, not because a pregendered 'person' transcends the specific paraphernalia of its gender, but because gender is not always constituted coherently or consistently in different historical contexts, and because gender intersects with racial, class, ethnic, sexual, and regional modalities of discursively constituted identities. As a result, it becomes impossible to separate out 'gender' from the political and cultural intersections in which it is invariably produced and maintained." Butler, *Gender Trouble*, 4–5.

If egalitarians think genders should be equal, complementarians think genders should maintain distinct roles. They ascribe those roles to the Bible, but in fact the roles seem to mimic a stereotype of the mid-twentieth-century white American family.[52] Complementarians feel the erasure of gender roles leads down a detrimental path for both. They emphasize man as a heroic figure and woman as a "helpmeet."[53] Man is the warrior and provider. Woman the keeper of the house. Man leads, and woman assists. From a New Testament verse prohibiting women from speaking or teaching in church, complementarians draw severe limits on women in ministerial leadership today. Though the Bible does not extend the prohibition of leadership to governance (indeed, the Bible has counterexamples of women in civil leadership), the prohibition of leadership underwrites skepticism of female politicians in the United States today.

As a leading figure in complementarian thought, Calvinist theologian John Piper couched his defense of the doctrine in concern for women. "[C]omplementarians acknowledge and lament the history of abuses of women personally and systemically, and the present evils globally and locally in the exploitation and diminishing of women and girls," said Piper, and, "complementarians lament the feminist and egalitarian impulses that minimize God-given differences between men and women and dismantle the order God has designed for the flourishing of our life together." The problems are the "impulses of a sex-blind, gender-leveling, unisex culture."[54]

In his view, woman is a seditious trickster. She might influence her children to view women as equals, so the husband must carefully raise children in "the instruction of the Lord." Here again we see Beauvoir's opposition between the Other and the Absolute Subject, though for Piper, the Absolute position can be God or the husband. Feminism oppresses women by tricking them into becoming masculine. Feminism makes men dysfunctional by obfuscating roles. In short, the role of the woman is to submit. There aren't two or more legitimate views but instead only God's viewpoint and the sinful viewpoint. In fact, if a woman holds egalitarian views but still submits to her husband, complementarians say she's a dangerous hypocrite. It's not enough

52. I say selectively, because complementarians do not expect women to follow Genesis's example of Sarah calling Abraham "master," nor do they require women who are assaulted to follow Levitical rules for marrying the assailant. Actually subscribing to their supposed values would make such submission impossibly unrealistic.

53. This term draws on the wording of Genesis 2:18 in the King James Version along with the interpretation of Eve as one presented to aid Adam's governance of the garden.

54. Piper, "God Created Man Male and Female."

to submit in act. In an Orwellian sense, she must be thoroughly convinced in her own mind in order to avoid God's wrath.

The Quiverfull movement takes complementarianism up a notch and shows how gender must be performed. We briefly discussed the movement's entanglement with homeschooling, but the familial and sexual panopticon as well as the fantasy of combat against secular pluralism are worth considering here. The wife must convince herself she enjoys submitting to the husband, and the husband justifies domination by saying he submits to Christ. The children see it all as normal. The key feature of the Quiverfull movement is the rejection of contraception.

In the late seventies, a self-proclaimed radical feminist converted to evangelicalism and soon became a figurehead for anti-feminism. Sometimes called the "queen of homeschooling," Mary Pride was never as widely recognized as the conservative activist Phyllis Schlafly but was remarkably influential within a niche, ideological market. In 1985, Pride published *The Way Home: Beyond Feminism, Back to Reality,* arguing that women flourished in the home under the authority of their husbands. "Christians have accepted feminists' 'moderate' demands for family planning and careers while rejecting the 'radical' side of feminism—meaning lesbianism and abortion," she wrote. "What most do not see is that one demand leads to the other. *Feminism is a totally self-consistent system aimed at rejecting God's role for* woman . . . And those who pick up its philosophy are buying themselves a one-way ticket to social anarchy."[55] Childbearing was among the highest of virtues. Pride armed herself with Scripture, and it was her use of Psalm 127:3–5 which would deliver a new name to the anti-contraception movement: "Children are a heritage from the Lord, offspring a reward from him. Like arrows in the hands of a warrior are children born in one's youth. Blessed is the man whose quiver is full of them. They will not be put to shame when they contend with their opponents in court."[56] On a single page, Pride would seamlessly connect the terms *pederasty, homosexuality, divorce, life-style, careerism,* and *the moral safety of the child.*[57] In turn, each of these were extensions of sex-positive philosophies infiltrating the church: "*The new evangelical perspective on sex is an unwitting denial of God's basic plan for marriage and leads directly into role obliteration.*"[58] The

---

55. Pride, *The Way Home,* xi–xii.

56. Ps 127:3–5 (NIV).

57. See for example, Pride, *The Way Home,* 11.

58. Ibid., 25.

roles fell apart with birth control, which contravened God's instruction in Genesis to be fruitful and multiple. The quiver played several parts. It's a womb but also an armory.

Who would dare bar from the world the young souls with which God shall bless us? In *A Full Quiver: Family Planning and the Lordship of Christ* (1990), Rick and Jan Hess likened the individual using contraception to one who'd reject God's offer of wealth or good health. It's not only ill-advised but a rejection of God's Word. Infertility is an "empty quiver" that can be fixed with prayer. Others likened contraception to a demonic trick or rebellion. Like many evangelical movements especially after the advent of dispersed, online self-radicalization, the decentralized movement's size and scope of influence is difficult to gauge. However, there's a wide variety of resources proselytizing for those who wish to self-radicalize. Print literature, websites, and organizations foster the idea that contraception is not only rebellion against God's will to life but, moreover, surrendering amidst spiritual warfare. To out-reproduce all other faiths is to win—at least on the assumption that the poor children won't turn apostate.

The enjoyment of submission is what makes this still-small movement a vignette for broader evangelical ideology. Pride rallied around the battle cry, "My body is *not* my own."[59] It's a desire to be caught up in a greater cause—the greatest cause. In a profile of the Quiverfull movement, journalist Kathryn Joyce described adherents as "domestic warriors in the battle against what they see as forty years of destruction wrought by women's liberation: contraception, women's careers, abortion, divorce, homosexuality and child abuse, in that order."[60] The desire for submission is a recurrent theme for the women profiled, such as when one mother called for a "return to patriarchy, to father-led families" before insisting, "Patriarchy may be a loaded word for some, but it's not for me." Pride herself likened spiritual submission to a military ideal, and military terminology remains common. Quiverfull families are cells, Christ is the commander in chief, the husband a lower commander, and the wife a private following him into battle. A Quiverfull mother of nine children called the home a battle station. As a strategic zone, the home exceeds the tactical power of canvassing for right-wing candidates. Fittingly, the children are not agents but instead ammunition. They are the arrows of the quiver flying to strike the enemy.

59. Ibid., 57.
60. Joyce, "Arrows for the War."

Enemy targets are nebulous in many cases. The movement finds no trouble in labeling feminism, secularism, and liberalism as enemies, but its emphasis on out-reproducing barely conceals racial or ethnocentric aims. They're not trying to out-reproduce liberal Christians (an oxymoron for the Quiverfull believer) so much as they're trying to stave off in America the demographic shifts seen in Europe. The Muslim or Arab immigrant in Europe is a warning for America's future. Reagan's "welfare queen"[61] comes to mind as an inverted ideal for the Quiverfull mother. Bearing so many children without the necessary financial resources is not wrong so long as the child is produced for the white, conservative, heteronormative, and Protestant cause.

From the moment the Anglican Church authorized contraception at the 1930 Lambeth Conference, Quiverfull writer Rachel Scott claimed, the United States entered a seventy-year battle for the soul of this nation which ended with the reckoning of 9/11. Just as Jerry Falwell pinned blame on "the pagans, and the abortionists, and the feminists, and the gays and the lesbians," Quiverfull pinned it on birth control. The catastrophe was a pivotal moment in this procreative-militarist group, for 9/11 reanimated the biblical accounts of Assyrian and Babylonian invasion as a catastrophe God must use to call a people back to faith. They see only three options for how this all ends. First, secularism might decrease childbirth so much that the Arab or black other could destroy America. Second, Christians might out-reproduce everyone and create a homogenous, theocratic heaven on earth. Or third, Christ might cut the whole Earth experiment short with an apocalypse. There's no fourth option, and either of the latter two should suit this movement. The fantasies of submission and domination, myths of masculinity and the eternal feminine, sexuality, violence, and gender performance all overlap. If the man is the commander, the home and the woman a battle station, and children the ammunition, then we have arrived at a troublingly simple formula: heterosexuality is a weapon.

---

61. On his 1976 campaign trail, Reagan began invoking the welfare queen figure as a way to evoke anti-black sentiments without explicitly mentioning color. Reagan's famous example in a campaign speech described one particular case of fraud and let the audience's imagination do the rest: "In Chicago, they found a woman who holds the record. She used 80 names, 30 addresses, 15 telephone numbers to collect food stamps, Social Security, veterans' benefits for four nonexistent deceased veteran husbands, as well as welfare. Her tax-free cash income alone has been running $150,000 a year." ("'Welfare Queen.'")

Shock and Aftershocks

Resistance to birth control is another metonymic cause for this purity ideal. It taps into fears and fantasies about a world that changed after the sexual revolution. Our data suggests sex changed much less than our openness to speaking about sex. However, in purity fantasies it wasn't our way of speaking but instead reality itself that changed so dramatically. In this fantasy, the Stonewall riots were not the expression of a desire for equal treatment but the beginning of an identity politics demanding special treatment. Feminism was not egalitarian but authoritarian. Sex education in schools, contraception, no fault divorce, same-sex marriage, and online dating are all seen as part of a decadent culture in decline. Nietzsche's view of Christianity's decadence returns with a vengeance here, for it is not too little Christian morality that leads to the death of God, as conservatives imagine, but instead too much.[62]

How could we possibly reach the point where sexually active persons rejoice over the deprivation of contraception? What type of fantasies justify this desire? After the Supreme Court decided *Burwell v. Hobby Lobby Stores, Inc.* (2014) in favor of the latter, closely held corporations were not required to provide no-cost contraception to female employees. The ruling found that such a requirement stipulated by the Department of Health and Human Services violated the Religious Freedom Restoration Act (1993). The act prohibited "Government [from] substantially burden[ing] a person's exercise of religion"[63] unless the state can demonstrate a compelling governmental interest in doing so. Even then, government could only impose this burden if it were the least restrictive means of securing a state interest. Of the nine Justices on the Court, five agreed that Hobby Lobby's rights (the religious rights of a closely held *corporation*) had been violated, which reflected not only the partisan split on the court but also a broader cultural split on the ethics or desirability of birth control.

Two-thirds of women of reproductive age use contraception at any given moment,[64] so if not for patriarchy one might think its availability

---

62. "Unconditional honest atheism (and it is the only air we breathe, we more spiritual men of this age!) is therefore *not* the antithesis of that ideal ... it is rather only one of the latest phases of its evolution, one of its terminal forms and inner consequences—it is the awe-inspiring *catastrophe* of two thousand years of training in truthfulness that finally forbids itself the *lie involved in belief in God.*" Nietzsche, *On the Genealogy of Morals,* 160.

63. As quoted in *Burwell v. Hobby Lobby Stores, Inc.,* 573 U.S. ___ (2014).

64. Jones, Mosher, and Daniels, "Current Contraceptive Use in the United States."

would be less controversial. The 2010 Affordable Care Act left too much of the decision-making power around no-cost contraception to the Department of Health and Human Services, rendering its birth control mandate vulnerable to future administrations with alternative aims. DHHS took a broad approach to decrease the out-of-pocket costs, but birth control, particularly Plan B and IUDs, had become politically contested as abortifacients by the pro-life movement. In this fantasy, certain types of contraception could be synonymous with mass murder. If we take a longer view of contraception, it looks less and less like a concern over fetal rights and more a constant reaction to other reactions.

The Food and Drug Administration approved the pill for contraceptive use in 1960, and access expanded to all fifty states after the Supreme Court's ruling in *Griswold v. Connecticut* (1965). At least, married women had a right to birth control—unmarried women wouldn't be granted the same right for seven more years. To challenge a nineteenth century law banning use or distribution of contraceptives, Planned Parenthood League of Connecticut executive director Estelle Griswold (following the work of earlier activists such as Margaret Sanger) opened a clinic and was arrested for her activities. Her defense before the court was telling at the time. She argued the state was violating a right to privacy, a right which reappeared in *Roe v. Wade* (1973). Between *Griswold* and *Roe* was the 1967 Summer of Love. Just in the four years before *Roe*, the percentage of Americans who believed extramarital sex was "not wrong" doubled to nearly half the population.[65] The more open sexual culture, the successes of second wave feminist thought, the growing acceptance of women in the workplace, the rise in divorce rates—all of these served to create a sense of cultural motion which might be stopped by an actor-turned-president and his religious affiliates.

Political scientists Robert Putnam and David Campbell conceptualized the current disassociation from organized religion among the "nones" as a second aftershock. The initial shock of the sexual revolution in the sixties and seventies created fertile space for the initial aftershock of the eighties and nineties. Even the youth grew more conservative in the first

---

65. "The best evidence is that the fraction of all Americans believing that premarital sex was 'not wrong' doubled from 24 percent to 47 percent in the four years between 1969 and 1973 and then drifted upward through the 1970s to 62 percent in 1982. Relevant surveys prior to 1969 are even rarer—silent testimony to how uncontested the norm of premarital chastity was in the 1950s—but scattered evidence suggests that virtually all the change in the norm came in one burst of liberation in the late 1960s and early 1970s." Putnam and Campbell, *American Grace*, 92–93.

aftershock.[66] The Religious Right saw itself tasked by God with the preservation of family values, and conservatism—ever more successful when it finds itself embattled—was lucky to find its new enemy in Clintonian liberalism after the fall of the Berlin Wall. By the nineties, more than a decade had solidified the Republican-evangelical alliance. Purity culture, abstinence pledges, homeschooling and private schools, and the increasingly sophisticated media of the Christian industrial complex were adjuncts of the coalition. It was indeed a backlash to liberation. Its cultural enemies were the devil that the movement needed to survive. What the coalition didn't foresee was the inevitable result of its success. Out of fear their children would succumb to secular culture, late Boomer and Gen X evangelical parents pushed an overdetermined religiousness that would drive a second backlash. This is what Putnam and Campbell called the second aftershock of Millennial disaffiliation. In the fifties, nearly all Americans reported an affiliation with a specific faith.[67] In record numbers their Millennial grandchildren would leave the faith altogether.

The superego prohibits desire, and then the prohibition generates desire. In the same way a parent's command "Don't reach for the cookie jar" generates the child's interest, repressive injunctions return in a different guise. Purity culture was designed to think of sex and little else, and sex was tied up in odd notions of reward, righteousness, roles, and warfare. Purity culture cannot teach consent, for consent would prepare the adolescent to break God's rules, but it surely teaches shame and aggression. The aggression is born of petty, substitute enjoyment and the sense that they've missed out. It's a culture of resentment and enjoyment.

66. "On homosexuality, abortion, and marijuana, as the Sixties receded in the rearview mirror, views among younger Americans in the 1970s and 1980s actually moved in a conservative direction. Among eighteen to twenty-nine-year-olds the view that homosexuality was 'always wrong' rose from 62 percent in 1974 to 79 percent in 1987, and opposition to legalization of marijuana rose from 50 percent in 1976 to 80 percent in 1990." Ibid., 117.

67. "Historically, whatever their degree of religiosity, almost all Americans have identified with one religion or another. In response to standard questions in the 1950s about 'what is your religious preference?' roughly 95–97 percent responded either with a specific denomination (Methodist, Baptist, and so forth) or with a religious tradition (Christian, Jewish, etc.). Only a very small fraction responded by saying 'none' or 'nothing in particular.' The shock of the long Sixties had increased the national incidence of nones from about 5 percent to about 7 percent, and it remained virtually unchanged until the early 1990s." Ibid.,122.

It produced adherents who do not, in fact, adhere. This is the power of fantasy—nobody truly buys it, but all will suffer.

4

Against Reality

The Persecution Complex, Media, and Propaganda

"In an ever-changing, incomprehensible world the masses had reached the point where they would, at the same time, believe everything and nothing, think that everything was possible and that nothing was true."

—HANNAH ARENDT

"It would not be impossible to prove with sufficient repetition and a psychological understanding of the people concerned that a square is in fact a circle. They are mere words, and words can be molded until they clothe ideas and disguise."

—JOSEPH GOEBBELS

Martyrs

The book opened with several definitions of martyr tailored to a Christian audience before claiming: "It is said that there are more Christian martyrs today than there were in 100 AD—in the days of the Roman Empire . . . An estimated 164,000 will be martyred in 1999."[1] The number depended on readers finding it plausible that someone was martyred for their faith every three minutes. This was the introduction to the book *Jesus Freaks* (1999), collaboratively written by Christian music trio DC Talk and advocacy group The Voice of Martyrs. Modeled on John Foxe's book of martyrs, *Jesus Freaks* collected ancient and modern tales in a

---

1. DC Talk and The Voice of Martyrs, *Jesus Freaks*, 15.

package designed for youth consumption. The book followed the audacious estimate above with this tale.

> She was 17 years old. He stood glaring at her, his weapon before her face.
>
> "Do you believe in God?"
>
> She paused. It was a life-or-death question. "Yes, I believe in God."
>
> "Why?" asked her executioner. But he never gave her the chance to respond.
>
> The teenage girl lay dead at his feet.
>
> *This scene could have happened in the Roman coliseum. It could have happened in the Middle Ages. And it could have happened in any number of countries around the world today. People are being imprisoned, tortured, and killed every day because they refuse to deny the name of Jesus.*
> *This particular story, though, did not happen in ancient times, nor in Vietnam, Pakistan, or Romania. It happened at Columbine High school in Littleton, Colorado, on April 20, 1999.*
> *Do you believe in Jesus?*[2]

The story fell into doubt too late for retraction. The girl to which the authors refer was Cassie Bernall, though a similar story was told of another student victim, Rachel Joy Scott. One victim, Valeen Schnurr, did answer that she believed in God after she was shot, and she survived her wounds. Eyewitnesses at the Columbine massacre suggested Bernall's death followed a different exchange. In this callous version, Bernall hid under a table in the school's library until one of the assailants found her, shouted "Peekaboo," and shot without querying her faith.[3] But the image of the martyr took root quickly. By year's end, Bernall's story was canonized in *Jesus Freaks* and the award-winning Michael W. Smith song "This Is Your Time." Her martyrdom was retold in sermons across the globe as an exemplar of faith in the face of ultimate consequence. Nearly two decades later, the Christian film studio Pure Flix would present a similar story through Scott's death instead in the film *I Am Not Ashamed* (2016). The girls had no say in being used this way. No, their memory was rewritten without their permission. Why

2. Ibid., 17.
3. Wilkinson, "After Columbine."

was martyrdom such an attractive fantasy? Why is the narrative of loss and constant persecution so enjoyable?

When you're powerful, playing the victim justifies aggressiveness. This has been the lesson throughout this book, but it bears repeating: you'd think suffering was something the subject puts up with as the price for sadism, but what if suffering is the goal? The white evangelical imagination we are exploring is first of all narcissistic, a type of perverse trait overlaid atop broadly neurotic subjects.[4] Whereas the obsessional neurotic desires to submit to the desire of the other, the perverse subject desires to *be* the object desired. When the perverse character provokes anxiety in the other, as Lacan said, "It is not so much the other party's suffering that is being sought in the sadistic intention as his anxiety."[5] We see this all the time when the Right delights in "triggering" the other. Freud explored a similar feature in melancholia. The melancholic ego admits guilt and accepts punishment."[6] Guilt can arise from the ego or the superego, but guilt usually results from a conflict between the two.[7] Fundamentalism is the religious form of obsessional neurosis, but its doctrinal content and communicative style is perverse (disavowing constantly what it knows to be true, imagining itself as the object of God's desire) or melancholic (submissive to punishment for deserved guilt). It wants an authoritarian ruler, but it wants to submit from the position of the heir to the throne.

To put it all together, the sadism through which this faith ravages the world is the by-product of its unconscious desire to suffer itself. Desire must be constantly invigorated with fantasy, which is why stories of martyrdom are attractive. In the aftermath of Columbine, a Southern Baptist news service reported a student saying, "God has laid it on my heart that I'm going to be martyred. When I told one of my friends, he said, 'That's awesome. I

4. I want to be clear on this, because I'm claiming the expression of sadism is not natural to the white evangelical so much as it is the obverse of the narcissistic desire of seeing itself as the ultimate object of desire. More specifically, it wants to see itself (its righteousness as saved and special subjects) as the object of God's desire. Lacan explained that "to recognize oneself as the object of one's desire is always masochistic." Lacan, *Anxiety*, 107.

5. Ibid., 104.

6. My descriptions of the obsessional and melancholic responses are drawn from Freud, *The Ego and the Id*.

7. The obsessional neurotic experiences guilt when she realizes her superego begins recognizing her id's desire and results to repression. The melancholic's superego, however, identifies with the object of masochism.

wish it could happen to me.'"[8] The student's expression mirrored the New Testament's warning that the righteous will suffer persecution. Consider it pure joy![9] False narratives of persecution are good news, for it confirms what they pretend to believe and yet deeply know to be false.

As a symptom or hint, persecution fantasies are reverse revenge fantasies. The film *God's Not Dead* (2014) expressed this sadomasochism in a travesty of art. The film deployed every imaginable stereotype of atheism. The plot revolved around freshman Josh Wheaton's (no doubt a reference to a famous evangelical college by the same name) confrontation with the professor of an Introduction to Philosophy course. On the first day of class, Professor Radisson listed philosophers across the whiteboard: Bertrand Russell, Albert Camus, David Hume, Michel Foucault, Friedrich Nietzsche, and so on—also Ayn Rand.[10] What did they all have in common? All are atheists, so all students would need to begin the class doing something no college student would ever be asked to do. They were to write "God is dead," or else defend God's existence in classroom trial.[11] Allow me to spoil the ending. After losing his girlfriend (a relationship that began as a student-teacher affair, presumably due to moral relativism), a car struck Professor Radisson. A pastor arrived on the scene to deliver last rites, which in Protestantism is the sinner's prayer. He converted to Christianity only moments before death while lying in the street. The pastor told the dying professor he's lucky, since he's about to know more about God than the pastor knows.

Christopher D. Rodkey introduced the term *reverse revenge fantasy* here to indicate a dynamic interchange: (1) white evangelicalism imagines itself as an underdog, (2) while holding all the power, therefore (3) it

---

8. Rosin, "Columbine Miracle."

9. For example, "In fact, everyone who wants to live a godly life in Christ Jesus will be persecuted," 2 Timothy 3:12 (NIV). See also, "Consider it pure joy, my brothers and sisters, whenever you face trials of many kinds, because you know that the testing of your faith produces perseverance," James 1:2–3 (NIV).

10. Isn't Rand's inclusion in a philosophy course an unfortunate hint that a director knows so little of the field?

11. To me, the scene recalled an experience from childhood verging on a type of social martyrdom fantasy. Beginning in 1990, the event was called "See You At the Pole." The idea was for the Christian students at a school to arrive early to school and gather around the flagpole in prayer for the students, the nation, or whatever. In theory, we were supposed to generate debate or discussion with fellow students who inquired about our peculiar faith. The concept depended on children's direct trust in adults who told them their faith was on the defensive and must transform into a bolder declaration. But what was the adult enjoying by refusing to recognize Christianity's hegemony in the United States?

fantasizes about cruelty in such a way that this cognitive dissonance gets downplayed.[12] The fantasy seeks power while professing faith in a Messiah who said the meek shall inherit the earth. Rodkey argued this film betrays the true desire of the evangelical. Professor Radisson persecuted the student in precisely the same way an evangelical wishes she could persecute a secular professor. Fantasy isn't simply a matter of desiring that the world be such and such a way, for fantasy already includes enjoyment as part of its matrix. Revenge fantasies also drive religio-political dynamics. After all, don't many select a candidate at the ballot box purely for revenge?

Persecution is not always a fantasy. Martyrdom counts many heretics and dissidents among its casualties. Christianity was born in a period of sporadic persecution alluded to in the New Testament and witnessed intermittently. Early on, Tacitus accused Nero (r. 54–68 CE) of persecution, though evidence and its extent is unclear. Persecution was briefly organized in the late Roman period under Decius (r. 249–251 CE) and Diocletian (r. 284–305 CE), but Roman persecution takes an undeservedly outsized space in the Christian imagination. Recall how the opening section of *Jesus Freaks* glossed over a detailed account of persecution and left the reader to fill in the gaps of what is meant by more martyrs today than in the Roman period. Of course, the book's name comes from the title track of DC Talk's Grammy award-winning album *Jesus Freak*. The title song's first verse imagined a shirtless, tattooed street preacher boldly declaring his faith to a city, while the second verse drew a parallel to John the Baptist's crazed look as an itinerant preacher in the wilderness until his beheading. Likening the two figures confers a spiritual authority on the odd figure of the street preacher. The chorus delivered the term linking the two: "What will people think when they hear that I'm a Jesus freak?" The album was one of the most successful works of Christian media in recent decades, which suggests it tapped into a zeitgeist of enjoyment in the persecution fantasy that was entirely fictional.[13]

---

12. Rodkey, "God's Not Dead as Reverse Revenge Fantasy."

13. The premise was a farce, and I'm indebted to Adam Kotsko for this observation. The term "Jesus freak" was deployed for a brief period to describe the charismatic Jesus People, who, disillusioned with excesses of the hippie movement, gained converts on the West Coast in the late 1960s and early 1970s. The movement fizzled by the 1980s, as did the term "Jesus freak." By the time of DC Talk's album, it was not a common pejorative. Kotsko rightly described the redeployment of the term as part of a "fake culture" wishing to believe its outsiderness was the result of a mainstream culture that does not wish to understand evangelicals. See Kotsko, "On Having a Fake Culture."

Evangelicals resuscitated a dormant term to fantasize their oppression under conditions in which they held power. This is the reverse revenge fantasy at work. They created an epithet for themselves. It indirectly lamented the politically correct time in which they lived, a time wherein they were no longer allowed to openly express epithets at minority groups.[14]

Revanchism and Revisionism

A persecution complex justifies violence as if it's preemptive defense. Less than half of white evangelicals say gays and lesbians face much discrimination today.[15] Less than half believe Muslims face discrimination, but more than half feel Christians face discrimination.[16] The same question about discrimination against Christians drew agreement from only four in ten nonwhite Protestants and less than a quarter of unaffiliated Americans. In another study, the question of whether immigrants, African Americans, and gay and lesbian people face discrimination drew agreement from only 40 percent of white evangelicals. In contrast, a mere 8 percent of black

---

14. Incidentally, former DC Talk member Michael Tait stars in *God's Not Dead* with his song of the same name. The chorus lyrics read "My God's not dead, He's surely alive, He's living on the inside, Roaring like a lion." This too works as a disingenuous reclamation of something that was not happening. The song parallels the film's impossible plot (a student would not normally be asked to write "God is dead"), but it also evokes Nietzsche. It does not engage the actual point made by Nietzsche in the parable of the madman, but instead the song reduces Nietzsche's famous phrase to a banal atheism.

15. I draw these numbers from polling conducted in response to the series of "bathroom bills" pushed by Republicans to ostracize transgender people. On that question, 50 percent of white evangelicals support such legislation to mandate people use restrooms corresponding to sex assigned at birth. I actually see that number as lower than one might expect. On the subject of discrimination against gay and lesbian people, "White evangelical Protestants stand out as the only group in which less than a majority (46%) believe gay and lesbian people face a lot of discrimination today. Majorities of white mainline Protestants (52%) and white Catholics (54%) and at least seven in ten nonwhite Protestants (70%), members of non-Christian religious traditions (70%), and unaffiliated Americans (73%) say gay and lesbian people experience a great deal of discrimination in the U.S. today. Opinions about discrimination faced by transgender people follows a similar pattern." Cox and Jones, "Majority of Americans Oppose Transgender Bathroom Restrictions."

16. "White evangelicals are more likely to say Christians face a lot of discrimination than they are to say Muslims face a lot of discrimination (57% vs. 44%, respectively). White evangelicals are the only major religious group in which a majority say Christians face a lot of discrimination." Ibid.

Protestants felt none of these groups face discrimination.[17] More broadly, while nearly six in ten Americans believe African Americans still face a significant amount of discrimination, a third of Republicans agree.[18] This is the embattled view that sees equality as loss.

The persecution complex feeds conservative politics a feast of Nietzschean *ressentiment*. The outrage machine is moral in nature. It's disingenuous in its motives, and its rhetorical demands are so easily abandoned, yes, but it's moral in its presentation. The American Right can barely contain the moral disgust it feels for liberalism, and it shares this moral framework with the Left in a way I find refreshing. What I mean is this: the Right and Left frame their opponents as evil, whereas liberal centrists try to understand everyone's point of view. Liberals want to assume the best as if we all share a common moral framework. What sets the Right apart from the Left is, among other things, the vastly greater power held by the Right. What sets the Right apart from the liberal center is its ability to take a brutally clear moral stance, e.g. in opposition to egalitarian rights. When these two components are combined, we get the outrage machine.

Consider how Fox News, along with organizational steering from the Koch brothers, helped propel the Tea Party onto the national scene after Obama's election. Ten months after the inauguration, radio and FNC character Glenn Beck announced his intention to hold a rally the following year later on the National Mall. The date would be August 28, 2010, which drew no small amount of criticism. A movement animated by disgust at the first black president would hold its rally on the forty-seventh anniversary of Martin Luther King, Jr.'s "I Have a Dream" speech. The name of the event was barely even a dog whistle for those who could imagine Obama as nothing other than corrupt, socialist, Muslim, Kenyan, or un-American. Beck called the event Restoring Honor, a title with clear moral impulse.

By that time, Beck was already a risibly cartoonish figure. His fondness of the blackboard was infamous, playing as he did a professorial character charting conspiracy theories for his voracious audience. Comedians Jon Stewart and Stephen Colbert mocked the Restoring Honor rally by

17. Cox, Lienesch, and Jones, "Who Sees Discrimination?"

18. "Nearly six in ten (57 percent) Americans say blacks face a lot of discrimination in the U.S. today, while 39 percent say they do not. However, fewer than one-third (32 percent) of Republicans believe blacks face a lot of discrimination in society, compared to roughly two-thirds (65 percent) who say they do not. Majorities of political independents (58 percent) and Democrats (77 percent) agree blacks experience a great deal of discrimination." Public Religion Research Institute, "Who Sees Discrimination?"

proposing their own. Stewart announced a plan to hold a Rally to Restore Sanity, while Colbert (in his boisterous, conservative alter-ego) proposed a March to Keep Fear Alive. The eventual event, the Rally to Restore Sanity and/or Fear, was held two days after Restoring Honor and drew at least twice the crowds. However, while the liberal comedy world busied itself with its persistent hallucinations that all was well (if only we could be more civil!), Beck was tapping into a latent rage. It was a rage that swept the House of Representatives in the midterm election around the corner, and the rage mutated into its rational conclusion in Trumpism. Whether its persecution was real or imagined mattered precisely as much as whether the Obama "birther" conspiracy theory was a serious misunderstanding or a joke to swing elections. Such is the true genius of folk conservatism; it always serves at the behest of masters, and yet it chooses to see itself as the last bulwark against power.

The American conservative's protest against reality today is deeply rooted in older trends of white supremacist folk religion. Mistrust of expertise was baked into the distinct form of American Christianity emerging by the late nineteenth century. The Great Awakenings benefitted from and fomented the self-styled theologian who was a man or woman of the people and in no need of denominational authority. The circuit preacher riding from revival to revival across the American South and Northeast was the paragon of decentralized authority. The circuit preacher arrived at a town and announced the tent meeting, the revival gave the town a break from its daily repetition, the offering for the preacher was collected, and the preacher continued to the next town.

Christianity during the Revolutionary war was not the same as that of the post-Civil War period. There's a sect-church-sect pattern to American faith.[19] A movement begins as a splintering sect, evolves into an established denomination, and then begins to modernize. The modernization inevitably draws the ire of traditionalists and produces a gap or vacuum on the Right, out of which a new sect springs. The new sect will generally follow the same pattern of its predecessor. However, the Baptist style of governance has always resisted modernization. The voting rights of each member of a congregation, as well as the high degree of local church autonomy, stymies progress. It is precisely this decentralization of power and authority that create an environment amiable to regressive elements.

19. See Finke and Stark, *The Churching of America, 1776–2005.*

The Southern Baptist Convention, which split off from its northern Baptist coreligionists over the issue of slavery, stands as a prime example of progress-resistant revanchism today while counting itself the largest Protestant denomination in the United States. Likewise, white evangelicalism has no hierarchy adjudicating doctrinal matters, and its people shift effortlessly between churches if the teaching in one location disappoints. In contrast, the Episcopal Church, which emerged as an American Anglican alternative during the Revolutionary War, has a hierarchical structure that provided fertile ground for a groundswell of top-down and bottom-up progressive movement. The progressive Episcopal Church is on the decline with fewer than two million members (in contrast to the SBC's sixteen million). The pattern here is true across faiths, for it's often the most strict or reactionary that draws the largest crowds. Reactionaries might want to turn back the clock, but they do draw the crowds.

At the time of the Revolutionary War, a mere 17 percent of Americans were listed on the membership roles of a church,[20] though certainly a much larger portion of the population was Christian. The majority of Christians were dispersed among two hierarchical groups, the Anglicans and Presbyterians, and one less so, the Congregationalists. The bourgeoisie were often deists while remaining affiliated with traditional denominations. Modern reactionaries like to point to one smug slaveholder from the era as a type of anti-elitist hero, especially for a quote still inscribed into his monument in Washington, DC: "I have sworn upon the altar of God eternal hostility against every form of tyranny over the mind of man." While easily misinterpreted sans context to signal hostility to federal overreach, this quote was about theocracy. The tyranny of which he spoke was that of the Anglican and the Congregationalist who sought to establish a national faith. But it was not this paradox with regard to authority which would so irrevocably shift American Christianity to a more populist agenda. For that we must turn to America's original sin.

Just before the American Civil War, the northern preacher Henry Ward Beecher (1813–1887) called slavery "the most alarming and most fertile cause of national sin,"[21] even as southern ministers preached a po-

---

20. Church membership would rise to 37 percent by the Civil War and 62 percent by the 1980s. Yes, far more Americans were Christian than what is reflected in the membership roles, but perhaps these shifts upward suggest something about the mythic nature of the past projected by those who speak of America's legacy of Christian commitment. See ibid., 22.

21. Beecher, as quoted in Noll, *The Civil War as a Theological Crisis*, 2.

lar opposite message. The Presbyterian minister James Henley Thornwell (1812–1862) insisted God's providence in the emerging civilized world was surely a nod of approval, and he lamented the "fury and bitterness" of abolitionists.[22] He insisted as well, "We cherish the institution not from avarice, but from principle."[23] Others simply pointed to the clear approval of slavery in the text. Historian Mark Noll drew on this hermeneutical conflict, insisting, "In the uncertain days of late 1860 and early 1861, the pulpits of the United States were transformed into instruments of political theology."[24] Today's biblical literalists surely imagine the simplest "What does the plain text say?" hermeneutic is the oldest and truest method of interpretation, but of course this is impossible. Prior to the printing press and rising rates of literacy in the few centuries prior to the war, it wouldn't have made sense to appeal to what the Bible says.

As we saw in chapter 2, the doctrine of perspicuity supposed the Bible was simple enough for comprehension without advanced training in languages or cultural context. Perspicuity was the message of the nineteenth-century circuit preacher as well as the expertise-avoidant faithful today. It's first of all a tool for oppressing, not for reading. The need to justify slavery arrived at a key moment, one in which rising literacy and many Bibles in circulation conjoined with prejudice. Racism disguised itself as a hermeneutic. As Noll explained:

> It was no coincidence that the biblical defense of slavery remained strongest in the United States, a place where democratic, anti-traditional, and individualistic religion was also strongest. By the nineteenth century, it was an axiom of American public thought that free people should read, think, and reason for themselves. When such a populace, committed to republican and democratic principles, was also a Bible-reading populace, the proslavery biblical case never lacked for persuasive resources.[25]

The argument over interpretation erupted into a temporary war of arms, but the legacy of the debate—interpretation as a political weapon—entrenched itself for the long haul.

The post-war period saw another innovation of American Christianity. For the first time, the literature began using phrases like "personal

---

22. Thornwell, "Rights and Duties of Masters," 538.
23. Thornwell, as quoted in Noll, *The Civil War as a Theological Crisis*, 2.
24. Noll, *The Civil War as a Theological Crisis*, 1.
25. Ibid., 34.

relationship with Christ" or "personal savior." Describing Jesus in very personal terms became very popular in the 1970s and 1980s, but it began in the final decades of the nineteenth century.[26] The anti-elitism of Christianity bore a selection of tools useful for an alternate reality: the personalization of faith, the literal reading of the Bible, and the rejection of the trained clerics or scholars. The stage was set for the fundamentalism of the early twentieth century, which would evolve into a more clandestinely hostile (and equally reactionary) evangelicalism by the nineteen twenties and thirties.

White evangelicalism is revanchist—its convictions are repetitions in disguise. It wants to recover what it lost without admitting its aims. Biblical literalism was also the tool defending segregation in the civil rights era, and it would reassert itself again with the Religious Right. Reagan's dog-whistle "welfare queen" wasn't so different from Thornwell's admonition that the slave submit with "cheerful obedience to the lawful commands of his master."[27] The climate denial of the 1990s to present is not different in kind than the nineteenth-century millenarians predicting the apocalypse divined from a biblical timeline. The rejection of the university professor or the "liberal mainstream media" is not so different from the old revival preacher criticizing the clergy's expertise in favor of reading the Bible for oneself. Wishing nonstop for deception, and twisting the human impulse to trust the subject-supposed-to-know, this faith projects its own biases upon the desires of God to make them one and the same.

The Propaganda Machine

Between the invention of writing more than 5,000 years ago and the turn of the twentieth century, the printing press was the greatest revolution in communication. The presses of Europe and Asia gave us the book, the pamphlet, and the newspaper for our information and our deception. The communicative technologies of the twentieth century were qualitatively different. Enter the radio, the television, and the internet. Like the internet, the radio owed its rise to military purposes. Radio experimentation began at the close of the nineteenth century, but its use accelerated drastically

---

26. I originally learned of this through my study of nineteenth-century theological literature, though my claim here is based on an Ngram demonstrating the appearance of these terms in this period. If the reader doubts the novelty of the "personal savior," you need only run various versions of these terms on the Ngram yourself.

27. Thornwell, "Rights and Duties of Masters," 541.

during the First World War. Between the two wars, we learned there was an audience for vitriol over the radio.

During the Great Depression, the Catholic priest Father Charles Coughlin (1891–1979) prefigured the clamor of today's AM political talk. He began his radio career in 1926 with a children's catechism course and soon expanded to sermons for adult audiences. His scope shifted after the 1929 stock market crash, and Coughlin's audience rose to tens of millions as he intertwined the theological, the economic, and the political. He was supportive of President Roosevelt's New Deal at first, but Coughlin's message grew more populist and hostile in the mid-thirties.

His barely coded term *international banksters* gave way to evermore explicit anti-Semitism. Coughlin insisted, "We have lived to see the day that modern Shylocks have grown fat and wealthy, praised and deified, because they have perpetuated the ancient crime of usury under the modern racket of statesmanship." He promoted the militia-style anti-Semitic group Christian Front and its "Buy Christian" message in 1938. By the time he endorsed "America first" nativism in 1941, he was toxic. Coughlin was seen as so anti-Semitic that even the America First Committee (which was rallying against American intervention in Europe) was less than thrilled with the influx of support from his crowd. While Roosevelt's Executive Order 9066 brutally targeted those of Japanese descent for internment camps, Pearl Harbor's attack provided Coughlin the opportunity to ferociously decry the Jews who were tricking the United States into war. Coughlin's anti-Semitism had finally provided long-suspicious government authorities a justification to target him. In 1941, the State Department denied him a passport on the grounds of being a "reported pro-Nazi." The following year, Archbishop Edward Mooney demanded Coughlin retire from his publishing and radio career and focus on his parish duties in Michigan.[28]

Many elements here prefigure the rise of the right-wing radio and television personality today. We see the reactionary nature, the shifting social demands, the anti-Semitism and xenophobia, and the conflation of conservative theology and semi-fascist politics. Above all his audience ate up the fantasy of persecution. Coughlin could have been Rush Limbaugh, Alex Jones, or Jordan Peterson if born a few decades later. Agencies were willing to target an ideologue who'd have free rein today. The Second World War gave the government leeway with the public to crack down on

---

28. Quotes from US Holocaust Memorial Museum, "Charles E. Coughlin."

broadcasts and publications that appeared to rhyme in theme with European anti-Semitic propaganda.

From the post-war period to the 1980s, another factor tampered the excesses of media extremism. The fairness doctrine was eliminated merely nine years before the launch of Fox News. To this day, the possible return of the fairness doctrine is a threat in conservative fantasy and a cure-all in liberal fantasy. The looming danger of news media, with its ability to stir up public opinion against any target, was clear in the Depression. Broadcasters could spin editorials out of thin information until audiences no longer heard a difference between the anchor and the carnival barker. From 1941 to 1949, the Federal Communication Commission relied on the Mayflower Doctrine to mitigate the threat. Initially the Mayflower Doctrine prevented editorialization of the news, but the FCC eventually relaxed enforcement so long as editorialization was matched by another point of view.

Broadcasters and the FCC needed a clearer set of guidelines, thus in 1949 the Mayflower doctrine was replaced by the fairness doctrine. FCC Communication Report's most salient demands were that (1) licensee stations "devote a reasonable percentage of their broadcasting time to the discussion of public issues of interest in the community," and (2) the public should have "a reasonable opportunity to hear different opposing positions on the public issues of interest and importance in the community." The concern was free speech; without balance a broadcast license was just a mouthpiece for special interests. The FCC took a quixotic view of the broadcaster's responsibility to the community at the position's summary, wherein "the licensee is a trustee impressed with the duty of preserving for the public generally radio as a medium of free expression and fair presentation."[29]

If the aim was free speech, the opposition counterattacked on those grounds. The fairness doctrine survived its first serious test after an author named Fred J. Cook published a scathing critique of Republican presidential candidate Barry Goldwater. His book drew the ire of Christian Crusade radio evangelist Billy James Hargis broadcasting out of Red Lion, Pennsylvania. Hargis excoriated Cook, who demanded an opportunity to respond on-air, and the station denied him the opportunity. The FCC sided with Cook, and the case worked its way up the appeals process until *Red Lion Broadcasting Co., Inc. v. FCC* (1969) reached the Supreme Court. The first amendment's free speech provision took center stage in the case in a peculiar way. On the one hand, citizens did not possess a right to radio

---

29. Federal Communications Commission, "Fifteenth Annual Report," 33.

licenses. On the other, licensees had no First Amendment right to present a uniform view. The spirit of the amendment aimed for an informed public, and it was first of all a right of the public, not the broadcaster. Holding that "there is an affirmative obligation of the broadcaster to see that both sides are presented,"[30] the Supreme Court's decision was unanimous in favor of the FCC. The fairness doctrine withstood its first test.

The critics closed in over the decades as the Supreme Court waffled, applying the doctrine to a television station in the sixties but refusing to apply it to a newspaper in the seventies. In 1987 the FCC's four voting members unanimously killed the fairness doctrine. The FCC licenses stations, not networks, so it's difficult to gauge how it might have affected conservative networks like Fox News. Stations certainly benefited by being able to carry FNC without presenting a serious side, and the people certainly lost.[31] Instead of mapping direct results, we can say the doctrine's death was part of a changing legal landscape increasingly lenient to extremists just as they saw themselves increasingly marginalized. Now the persecution fantasy was free to lash out and counterattack.

The loss of the fairness doctrine meant stations needn't fear legal repercussions or take social responsibility. While networks benefited indirectly, other right-wing media voices benefited much more directly. After a four-year stint on a local Sacramento radio station, Rush Limbaugh became the most prominent, early beneficiary of the FCC's decision when his national broadcast of political commentary began the year following the fall of the fairness doctrine. Millions of listeners tune in weekly for his vociferously conservative slant. His programming model demonstrated a rage-mongering potential for the conservative movement. Numerous personalities on radio and internet broadcasts—Hugh Hewitt, Laura Ingraham, Glenn Beck, Sean Hannity, Mark Levin, Michael Savage, and Alex Jones—saw the bombastic style and modulated Limbaugh's style of wit with their own idiosyncrasies of violence, conspiracy theories, and so on. The liberal center

30. *Red Lion Broadcasting Co., Inc. v. FCC*, 395 U.S. 367 (1969).

31. As explained by the FCC, "*We license only individual broadcast stations.* We do not license TV or radio networks (such as CBS, NBC, ABC or Fox) or other organizations with which stations have relationships (such as PBS or NPR), except to the extent that those entities may also be station licensees. We also do not regulate information provided over the Internet, nor do we intervene in private disputes involving broadcast stations or their licensees. Instead, we usually defer to the parties, courts, or other agencies to resolve such disputes." Federal Communications Commission, "The Public and Broadcasting."

and the Left failed in their attempt to replicate the model. Perhaps the most significant example of progressive radio, Air America, folded after a brief run from 2004 to 2010. Many of its contributors—Thom Hartmann, Rachel Maddow, Al Franken, Marc Maron, and even Ron Reagan (son of President Reagan)—went on to various radio, television, and political careers. However, the appetite for a Center Left angle never mirrored the Right.

After decades in the making, the greatest right-wing media success story launched in 1996. What we need to understand about Fox News Channel is that, as an apparatus, it eliminates the need for state media. In theory, state media would switch perspectives if democracy were to shift power back and forth between parties. However rare that is in practice, this doesn't happen at all with privatized propaganda. Even worse, it's designed to be an enclosed news source. With its mesmerizing lights and sounds, a cast of characters chosen to please the prejudices of geriatric whites, and the constant scandal-mongering, it's the trusted voice even if the viewer has access to serious news sources. In an age with more options than ever, an all-encompassing conservative ecosystem negates the advantage of information access. Every story is a crisis reminding every viewer they are persecuted and despised, so they seethe with rage.

The architect was Roger Ailes, and when profiling him, journalist Tim Dickinson summarized his career as an effective operator: "As a political consultant, Ailes repackaged Richard Nixon for television in 1968, papered over Ronald Reagan's budding Alzheimer's in 1984, shamelessly stoked racial fears to elect George H. W. Bush in 1988, and waged a secret campaign on behalf of Big Tobacco to derail health care reform in 1993."[32] Ailes was not yet thirty years old when he boldly told Nixon "the camera doesn't like you." Nixon knew this to be true but lamented, "It's a shame a man has to use gimmicks like this to get elected." His reply to Nixon might as well have been a prophecy of all havoc he wrought upon us from that day in 1967 until his death in 2017. Ailes told the crook: "Television is not a gimmick."[33]

Television is Not a Gimmick

It's absurd to think people want dispassionate information. People desire to see familiar faces and hear words giving coherence to affects. They want feelings verified, and this is what Ailes understood. Republican operative

32. Dickinson, "How Roger Ailes Built the Fox News Fear Factory."

33. McGinniss, *The Selling of the President*, 63.

Lee Atwater once said Ailes had two speeds: "Attack and destroy."[34] When Nixon needed a way around traditional media, Ailes designed a traveling road show that mimicked a legitimate newscast, complete with preselected partisans who'd ask friendly questions.[35] That's how he learned to mimic legitimate news. After a brief hiatus in which he tried his hand as a producer on Broadway, Ailes reentered the political-media field in the seventies with a new right-wing television channel called Television News Inc.[36] It collapsed after only a year, but for that year its motto was "fair and balanced." A frustrated channel director called it a propaganda machine.

By the late eighties, Ailes was the GOP kingmaker. His deep conviction was that politics was emotional. He was right. The infamous "Revolving Door" Willie Horton ad was a perfect example. To sink the campaign of 1988 presidential candidate Michael Dukakis, Ailes ran the blatantly anti-black ad attempting to link Dukakis's record as governor to Horton, who assaulted a couple while released on furlough from prison. The ad originally included a prison scene with multiple black men, and Ailes expertly intuited that so many black men would make the dog whistle to white audiences too obvious—better to focus on only one black male and leave the rest to racist anxiety.

With the end of the Cold War, the conservative-capitalist alliance needed new enemies (real or fantasized) to charge its ranks. In the early nineties, Republican voters were hungry for scandal and fed on a stream of outrage over a centrist, Clintonian "third way" liberalism. The party was on the defensive, and, as political theorist Corey Robin has expertly shown,

34. Stengel, "The Republicans."

35. Dickinson describes the tactic as such: "The 'only hope,' he recalled, 'was to go around the press and go directly to the people'—letting the campaign itself shape the candidate's image for the average voter, 'without it being interpreted for him by a middleman.' To bypass journalists, Ailes made Nixon the star of his own traveling road show—a series of contrived, newslike events that the campaign paid to broadcast in local markets across the country. Nixon would appear on camera in theaters packed with GOP partisans—'an applause machine,' Ailes said, 'that's all that they are.' Then he would field questions from six voters, hand-selected by the campaign, who could be counted on to lob softball queries that played to Nixon's talking points. At the time, Nixon was consciously stoking the anger of white voters aggrieved by the advances of the civil rights movement, and Ailes proved eager to play the race card." Dickinson, "How Roger Ailes Built the Fox News Fear Factory."

36. The outfit generated inexpensive clips for distribution to subscribing stations, but, importantly—brilliantly, even deviously—local stations had no obligation to reveal the source. The local stations were able to cut costs, though the true cost was a public unaware of the explicit biases channeled through their nightly news.

conservatism thrives on the underside of power.[37] "Right now Bill Clinton has 15,000 press secretaries,"[38] said Ailes of the media a decade before Clinton would say the GOP wielded a "destruction machine." To make the media itself an enemy was a stroke of genius in the battle against reality. Around this time, New Corp. CEO Rupert Murdoch was testing the waters for a right-wing counterpart to CNN, which had shown the potential of a news-only network. What was needed was a business model and leadership. The new model was Astroturf: why not generate a built-in audience by paying distributors per subscriber?[39] At the time, Ailes was splitting his time between his work as a tobacco lobbyist, producing for Limbaugh, and heading the CNBC business network when Murdoch sold Ailes on the new venture. In October 1996, America suddenly had access to a channel branding itself as "fair and balanced."

The broadcast content mirrored emotional tactics learned from the Nixon campaign. The figure of the liberal has always served as a punching bag on Fox News programming. The program *Hannity & Colmes* premiered on the network's first day, pairing conservative Sean Hannity with liberal Alan Colmes. Without attention to Colmes's centrism, the ideologues invited as guests, or the topical agenda, the viewer saw only two opposites in a balance.[40] Hannity and Bill O'Reilly, who was also on air from the first day, were always the true id of Fox News. Isn't it much like the old Freudian kettle logic?[41] Fox News is not biased; or it's only biased sometimes; or it's a counter-bias to mainstream media bias. It's an outsider never taken seriously,

---

37. See Robin, *The Reactionary Mind.*

38. Fineman, "Bush."

39. Whereas cable providers typically pay to use a channel, the new Fox News would pay distributors per subscriber. Murdoch's biographer Neil Chenoweth described the pay to play model marvelously when he wrote, "[Murdoch] was prepared to shell out half a billion dollars just to buy a news voice." The audience was built-in. Dickinson, "How Roger Ailes Built the Fox News Fear Factory."

40. Colmes's actual status as a prop was underlined when, after a twelve-year run, the duo's show became *Hannity* in 2009. When pressed, the network has claimed "fair and balanced" only applies to its daytime news shows, not its evening opinion shows. It is all belligerent propaganda, of course, but the excuse works effectively for those who desire their own deception.

41. In the joke, when one man borrows a kettle from the other and returns it with a hole busted in the kettle's base, the owner is upset. The borrower defends himself: *First, the kettle had a hole in it already; second, I gave it back undamaged; third, I never borrowed that kettle.* See Freud, *Jokes and Their Relation to the Unconscious,* 62.

or it's the leader of the ratings pack. It's the dreadnought crushing the enemy fleet or the last, lonely soldier bravely facing the onslaught.

The viewer needs to identify with the duplicity and deception. The network's self-styled us-against-the-world attitude merges seamlessly with the Christian persecution complex. Consider the annual, imaginary War on Christmas. Normally the first flare lights up briefly in the summer when FNC hosts highlight a corporate memo altering holiday season policies. By November, the viewer is reminded daily of the liberal secularist's rejection of "Merry Christmas" and Christian iconography, preferring "Happy holidays" and pluralistic imagery instead. The viewer enjoys the specter of oppression. The imaginary War on Christmas simultaneously weaponizes the viewer's fleeting attention and taps into her unconscious knowledge. She enjoys feeling anger at the secularist's assault on her tradition and yet represses knowledge that no such attack exists. The pleasure of the martyrdom fantasy with which we opened this chapter is the nightly, affective intensity of the propaganda viewer.

The result is the "Fox effect." Viewers' emotions are weaponized against them and drive measurable results for GOP campaigns.[42] The share of the public getting news from network television has declined to approximately half the population,[43] which I consider good news since, after all, television isn't much for news. FNC is the most visible threat, but in some ways it provides a punching bag distracting us from the equally dangerous problem posed by Sinclair Broadcasting Group. Currently reaching four in ten homes in the United States, Sinclair's underhanded methods include frequent statements aired on local television that come directly from headquarters. Owning multiple brands in the same market lets viewers feel like they are choosing sources wisely while, in fact, they are being served the same message on different stations. For instance, in the swing state of Michigan there

42. Gregory J. Martin and Ali Yurukoglu found that without the "Fox effect" the Republican presidential vote share would have dropped 0.46 percent in 2000. But in 2004, the effect boosted Republican advantage to 3.59 percent. By 2008, the advantage grew to 6.34 percent. See Martin and Yurukoglu, "Bias in Cable News." Further, in the 2016 election, Pew found that four in ten Trump voters listed FNC as their main source of news. Among Clinton voters, CNN ranked the highest at 18 percent, followed by MSNBC at 9 percent. Both Trump and Clinton voters listed Facebook as their third source (7 percent and 8 percent respectively), though the sources behind Facebook news items doubtlessly varied. See Gottfried, Barthel, and Mitchell, "Trump, Clinton Voters Divided in Their Main Source for Election News."

43. Gottfried and Shearer, "Americans' Online News Use Is Closing in on TV News Use."

are multiple stations owned by Sinclair but which are branded as NBC, ABC, CBS, and Fox. A viewer would be unaware that her local television anchors are parroting messages delivered not only on the other local stations she considers unreliable but also on other stations across the nation.[44] Beyond the television, the question now is whether Americans will have the capability of discerning credible and fake sources online.

Unfortunately, the pick-and-choose nature of media today led to a general mistrust of information rather than more cautious selections. In early 2018, a concerning survey found nearly seven in ten US adults had "not very much confidence" or "no confidence at all" in the media. Four in ten Democrats and a staggering nine in ten Republicans reported these views.[45] Mistrust in information and reality is indeed a heightened problem on the Right. A 2012 survey drew laughs when it showed viewers of comedian Jon Stewart's *The Daily Show* were more informed on a narrow set of foreign and domestic issues than FNC viewers. In fact, the latter were less informed than those who reported consuming no major source of news at all.[46] The results were a tragedy. It was proof of conservative media's ridiculous protest against reality, an indictment that made absolutely no difference as it marched forth on a mission to transform reality. Just as Ailes told Nixon television was no gimmick, the network helped carry the first reality star president to victory. In turn, the reality star co-opted the term "fake news" and deployed it against reality while digesting FNC's morning talk show and evening opinion shows—not the President's Daily Brief—as his own chief source of news. The circular and insular nature of the relationship is isolated from reality even as it transforms that very reality. This is not a joke but instead a catastrophe.

The Cue and Supremacy

Flows of misinformation rely on media apparatuses to funnel propaganda. Eight in ten white evangelicals report "not very much confidence" or "no confidence at all" in the media.[47] Research as early as 1960 demonstrated media's direct effect on public opinion, but today we live in such a hyperreality of options to fit our feelings. In her research on the relationship

44. Kolhatkar, "The Growth of Sinclair's Conservative Media Empire."
45. Marist Poll, "Trust in Institutions Poll Findings."
46. Cassino, Woolley, and Jenkins, "What You Know Depends on What You Watch."
47. Marist Poll, "Trust in Institutions Poll Findings."

between climate change denial and viewership of Fox News, CNN, and MS-NBC, Lauren Feldman explored the role of the host in disseminating cues.[48] The cue is not simply the misinformation but the style of misinformation. When discussing climate change, the host's smirk or tone leads the viewer just as much as the misinformation.

Indirect cuing mirrors methods used in the Nixon administration's so-called Southern Strategy, the successful effort to draw southern racists away from the Democrats. For example, Nixon's "silent majority" overtly called for American patriots to reject anti-Vietnam War activism. Wasn't it also a dog whistle to those in the majority who saw how American minorities were gaining ground? In his interview with the *New York Times*, Nixon's strategist Kevin Philips explained the Southern Strategy by boldly declaring the Republican party would never again win more than 10 to 20 percent of the African American vote. Those votes wouldn't be needed if enough whites were drawn into the GOP.[49] The administration's domestic policy advisor John Ehrlichman described the strategy as such:

> The Nixon campaign in 1968, and the Nixon White House after that, had two enemies: the antiwar left and black people. You understand what I'm saying? We knew we couldn't make it illegal to be either against the war or black, but by getting the public to associate the hippies with marijuana and blacks with heroin, and then criminalizing both heavily, we could disrupt those communities. We could arrest their leaders, raid their homes, break up their meetings, and vilify them night after night on the evening news. Did we know we were lying about the drugs? Of course we did.[50]

48. The cue is not simply the words uttered by the host. It's the tone, the smirk, and the selection of guests entertained as authoritative. While a Democrat's perception of climate change was unchanged by high levels of viewing Fox News, CNN, or MSNBC, Feldman demonstrated that Republican viewers were much more open to climate science if they watched the latter two rather than Fox News alone. One might expect as much, since Republicans who watch all three are presumably less conservative than those who watch Fox News alone. But Feldman found that even highly conservative viewers of all three networks accepted the consensus on global warming at roughly equal pace with Democrats. She concluded her report with a related problem of cuing quantity: "Notably, Fox also provided substantially more coverage on climate change than the other two networks, thereby amplifying doubt about global warming within the cable news landscape." Feldman et al., "Climate on Cable, 23.

49. Boyd, "Nixon's Southern Strategy."

50. Journalist Dan Baum recalled this frank admission from Ehrlichman in an interview discussed in Baum, "Legalize It All."

Nixon's advisor Lee Atwater put the policy in even more blatantly vile terms:

> You start out in 1954 by saying, "N*****, n*****, n*****." By 1968 you can't say "n*****"—that hurts you, backfires. So you say stuff like, uh, forced busing, states' rights, and all that stuff, and you're getting so abstract. Now, you're talking about cutting taxes, and all these things you're talking about are totally economic things and a byproduct of them is, blacks get hurt worse than whites . . . "We want to cut this," is much more abstract than even the busing thing, uh, and a hell of a lot more abstract than "N*****, n*****."[51]

This is how vague, abstract cues resonate. It's how the Reagan administration moored supply-side economics and right-wing religious dogma to the white fantasy. Suddenly, support for lower taxes on the wealthy or opposition to abortion were stitched together. By the end of the 1980s, it didn't mattered whether constituents wished for the days when a racial epithet could be yelled aloud or if instead constituents were single-issue voters against abortion access—whatever the cause, they would be voting for industrial deregulation and lower taxes for the wealthy.

White working class anxiety was a misnomer, but there was no other way to politely equivocate after November 2016. While I do not consider the results absolutely conclusive on the question of whether Trumpism was driven partly by "white working class anxiety" or purely "white anxiety" alone, the evidence points more toward the latter. The election demonstrated the power of decades of dog whistles and cues that could now drop the pretense and express white supremacist and authoritarian desire openly.[52] For the 81

51. Transcript from audio of 1981 interview of Atwater by Alexander Lamis in Perlstein, "Exclusive."

52. In late spring of 2016, with nearly half of all primaries already held, when the median household income for primary voters going for Trump was $72,000 while Sanders and Clinton drew support from those with a median of $61,000. The median household income in the United States at that time was $56,500. Using data from the 2016 National Election Study, political scientist Robert Wood showed that while those in the top 96–100 percentile of income earners were less likely than usual to vote Republican, there was not a terribly significant difference in middle and lower income brackets. The possibility a voter's predisposition for authoritarianism correlated to support for Trump was another popular (and quite understandable) theory. However, when testing for authoritarian tendencies and comparing them against tests for symbolic racial bias, a stark difference emerged. Testing for unconscious racism must be done indirectly so as not to trigger defenses, so respondents were asked given wording with slightly veiled prejudice, e.g. "Irish, Italians, Jewish and many other minorities overcame prejudice and worked their way up. Blacks should do the same without any special favors," or "It's really a matter of some people not trying hard enough; if blacks would only try harder they could be

percent of white evangelical voters who supported Trump in the general election, the emphasis truly was on the whiteness. The persecution fantasy augmented the sense that a hierarchy was being upset.

Decades of preaching on traditional family values decayed into a tragic parody. All it took was a figure speaking aloud the bigotries they'd barely concealed with faith. Only two months before the election, Public Religion Research Institute showed a remarkable shift on the question of whether "an elected official who commits an immoral act in their personal life can still behave ethically and fulfill their duties in their public and professional life."[53] In 2011, 44 percent of Americans assented to this statement. By 2016, assent grew to 61 percent. Every category tested increased in their affirmation over these five years with the exception of the religiously unaffiliated. In effect, only the unaffiliated care *more* now about an official's private ethics. What drew attention, though, was the sharp turn taken by white evangelicals. They dropped the facade of moralism. Whereas only 30 percent had felt a privately immoral official could ethically fulfill their duties, by 2016 an impressive 72 percent suddenly agreed. I don't want to call this hypocrisy, which is a boring and always-wrong interpretation of motives. We already knew the values were duplicitous. What was interesting was that the faithful began openly vocalizing their own duplicity. They acknowledged their values were never so important, and, to say it all, this shift toward admitting their farcical long game emerged in order to support a character who barely even pretended to hold their religious values.

In *The Origins of Totalitarianism*, Hannah Arendt explored propaganda in the fascist and communist regimes. Misinformation isn't about convincing the public of falsehood but about exhausting their ability to care about the truth. The longer form of this chapter's opening quote from Arendt reads:

> In an ever-changing, incomprehensible world the masses had reached the point where they would, at the same time, believe

---

just as well off as whites." Wood examined the effect of moving higher on the authoritarian and symbolic racial scales. The latter clearly had the more consequential effect. A shift from the fiftieth to seventy-fifth percentile on authoritarianism induced a 3 percent increase in likelihood to support Trump, whereas the same shift in racism created a 20 percent jump. See Silver, "The Mythology of Trump's 'Working Class' Support" and 2016 American National Election Study discussed in Wood, "Racism Motivated Trump Voters More than Authoritarianism."

53. Public Religion Research Institute, "Backing Trump, White Evangelicals Flip Flop on Importance of Candidate Character."

everything and nothing, think that everything was possible and that nothing was true. The mixture in itself was remarkable enough, because it spelled the end of the illusion that gullibility was a weakness of unsuspecting primitive souls and cynicism the vice of superior and refined minds. Mass propaganda discovered that its audience was ready at all times to believe the worst, no matter how absurd, and did not particularly object to being deceived because it held every statement to be a lie anyhow. The totalitarian mass leaders based their propaganda on the correct psychological assumption that, under such conditions, one could make people believe the most fantastic statements one day, and trust that if the next day they were given irrefutable proof of their falsehood, they would take refuge in cynicism; instead of deserting the leaders who had lied to them, they would protest that they had known all along that the statement was a lie and would admire the leaders for their superior tactical cleverness.[54]

The rate of lying in the Trump administration might be an outlier, but the white evangelical's love of the liar is nothing new. The strategy of organizing men and women to work against their interests invariably turn to tactics of truth exhaustion. For instance, during the civil rights era and the party realignment, the conservative movement depended on seeing every black protestor as an "outside agitator." No African American could hold a genuine concern in their liberation, for this would require the white racist to consciously admit her own lifestyle was built on the oppression of others. The figure of the outside agitator mitigated the cognitive dissonance. The trope's effectiveness did not depend on the white racist's genuine belief. It only needed the racist's ambivalence. The same phenomenon drove the Religious Right to see secularism as attacking Christians on all fronts and at all times. The subject both knows and chooses to repress, but this standard feature of human psychology can be exploited especially within southern white culture wherein disingenuousness is a key component of normative communication.

They absorb slogans to enjoy, not to learn, and to reinforce the fragile ego, not to gather data for systematic worldview construction. Let's conclude by returning to a telling moment in the film *God's Not Dead*. The plot launched as the student discussed with his pastor the challenge of an atheist professor to write "God is dead" or else defend God's existence. The pastor told him to consider the gravity of his role: he was quite possibly the

---

54. Arendt, *The Origins of Totalitarianism*, 382.

only person who could ever tell his classmates about Jesus Christ. Set in the United States, even a moment's reflection would dismantle the risible impossibility of students never having heard of Christianity. Why were the filmmakers so bold as to include this dialogue? They correctly ascertained the audience's ability to immediately disavow their power as part of an overwhelmingly dominant faith. When the status of power feels uncomfortable, it inverts itself into a persecution complex. It's why conservative documentary filmmaker Dinesh D'Souza finds wild success with claims that, actually, liberals are the real fascists. White evangelicals imagine they'd respond to persecution bravely like Dietrich Bonhoeffer, the minister who refused to acquiesce to Hitler and died for his role in a failed resistance plot. They told themselves they had eyes to see. So, when news of ethnically and politically motivated camps for children broke in the summer of 2018, how did the white evangelical end up responding?

5

Against Society

Populism, Fascism, and Hierarchies of Contempt

"Desire can never be deceived. Interests can be deceived, unrecognized, or betrayed, but not desire. Whence Reich's cry: no, the masses were not deceived, they desired fascism, and that is what has to be explained."

—GILLES DELEUZE AND FÉLIX GUATTARI

"[T]he conservative position stems from a genuine conviction that a world thus emancipated will be ugly, brutish, base, and dull. It will lack the excellence of a world where the better man commands the worse."

—COREY ROBIN

Illusions of Insurrection

The greatest myth entrenched in the minds of liberals and conservatives alike is that we all share a basic vision of a common good. We merely disagree on the technical details of how to reach that common good, so the myth goes. We need only come to the table, find agreement, and maintain civility while refusing to call anything wicked. We see cruelty and ignore it, preferring only to see misguided benevolence. Hanlon's razor ("never attribute to malice that which is adequately explained by stupidity") is true often enough, so we figure all problems would disappear with enough consciousness-raising. The capitalist machine depends on this myth. Our topics thus far have been a history of white evangelicalism's past. Now in conclusion, we need to stretch beyond the confines of the faith to see the omens of hierarchy and contempt built into white evangelicalism as a political project. This chapter serves as a study of reactionary movements on its own, but let us read the warnings of the faith's possible future.

A myth was born one day after the Obama administration announced its Homeowners Affordability and Stability Plan in February 2009. The plan would invest $75 billion to assist seven to nine million Americans, stymieing the cascading foreclosure crisis at the heart of the Great Recession. From the floor of the Chicago Mercantile Exchange, reporter Rick Santelli fielded questions from the hosts at CNBC. "You know, the government is promoting bad behavior," he began before suggesting the administration should conduct an online poll to gauge whether Americans desired to subsidize "the losers' mortgages." He invoked old tropes of personal responsibility and carelessness to suggest property *should* be repossessed and given to "people that might have a chance to actually prosper down the road," for we should "reward people that could carry the water instead of drink the water." The traders behind him cheered in agreement, and Santelli soaked in the attention with arms raised. He directed his voice to the floor, shouting "How many of you people want to pay for your neighbor's mortgage that has an extra bathroom and can't pay their bills? Raise their hand." The audience booed as he added, "President Obama, are you listening?" He red baited with an allusion to communism in Cuba. "We're thinking of having a Chicago Tea Party in July," he cried. "All you capitalists that wanna show up to Lake Michigan, I'm going to start organizing."

The CNBC hosts grew impressed with the energy in the crowd. One host requested, "Can you do that one more time? Just get the mob behind you again—I loved it." Another host suggested Santelli couldn't just jeer up the crowds at will. Santelli recognized the painfully awkward nature of the request and steered the conversation toward his dubious belief that this crowd (a collection of bankers and traders) represented "a pretty good statistical cross-section of America." Santelli invoked the moral authority claim of Nixonian conservatism as he called the bankers "the silent majority." Fantasy isn't killed by irony.

By the end of the day, the web domain ChicagoTeaParty.com, which had lain dormant since its initial registration, had been updated with the Santelli rant. This particular domain had been registered on November 3, 2008, merely one day prior to the election of Obama.[1] Likewise, the Koch brothers' Citizens for a Sound Economy (a precursor to later

1. See http://whois.domaintools.com/chicagoteaparty.com.

organizations Americans for Prosperity and Freedomworks) first registered USTeaParty.com in 2002. Writing for *Playboy* magazine of all places,
Mark Ames and Yasha Levine drew controversy for suggesting Santelli's
rant was planted as part of a well-plotted astroturfing campaign giving
the illusion of populist insurrection, a claim Santelli denied. The article
disappeared after a threat of a libel suit, and the nature of background
preparation or Santelli's knowledge remains unclear, but the accusation
was one part of the liberal confusion over the nascent reaction to Obama.
Was this a quasi-populist reaction, a capitalist conspiracy, or a confusion
of interests mixed with genuine anger? Should it be treated as ridiculous
or loathed as a destruction machine?[2]

Soon the Tax Day Tea Parties popped up across the United States with
funding and organizational support from the conservative donor class and
exposure from Fox News. Glenn Beck credited Santelli's rant as the movement's genesis. At most, Santelli gave the Tea Party its rhetorical cover. The
reality was more complex. It was many things: retribution for the election
of the first black president, blowback from the financial collapse, and a consequence of unlimited funding after the Supreme Court's *Citizen's United*
decision. It was also the culmination of years of activism, the resonance of
racial resentment and anti-tax dogma, and an upsurge of libertarian power.
Plutocrats had turned the slashing of top marginal tax rates into a moral
crusade for serfs who felt they too might be robbed by "losers" if and when
they chose to rise as entrepreneurial "winners." Though acronyms abounded
on the poster boards ("Taxed Enough Already" becoming a standard), its
nomenclature harkened to the 1773 spill in Boston Harbor. They felt more
conservative than Republicans, and right from the start many Tea Party-
sympathetic voters incredulously claimed no affiliation to the GOP. They
undertook a righteous mission as patriots reclaiming their country.

What began as a much-needed lifeline of energy for the GOP after the
2008 loss became its own nightmare once the Tea Party seated its caucus
after the 2010 midterm. Legislative maps were gerrymandered according
to a new census, increasingly safe districts provided fertile ground for
insurgent right-wingers to primary moderates. As the surge turned into
a purge, the party drifted deeper into extremist clamor. It roared loudest
in protest against the Patient Protection and Affordable Care Act, which

---

2. I want to credit Paul Elliot Johnson, whose work on the Tea Party initially drew my
attention to several of the lesser-known historical elements I explored in the paragraphs
above. See Johnson, "Imagining American Democracy."

conservatives—ever the more effective sloganeers and fantasy engineers—
nicknamed Obamacare. Liberals abandoned any real public option immediately, but the Tea Party took voting against one's interests in a new
direction with Obamacare. As many as 40,000 Americans per year were
dying from lack of healthcare while costs skyrocketed. The fixes would be
difficult, but they weren't a mystery. According to the World Health Organization, the United States had dozens of examples of more effective national health care systems from which to choose. So whereas voting against
one's interests typically referred only to economic advantages, we suddenly
saw people eagerly voting away access to healthcare.

Where was the white evangelical in all this libertarian noise, which
seemed bereft of God-talk? As discussed in the previous chapter, Putnam
and Campbell's survey of American religion drew widespread attention
to the rise of the "nones," those with no overt religious affiliation. What
drew my attention, though, was an addendum providing some of the ear-
liest longitudinal research on the Tea Party phenomenon. Original data
was gathered in 2006 and re-queried in 2011. Whereas Tea Party rhetoric focused on the size of government, debt, or taxation, and whereas it
claimed no partisan loyalty to a major political party, Putnam and Campbell demonstrated the self-deception involved. Views on the government's
size or scope, like views of debt, were not the identifying markers in the
data. Two factors stood out more than anything else that, in 2006, would
predict Tea Party affiliation five years later. The strongest predictor was
prior affiliation with the Republican party, which laid to rest any claim of
independence.[3] The second predictor was a desire for theocracy. Respondents' theocratic tendencies were gauged via three questions of "whether
our laws and policies would be better if we had more 'deeply religious'
elected officials; whether it is appropriate for religious leaders to engage in
political persuasion; and whether religion should be brought into public
debates over political issues."[4] Anti-black, anti-choice, and anti-immigrant
views were all in the mix of identifiers as well, but as the movement ebbed
and its animus later flowed into Trumpism, we saw how theocracy covered
for white nationalism.

When considering the condition of the United States and the Western
world, I often return to a classic question posed by Baruch Spinoza and
Wilhelm Reich and repeated by Gilles Deleuze and Felix Guattari.

3. Putnam and Campbell, *American Grace*, 572.
4. Ibid., 574.

The fundamental problem of political philosophy is still . . . "Why do men fight *for* their servitude as stubbornly as though it were their salvation?" How can people possibly reach the point of shouting: "More taxes! Less bread!"? . . . after centuries of exploitation, why do people still tolerate being humiliated and enslaved, to such a point, indeed, that they *actually want* humiliation and slavery not only for others but for themselves?[5]

Indeed, how do the liberals desire nothing more than incremental reforms while leaving the oppressive vectors of late capitalism untouched? How does the conservative pauper wish to lower taxes on the wealthy while depriving themselves of living wages or healthcare? More precisely, how does one enjoy not only cruelty but suffering as well? Reich's claim was that fascism was not simply a form of government with these or those features but "only the organized political expression of the structure of the average man's character . . . *the basic emotional attitude of the suppressed man of our authoritarian machine civilization and its mechanistic-mystical conception of life.*"[6] Whence comes the *jouissance* of sadism and masochism incurred when society is burned down?

The Unite the Right rally should have been a turning point, but instead it showed us how much further we could sink. After a statue of Confederate general Robert E. Lee was slated for removal, white supremacists gathered from across the United States on the evening of August 11, 2017. They bore down upon Charlottesville, North Carolina with Confederate and Nazi flags and chanted "White lives matter!" and "You will not replace us!" As the night went on, the slogan mutated to "Jews will not replace us." The cartoonish nature of grown white men performing anger while wielding tiki torches turned quickly to horror as they marched near a church holding an interfaith prayer gathering. There were no casualties that night. The next day was different. Early Saturday afternoon, a white supremacist drove his car through a packed crowd of anti-racist demonstrators. Nineteen were injured, and Heather Heyer suffered fatal injuries.

Unwilling to judge barbaric violence or bigotry, the president equivocated: "I am not putting anybody on a moral plane, what I'm saying is this: you had a group on one side and a group on the other, and they came at each other with clubs and it was vicious and horrible and it was a horrible thing to watch, but there is another side." He claimed it was the Left who attacked,

5. Deleuze and Guattari, *Anti-Oedipus*, 29.
6. Reich, *The Mass Psychology of Fascism*, xiii.

casting the blame as he did on "both sides." When given another chance to elaborate or retract, he doubled down with frightening ease. "Excuse me, they didn't put themselves down as neo-Nazis," he said of those carrying Nazi and neo-Nazi flags. "And you had some very bad people in that group. But you also had people that were very fine people on both sides."[7]

It came as no surprise to me that white evangelicals continued to support a leader defending Nazis. It was all too normal now. All theology is political, just as all politics is theological. As famously described by the German jurist Carl Schmitt, who also had a shameful relationship to fascism, "All significant concepts of the modern theory of the state are secularized theological concepts not only because of their historical development . . . but also because of their systematic structure, the recognition of which is necessary for a sociological consideration of these concepts."[8] Just as God was sovereign, so too became the nation-state. Just as God declared the exception to natural law via miracle, so too the executive declares the exception via the order. Just as baptism marked inclusion, so too the social security card delineates those who are saved by citizenship or else damned.

The only thing unavailable today is repentance. That's what Walter Benjamin said when he described capitalism as the first case of a blaming cult rather than a repenting cult. A theology inevitably underwrites and justifies a political zone, which is precisely why it's so dangerous. It cannot forgive itself or the other. It was out of a need to denote a perverse, authoritarian theology that the theologian Dorothee Soelle coined the term *Christofascism*.

As we draw this study of white evangelicalism to a conclusion, it's equally important to analyze the white nationalism always lurking underneath it and now expressing itself openly. It's a threat that won't pass with a term limit on one administration or the election of another. It's a crude symptom of a desire that was, for far too long, allowed to cover itself with theological dogma and family values. For decades it felt incensed if you didn't respect the pious and self-righteous rhetoric it would so eagerly abandon at the first chance of an ethnostate. Liberals too easily dismissed conservative Christianity as a fool's faith rather than as a declaration of intent. We face a reckoning now, and we must rediscover the lessons of twentieth-century critical theory if we desire to understand the twenty-first and survive to the twenty-second. As Wilhelm Reich cried in another era, we must now ask

7. Transcript from Politico, "Full Text."
8. Schmitt, *Political Theology*, 36.

why the white evangelical desires now to be saved and then to damn, now to join the populist swell and then to desire fascism.

Populist Reactions

For a brief few years at the close of the nineteenth century, the United States had a populist party that eventually blended into a major political front. It gives us a few lessons on populist dynamics. For a century before the Civil War, silver slowly bled out of Western markets for a mix of reasons. Without a standard currency used across all states in the union, multiple local currencies and bank notes proliferated. As far back as 1792, the Coin and Mintage Act had established a gold-to-dollar ratio,[9] and ever after the conservative position favored gold over silver. Indeed, much of the transition to capitalism detailed by Karl Polanyi's *The Great Transformation* is a history of the misguided but orthodox view that markets needed gold like the body needs blood—no fiat substitute would do. But regardless of what some piece of legislation said, gold's trading value was always in flux. Many improvised or foreign currencies picked up the slack. The treasury introduced the greenback during the Civil War, a coin based on the Spanish dollar circulated widely, and many even used stamps as a currency. Use of foreign currencies winded down in the latter nineteenth century, and consequent market havoc required new methods. The 1890 Sherman Act triggered government silver purchases as a solution.

Within three years, prices were again in disarray as the Panic of 1893 crashed into a depression requiring a scapegoat. The gold standard crowd blamed the Sherman Act, and the emerging Free Silver movement demanded the minting of silver coins. Much like today, both ends of the spectrum mistrusted the fiat currency, but bullion too was problematic. If a coin's value as a precious metal rose high enough above its denominational value, it made more sense to trade a gold coin for its weight rather than its official rate. Coupled with sharp population growth in the latter nineteenth century, the government's indecisive monetary policy was a recipe for disaster, especially for agrarian communities. How were they supposed to pay their debts without proper denominations of coins small enough to actually use?[10] Free Silver figurehead William Jennings Bryan put it succinctly:

9. US Mint, "Coinage Act of April 2, 1792."

10. One perspective argues that this budding Free Silver movement sought inflation. The movement was largely made up of farmers with mounting debts, and inflation could

"How can we pay our debts without selling something and how can we sell anything unless there is money in circulation to buy with?"[11]

The People's Party (or Populist Party) formed around an agenda friendly to farmers and labor unions while hostile to corporations and bankers. The party officially lasted into the first decade of the twentieth century, but its most prominent years were 1892 to 1896 while rallying around the Free Silver issue. They called for the state to seize ownership of railroads and impose a graduated income tax. They wanted relief for farmers and an eight-hour working day for the industrial sector. They wanted pensions for sailors and soldiers and opposed government bail-outs of private corporations. They sought labor protections and a host of other working-class goals. Silver was merely one issue among many. The interpretation of the Free Silver movement as an inflationary debt trick is interesting here, because one reason populists were drawn to the Free Silver proponents was that it would stick it to East Coast bankers. This hostility to bankers—specifically on the East Coast—led naturally to charges of anti-Semitism.[12] All the standard elements of populism were here: the rural

---

reduce the real burden. However, another perspective points to the proliferation of subsidiary currencies and argues that the animating drive of the Free Silver movement was the inability to easily divide wages and the consequent inflation of prices. The population of the United States grew by 60 percent in only two decades between 1860 and 1880, but the government essentially attempted to freeze subsidiary currencies to pre-war levels. Subsidiary currencies included silver coins, the stamp, or the quartered greenback (literally a greenback cut into quarters). The latter's very existence perfectly captures the essence of the problem; there simply weren't enough smaller currency units in circulation. Especially in the American South and West, records indicate merchants or creditors rounded up to the next dollar when smaller units were unavailable for payment. The creditor certainly didn't want to round down, and the debtor farmers grew angry at debts arbitrarily inflated to all payment at all. The dollar was in circulation, but it was equal to more than one half day's wages. One can imagine the difficulty today of settling small, cash transactions if no coins or bills smaller than today's $50 bill were in circulation. See Gramm and Gramm, "The Free Silver Movement in America."

11. Bryan, "Life and Speeches of Hon. Wm. Jennings Bryan," 163.

12. There are various ways of interpreting the relationship between Free Silver populists and anti-Semitism. Naomi Cohen described the situation as such: "Before the Populist campaign, American Jews had noted and taken issue with the economic stereotypes used against them. They repeated frequently, but with little success, that the historical source for the character of Shylock was a Christian and not a Jew . . . Just because Populist rhetoric meant only more of the same, contemporary Jews were less concerned about the free silver campaign than the recent controversy over Populist anti-Semitism might lead one to expect. Jewish defensiveness, which usually climbed in direct proportion to the gravity of the situation was generally absent." Cohen, "Antisemitism in the Gilded Age," 199.

grief, the ethnic animosity, anti-intellectualism, an authentic proletarian base, genuine economic difficulty coupled with desperate economic theory, the floating signifier "Free Silver" rallying the crowd, and a clownish champion. The party threw its weight behind Democrat William Jennings Bryan in his second of three unsuccessful campaigns for the presidency. This was three decades before his appearance at the Scopes Monkey Trial, but his ability to work the crowds was already a political force.

At the Democratic convention in July 1896, Bryan delivered his fiery speech "The Cross of Gold." He spoke of the humble citizen accosted by the gold-standard crowd. Ever the bloviator, he described the contest between Free Silver and the gold standard this way (only decades after the Civil War, no less): "Never before in the history of this country has there been witnessed such a contest as that through which we have passed." Bryan saw himself as fighting the good fight, a defensive war against tyranny. He impugned the motives of the gold standard crowd by linking them to their English counterparts. Bryan's point wasn't subtle when characterizing the debate not as a difference of economic theory but as a fight against foreign dominion. He concluded by telling the naysayers, "you shall not press down upon the brow of labor this crown of thorns. You shall not crucify mankind upon a cross of gold."[13] Yes, he compared a cause accused of anti-Semitism to Christ being persecuted by Jews. By 1900, the Republicans pushed through the gold standard that would last until another of their own, Nixon, ended the policy in 1971.[14]

What then is populism, and why is it generally Right wing in the West today when for so long it shared more territory with the Left? *Populism* is a vague term with malleable political vectors. Is it genuine grief, a xenophobic rally, an ideological configuration to be exploited, an expression of the People? Political theorist Ernesto Laclau certainly took the latter term—*the People*—to be the traditional populist's master signifier. Compare the impotency of the Free Silver and Tea Party movements against the revolutionary Jacobins to see the way in which the *People* designates a point of desire prior to motion, which won't necessarily materialize. It isn't a platform but instead a type of chaotic logic. For Laclau, "populism has no referential unity because it is ascribed not to a delimitable phenomenon but to a social

13. Ibid., 247.

14. Nixon's decision here was a unilateral betrayal of the Bretton Woods monetary system, the very arrangement that lent such massive economic prosperity in the post-war years.

logic whose effects cut across many phenomena. Populism is, quite simply, a way of constructing the political."[15]

Kenneth Minogue framed populism as a tripartite structure: movement, ideology, and rhetoric. They ran in that order of importance in his theory. Movement is the thrust of popular will, veering in surprising directions and transforming the political landscape as if by accidental whims. Ideology plays a subservient role by sustaining movement, so ideology can be discarded as needed or reconfigured to direct motion. Witness the recent oscillations of the evangelical between free trade libertarianism and protectionist nativism, isolationism and militarily-expeditious neoconservatism, theocracy and crass conservatism. Each name packages the People—or real Americans, true Christians—into contradictory and resonating ideological spheres. Finally, the rhetoric is most dispensable and plays only an ancillary role of curating ideological affiliates. In other words, no party line, official press release, or morning policy tweet really means much. It can all be thrown out and reinvented. Rhetoric is disposable, never authentic expression.

Let's put the (too simplified) difference between Minogue and Laclau like so: does rhetoric/belief always follow material reality, or does rhetoric/belief play a role in determining material reality? Think of the old Marxian axiom that it is not consciousness that determines social being but instead social being that determines consciousness. Even if Marx is broadly correct (he is), to what extent is rhetoric a creative or destructive power? Contra Minogue, Laclau argued these three tiers of movement, ideology, and rhetoric are not at all hierarchical.[16] Each can change the other two, none serve some ultimate purpose, and each are enjoyed in their own way. At any moment, rhetoric can suddenly awaken new vectors. For example, didn't conservatives reject decades of free-market dogma the moment they saw a presidential tweet calling for protectionist tariffs? Didn't evangelicals abandon family values language the moment they needed to support an agenda led by someone who didn't match up? Rhetorical tropes are floating signifiers invested with libidinal energy, and they're quickly discarded when they no longer procure enjoyment.

The populist's ideology expresses both Marx's definition of ideology (they don't know it, but nevertheless they are doing it) and Sloterdijk's (they know very well they are doing it, but it must be done). Those who have read

15. Laclau, *On Populist Reason*, xi.
16. Ibid., 10–13.

my work before will know my affinity for Ernesto Laclau, so forgive the repetition of material here. For Laclau, what matters in populism is the co-alition around the *empty signifier* (the People, real Americans), which then draws into its orbit various *floating signifiers* (law and order, less regulation, all lives matter, pro-life) as needed. Unlike the empty signifier which can mean anything, the floating signifier means a very specific thing—though never what it claims. For the white supremacist, the call for "civility" is a key floating signifier meant to dismiss authentic grief and justify aggression. For the white evangelical, "biblical" is a floating signifier meant to dismiss alternative viewpoints and underwrite narcissism. Each of these floating signifiers deliver multiple coded messages at once. They must curate rage carefully if the project is not to veer off course into a genuine expression of radical politics beyond the control of traditional party power structures. Populist rhetoric is not foolish but instead disingenuous.

When considering how this works, I think of an individual I know who proudly expresses multiple animating features of populist reason. He is a blue-collar white male living in the South who delights in displays of misogyny and racism. He hides from himself his deep commitment to the Republican party with frequent criticism of "both sides." You likely know the type. This is the figure of vindictive populism—at once against society and against self, sadistic and masochistic. A staunch opponent of the Obama administration's healthcare plan, he eventually signed up just in time. The diagnosis of a serious illness was just around the corner. He continued to criticize the federally subsidized healthcare on which his life depended. He was overjoyed as the next administration took steps to sack the law, drive costs higher, and cut funding to the very program providing his own health-care. He's not wholly ignorant of the risks. He understands his side's political success might mean his death, and yet it all feels worth it to him. Whether his pleasure derives more from the deprivation of others' healthcare, the suc-cess of ideological commitments, or the enjoyment of self-harm is unclear. It may simply be that the insult of shredding Obama's signature domestic achievement is worth the risk of death. Whatever the possible explanations, this aggressively populist logic drives sadistic and masochistic tendencies. It's not merely misinformed; it's enjoying, and we must get better at recog-nizing counterintuitive locations of enjoyment.

Embattlement in the Reactionary Mind

Conservatism loves a hierarchy, and Corey Robin argues conservatism thrives most when in defeat. Its hero figures of the warrior and the businessman were mainstays in the Cold War era, but the fall of the Berlin Wall left an aimless frenzy in the nineties. What should one desire once everything is won? Neoconservative Irving Kristol said as much of the Soviet Union's collapse, which "deprived us of an enemy . . . In politics, being deprived of an enemy is a very serious matter. You tend to get relaxed and dispirited. Turn inward."[17]

Nostalgia sets parameters for conservative fantasy. Robin defines conservatism as "a meditation on—and theoretical rendition of—the felt experience of having power, seeing it threatened, and trying to win it back."[18] He follows this definition with two monstrous examples of perceived power loss on the part of the white male. In the first example, rape within marriage was not illegal anywhere in the United States until 1979. The legal justification traced back to 1736 with English jurist Matthew Hale's argument that marriage conferred a permanent, contractual consent. The Supreme Court upheld such logic as late as 1957 when deciding, "A man does not commit rape by having sexual intercourse with his lawful wife, even if he does so by force against her will."[19] To make rape illegal was to threaten men's license to abuse, and today we still see fragile identities threatened by any language around consent. Whether or not one believes women's stories about assault continues to work as a social, political shibboleth today, i.e., those preferring hierarchy and abuse will always dismiss the woman's story. The same logic was used against employees complaining of employer abuses, because, as Robin explains, "until the twentieth century that consent was interpreted by judges to contain implicit and irrevocable provisions of servitude; meanwhile, the exit option of quitting was not nearly as available, legally or practically, as many might think."[20] What was true of the worker was even more true of the abused wife, who until the latter twentieth century had no real option to end the contract of marriage. In the second example of power loss, slavery apologist and Vice President John C. Calhoun pinned the inevitable end of slavery on the horror of receiving abolitionist

17. Kristol, as quoted in Robin, *The Reactionary Mind*, 127.

18. Robin, *The Reactionary Mind*, 4.

19. Ibid., 5.

20. Ibid.

petitions in Congress in the 1830s. Robin described Calhoun's final major address as frantic over loss: "the mere appearance of slave speech in the nation's capital stood out for the dying Calhoun as the sign that the revolution had begun."[21] In these cases, the conservative position rallies around the relative deprivation (relative to the wife, the worker, the slave) and sees rising equality as a cost to itself.

> Though it is often claimed that the left stands for equality while the right stands for freedom, this notion misstates the actual disagreement between right and left. Historically, the conservative has favored liberty for the higher orders and constraint for the lower orders. What the conservative sees and dislikes in equality, in other words, is not a threat to freedom but its extension. For in that extension, he sees a loss of his own freedom. "We are all agreed as to our own liberty," declared Samuel Johnson. "But we are not agreed as to the liberty of others: for in proportion as we take others must lose. I believe we hardly wish that the mob should have liberty to govern us." Such was the threat Edmund Burke saw in the French Revolution: not merely an expropriation of property or explosion of violence but an inversion of obligations of deference and command.[22]

Nostalgia for an imaginary past defends hierarchy. Fictionalized nostalgia grabs those who see their declining status and prefer to blame a race or gender rather than a capitalist. After all, the blue-collar worker (even the white male) has much to gain from the demolition of hierarchy. Wasn't this Marx's point when he ended the manifesto saying proletarians have nothing to lose but their chains? It's no surprise the aristocrats of every age side with the conservatives and forge counterrevolutionary agendas, but why does the working person go along with it?

From slaveholders to neoconservatives, the Right always understood that any successful defense of the old regime must incorporate the lower orders. They need to feel invested in the system, because the star struck fan's awe at celebrity burns out in time. The masses must be able to symbolically identify with the ruling class. Or they need to feel like faux aristocrats in the family, the factory, and the field. The former path makes for an upside-down populism, in which the lowest of the low see themselves projected

21. Ibid., 6.
22. Ibid., 8.

in the highest of the high. The latter is a version of feudalism in which the husband or supervisor plays the part of a lord.[23]

The admonition to "pull yourself up by your bootstraps" confers (or forces) upon the individual the responsibility to change the practically unchangeable economic circumstances in which one is born. The rare instances of those who jump to a higher class serve as a figure reinforcing the shame upon the vast majority who do not.[24] The United States today bears additional tools to augment the myth of class mobility—the Protestant work ethic, the prosperity gospel, the rugged individualism, the company man, the hard-working parent. Class mobility is particularly poor in America, and yet is there anywhere else where the myth of class mobility is more pronounced? For example, when I teach course sessions on tax policy, it's common for my students to criticize inheritance or capital gains taxes, saying, "I plan on being rich, and I wouldn't want anyone taking what I worked hard to earn!" Even when students can articulate how exchange value or salaries have no relationship to the practical use value of the commodity or labor, many are still taken by this fantastic myth of meritocracy. The fantasy of class mobility, of becoming *bourgeois*, is enough to defend the aristocracy. How does this process of ideological adoption work?

When a police officer shouts "Hey! You there!," the designated individual is no longer merely a citizen but, suddenly, a subject keenly aware of a power dynamic. The address conferring a specific status is *interpellation*. Louis Althusser used this term to distinguish the ideological state apparatus from the repressive state apparatus. Marxist theory traditionally focused on the repressive apparatuses, the public institutions of the police, the army, the prison, the court, and so on. These repress (or suppress) dissident behavior and reinforce conformity. Their force is primary, and their ideological function is secondary. For instance, the army's primary purpose is to destroy things and kill people, but it needs ideological aid (appeals to the patriotism

23. Ibid., 35.

24. We can compare all such individualizing and moralizing shame tactics to the situation in pre-revolutionary France, wherein the members of the Third Estate could in theory accumulate enough money to purchase their way into the Second Estate nobility. The peasant farmer needed only to raise his son with a private education such that he could, with massive doses of luck and connections, become a lawyer or merchant. The old nobility wouldn't accept the newly ascendent as a true peer, but the figure of the newly minted noble provided the possibility (however remote) of class change. The remoteness of such possibilities—and this is particularly true of the bootstraps myth in a terribly low social mobility state—is erased from the calculations as if the single exception disproves the rule of class immobility.

of the soldier and the tax-paying society, clairvoyant fictions wherein force spreads freedom, etc.). On the other hand, the state's ideological apparatuses aim for private formation and only occasionally require repressive force. For example, the school exists to educate a child into a worker or citizen, though it disciplines when required. Althusser wrote a provisional list of ideological apparatuses: the religious organization, school, family, law, political party, trade union, media, and cultural expressions such as arts and literature. In that last category, he even mentions sport, which is interesting in our present context given the intertwinement of sport and nationalistic bravado (the anthem, the fireworks, the attention to soldiers in the audience). We can't enjoy a pastime without being reminded of the loyalty demanded by the state. There's no practice that isn't ideological, for "there is no practice except by and in an ideology."[25]

Given the role that the interpellation of whiteness and evangelical righteousness play in this book, it's important to see how nationalists expect all ideological apparatuses to support the goals of the state. To them, Christianity *must* be American. If an ideological apparatus doesn't support the state, it's denounced. When during the 2008 campaign reporters discovered Barack Obama's pastor Jeremiah Wright once uttered the words "God damn America!,"[26] no appeal to the Hebrew Bible's prophetic tradition curtailed the right-wing outrage. Wright's criticism was not countered on theological grounds at all. Conservatives didn't debate over the proper interpretation of American abuse of power in relation to what the Bible says of abuse of power. Instead, the Right's reaction went straight to the supposed un-American nature of Wright's sermon. White evangelicalism's reaction exposed the vacuity of its own biblical convictions. The blackness of Wright and his parishioner Obama created a dimension of rage which wouldn't have been so aggressively visited upon a white pastor preaching the same sermon.

It was as if Wright existed in a social space granted by the white state, so his use of an ideological apparatus for non-patriotic purposes was tantamount to treason. We see similar criticisms against the public university,

25. Althusser, "Ideology and Ideological State Apparatuses," 170.

26. After explaining a history of racist government policies, the section of Wright's sermon read: "The government gives them the drugs, builds bigger prisons, passes a three-strike law, and then wants us to sing 'God Bless America.' No, no, no. Not 'God Bless America.' God Damn America! That's in the Bible, for killing innocent people. God Damn America for treating her citizen as less than human. God Damn America as long as she keeps trying to act like she is God and she is supreme!"

which offends conservatives because of its perceived un-Americanness. The merits of a course's critique of colonialism, white supremacy, heteronormativity, or capitalism are never debated. Instead the Right charges the professor with sedition, of turning the student against the state. Or consider the fear of the gay or lesbian couple raising a child, which the conservative imagines will not be properly interpellated as a heterosexual subject. The charge against these religious, educational, or familial ideological apparatuses is always the same: you had but one job, and you are failing us.

Ideology is totalizing and unconscious.[27] Fantasy and rhetoric (disjointed, superfluous, and contradictory) are the Imaginary-register cover stabilizing ideology (networked, semi-coherent, and motivating) at the Symbolic register. This is Lacan's lesson for politics: the subject is always trying to justify the desires and dissatisfactions of the Real, they want to feel secured in the Symbolic, and they need to find a way to live with themselves at the Imaginary. We cannot effectively use words to argue against ideology, because ideology is about security, not truth. What the populist loves is an ideal ego-image, which is aspirational.[28] The populist desires to become whatever she's told to be, so, in a manner of speaking, what the populist loves is narcissism.

Before the Red Scare and the Goldwater campaign, there weren't clear cases of right-wing populism in the United States.[29] We've seen examples of populist figures like Bryan and Coughlin throughout this book, but there weren't clearly Right wing movements behind these figures. Activists like Eugene Debs or W. E. B. Du Bois stand out as the organizers and intellectuals carrying genuine moral authority over the same time frame. Their work focused on authentic goals of liberation, whereas the Free Silver movement was a perfect example of how a largely rural and agrarian movement with

27. In Lacan's Real, Symbolic, and Imaginary registers, what Althusser calls the "imaginary relationship" linking the individual to the collective functions not at the level of the Imaginary but instead at the Symbolic. See Krips, *Fetish*, 80–81.

28. As Althusser described it, "The ideal ego corresponds with the self-image in terms of which a subject is interpellated and, more specifically, with an idealized image that a subject has of himself as it is reflected back from the site of the Other." Althusser, "Ideology and Ideological State Apparatuses," 75.

29. "There was no connection between populism and the discourse of the traditional Right, which was centred on the defense of unregulated capitalism and the discouragement of any kind of grass-roots mobilization. The first moment in which a conservative discourse with populist connotation arises is in the anti-Communist crusades of the 1950s, whose epicentre was McCarthyism but which had been preceded by a series of molecular processes on a variety of fronts." Laclau, *On Populist Reason*, 135.

economic grievances, overly simplistic solutions, and xenophobia still retained a disposition that was at least somewhat Left-populist in economic disposition while reactionary in its ethnocentrism. During the McCarthy period, the burgeoning right-wing impulse was anti-Communist, though it blurred the lines between communism and liberalism until it saw little difference between the two. In other words, populism is first of all a demand fitting nearly any political agenda. Unfortunately, today, it's difficult to imagine what a critical mass of left-wing populism would even look like.[30]

Time magazine's 2016 person of the year was Donald Trump, but it might well have been "the Populist" or "the Nativist." In addition to the United Kingdom's Brexit, right-wing and nativist movements across the Western world tested neoliberal dominance with a widespread backlash. What was happening in the United States was by no means unique. Some succeeded while others failed, but the moment raised the classic question: which is the symptom, and which is the cause? In particular, how does a conservatism or nativism built on markets and hierarchies of race, sex, and class fertilize a mass movement of workers campaigning for the rights of masters?

I don't have the answer. An all-encompassing definition of populism is impossible. "[I]nstead of starting with a model of political rationality which sees populism in terms of what it lacks—its vagueness, its ideological emptiness, its anti-intellectualism, its transitory character," Laclau shows instead that the goal should be "to enlarge the model or rationality in terms of a generalized rhetoric . . . so that populism appears as a distinctive and always present possibility of structuration of political life."[31] Populism is vague and underdetermined, more affective than rational, but it can always erupt at any moment within any political persuasion.

We can think of political affiliations as having these two logics, a *logic of difference* and a *logic of equivalence*.[32] A logic of difference seeks to define

30. Of course, the primary campaign of center-Left, democratic socialist candidate Bernie Sanders provided a possible road map, as does the ongoing efforts of the Democratic Socialists of America and similar groups. However, the vast majority of populist movements in recent years have been right-wing in the United States and Western Europe alike.

31. Laclau, *On Populist Reason*, 13.

32. "So we have two ways of constructing the social: either through the assertion of a particularity—in our case, a particularity of demands—whose only links to other particularities are of a differential nature (as we have seen: no positive terms, only differences); or through a partial surrender of particularity, stressing what all particularities have, equivalentially, in common. The second mode of construction of the social involves, as

how a movement, party, project, or people are different from another. In the logic of difference, an empty signifier such as the People designates not only those who are the People but also those who are not (the culturally, racially, sexually, or religiously other). In the logic of equivalence, separate interests are stitched together via common goals. For an example of the logic of equivalence on the Right, consider how Christian nationalism, abortion, libertarian tax policies, and white supremacy or anti-immigrant attitudes coalesce. For an example on the Left, we might turn to the recognition of intersectional structures oppressing minorities, the social safety net and minimum wage, or the power differential inherent in capitalism that leads to such pervasive sexual harassment in the workplace. The logic of difference defines the group against another, while the logic of equivalence shows how one goal amplifies another. Too much equivalence breaks down the urgency of crises. Too much difference makes an enemy of everyone outside the empty signifier. Contempt for everyone is the aesthetic of fascism.

The Specter of Fascism

To riff on the manifesto, a specter haunts the Western world today. Merely invoking the term invites upon myself the charge of hyperbole. We aren't allowed to say it without hearing snickering from someone who feels very safe and thinks we are too worried. "The premier demand upon all education is that Auschwitz not happen again," wrote the critical theorist Theodor Adorno. "Every debate about the ideals of education is trivial and inconsequential compared to this single ideal: never again Auschwitz. It was the barbarism all education strives against."[33] To claim we should arrange education to prevent this from happening again is somehow controversial today, because it means there's no neutral space. Either we're educating in such a way that fascist ideas are given space to grow and proliferate, or we're attacking those ideals. As democratic ideals collapse in

we know, the drawing of an antagonistic frontier; the first does not. I have called the first mode of constructing the social *logic of difference*, and the second, *logic of equivalence*. Apparently, we could draw the conclusion that one precondition for the emergence of populism is the expansion of the equivalential logic at the expense of the differential one. This is true in many respects, but to leave the matter there would be to win the argument too cheaply, for it would presuppose that equivalence and difference are simply in a zero-sum relation of exclusion of each other. Things are far more complex." Laclau, *On Populist Reason*, 77–78.

33. Adorno, "Education After Auschwitz," 191.

the Western world, we're confronted with the impossibility of neutrality in the classroom and in the public sphere. The current debate over whether white nationalists and neo-Nazis should be allowed to speak on the college campus obscures the terrifying reality already known to the teacher, for we often hear casual remarks from students who don't see how their train of thought dehumanizes their peer in the next chair. We feel pressure to resist ostracizing hostile ideals and to treat all sides as if they have equal legitimacy. The ideals of free inquiry and impartiality is why Carl Schmitt said liberalism only works in the "interim period in which it was possible to answer the question 'Christ or Barabbas?' with a proposal to adjourn or appoint a commission of investigation."[34]

Why investigate fascism in a book on white evangelical desire? I'm skeptical about the odds of convincing anyone who doesn't already understand the reasons, but let's consider a few. First, white evangelicals are a chosen sect. This was my claim from the introduction: chosenness is the only non-negotiable doctrine. Chosenness is ratified by God, which provides the theological justification for potentially any avenue of exclusion or violence. Second, its enjoyment of hierarchy, dominance, and submission to a strongman or familiar order—a familiarity tinged with nostalgia—is a fascist desire. Third, its apocalyptic vision already entails the destruction of the world and the bloodshed and/or damnation of all who won't submit to its theology. Fourth, as we've seen throughout this book, white evangelicalism grounds itself in centuries-old patterns of white supremacy. Though its overt anti-Semitism has waned, its supersessionism has not. Animosity can always return, especially when the Jewish people exist only as pawns in its apocalyptic vision and must still eventually face judgement. Its anti-blackness underwent no such dormancy.

Finally, the practical consequences of recent elections in America bear out the truth that white evangelicalism finds fascist aesthetics exhilarating. There's no clear daylight between the goals of the fascist, the conservative, and the white evangelical, and it's not surprising that the goals of the traditional Religious Right resonate with today's so-called alt-right. Just as Trumpism is the purest expression of the Republican project from the civil rights and Southern Strategy era onward—it is certainly not an aberration—so too our era of turmoil is the purest expression of white evangelicalism's fate. If this faith does not ultimately devolve into open, permanent fascism (as I suspect and hope it won't, since it can settle for

---

34. Schmitt, *Political Theology*, 62.

permanent, minoritarian rule), it will not be for lack of fascist sympathies. There's an appetite. Those who see themselves as already-forgiven have no use for shame or empathy.

What then is fascism? No one seems to know for sure. It's a bit like the unconscious in that way. When discussing "the desire of the masses for fascism," Foucault said it gets thrown around as a term of derision without any analysis of its content.[35] Is it the aftermath of a failed revolution? Benito Mussolini called the fascist state the "highest and most powerful form of personality, [it] is a force, but a spiritual force, which takes over all the forms of the moral and intellectual life of man." Fascism was spirit and rejection, a theory and a practice, a "will to power and to government." The word comes from the Italian *fascio*, meaning a bundle. The "fascist decalogue," the ten commandments for the Blackshirts, read more like a list of tautologies and platitudes for angsty youth—"Mussolini is always right," "The enemy of Fascism is your enemy," "Discipline is the sunshine of armies," and so on. But there's a lesson here: Italian fascism rose to power without adequately defining its ideological parameters. The aesthetic of brute strength drew the mob. The average American would probably describe it as totalitarian without remembering fascism emerged in democracies. It was bubbling to the surface in so many democracies well beyond Italy and Germany alone. It can win with less than 50 percent of the vote.[36]

For our purposes, I find political scientist Robert Paxton's definitions helpful and clear. Most troublingly, Paxton showed how all functioning democracies exist in a type of pre-fascism, a fertile space out of which fascist desire can spring.

> Fascism may be defined as a form of political behavior marked by obsessive preoccupation with community decline, humiliation, or victimhood and by compensatory cults of unity, energy, and purity, in which a mass-based party of committed nationalist

35. "In the affirmation of the desire of the masses for fascism, what is troubling is that an *affirmation* covers up for the lack of any precise historical analysis. In this I see above all the effect of a general complicity in the refusal to decipher what fascism really was (a refusal that manifests itself either in generalisation—fascism is everywhere, above all in our heads—or in Marxist schematisation). The non-analysis of fascism is one of the important political facts of the past thirty years. It enables fascism to be used as a floating signifier, whose function is essentially that of denunciation." Foucault, *Power/Knowledge*, 139.

36. Hitler, of course, came to power after receiving less than four in ten votes. He was awarded power by the victor, which should be an important lesson in how the worst evils can work through the democratic system rather than in opposition to it.

militants, working in uneasy but effective collaboration with traditional elites, abandons democratic liberties and pursues with
redemptive violence and without ethical or legal restraints goals of
internal cleansing and external expansion.[37]

It arrived in stages. The traits exist long before a fascist government.
First, a movement is created. Second, the movement roots itself in the existing political system. Third, the movement seizes power. Fourth, the movement exercises power. Finally, the movement either radicalizes or dies from
entropy.[38] According to Paxton, these stages show not only the spectrum of
fascist movement but, again, how the space of public debate and grievances
in society creates the fertile ground out of which fascist antipathy grows. If
a movement grows and marches onward from the first step, it will appeal to
a cluster of mobilizing passions.

- a sense of overwhelming crisis beyond the reach of any traditional
  solutions;

- the primacy of the group, toward which one has duties superior to
  every right, whether individual or universal, and the subordination of
  the individual to it;

- the belief that one's group is a victim, a sentiment that justifies any
  action, without legal or moral limits, against its enemies, both internal
  and external;

- dread of the group's decline under the corrosive effects of individual-
  istic liberalism, class conflict, and alien influences;

- the need for closer integration of a purer community, by consent if
  possible, or by exclusionary violence if necessary;

- the need for authority by natural leaders (always male), culminating
  in a national chief who alone is capable of incarnating the group's
  destiny;

- the superiority of the leader's instincts over abstract and universal
  reason;

- the beauty of violence and the efficacy of will, when they are devoted
  to the group's success;

37. Paxton, *The Anatomy of Fascism*, 218.
38. Ibid., 23.

- the right of the chosen people to dominate others without restraint from any kind of human or divine law, right being decided by the sole criterion of the group's prowess within a Darwinian struggle.[39]

The horror of fascism "lies in the fact that the lie is obvious but persists."[40] This was a lesson in *Dialectic of Enlightenment* (1947), Max Horkheimer and Theodor Adorno's examination of anti-Semitism and fascism in the midst of the Second World War. The lie required willing participation of those deceived. It helped if society was deprived of the faculties of critical thought.[41] Nazis did not start with Auschwitz. The first camps, Oranienburg and Dachau, opened to confine socialists, communists, and trade unionists long before the genocide began. They required the yellow Star of David first in Poland before enforcing it in the Reich. They tried segregation and street violence before *Kristallnacht*. They first tested Zyklon B on 600 Soviet prisoners. It began with gunfire and gas vans before the camps. Each of these "dress rehearsals" tested the limits of power and lowered the threshold for what would feel acceptable later.[42] We must not compare anything today to that unspeakable barbarism. We also must remember and never close our eyes to the pattern exhibited. People need a bit of time to reach the point of absolute cruelty, but it doesn't take so very long.

When news of the internment or concentration camps for immigrants hit in the summer of 2018, the argument in their defense was often that these were not concentration camps. To call it such was hyperbolic, they reasoned, for there were no mass executions! We learned that many Americans were perfectly fine with politically or ethnically motivated concentration camps so long as (for now) they are not also death camps. If Dachau opened nearly a decade before it became a location for gruesome violence, we need to ask: how long it would it take Americans to come around to the idea of genocide?

39. Ibid., 41.

40. Horkheimer and Adorno, *Dialectic of Enlightenment*, 208.

41. "But if the progressive ticket strives for something which is worse than its own content, the content of the Fascist program is so meaningless that, as a substitute for something better, it can only be upheld by the desperate efforts of the deluded. Its horror lies in the fact that the lie is obvious but persists. Though this deception allows no truth against which it could be measured, the truth appears negatively in very extent of the contradiction; and the undiscerning can be permanently kept from that truth only if they are wholly deprived of the faculty of thought. Enlightenment which is in possession of itself and coming to power can break the bounds of enlightenment." Ibid., 208.

42. For a discussion on these "dress rehearsals," see Paxton, *Anatomy of Fascism*, 158–64.

My working assumption is that reactionaries today would prefer an underclass of exploitable labor over camps. My claim is not that white evangelicalism is fated to such a future—certainly not. My claim is that it could march right into that future under certain circumstances. My claim is that its desire is an inherently violent desire that dismisses any pain it doesn't feel itself.[43] According to Horkheimer and Adorno, any attempt to appeal to rationality will prove futile, because the logic of fascism is domination and suffering.[44] The fascist subject desires her self-deception, for what she hates in the other is a projection of what she hates in herself.

Once we hear human beings labeled *vermin*, it's too late. This is the most dangerous point where the machine begins to turn. Anti-Semitism was worse in rural zones where Jewish populations were thin. The minority called vermin echoes in the authoritarian's heart, for "The portrait of the Jews that the nationalists offer to the world is in fact their own self-portrait."[45] At the same time, this hate merged into the regular political antipathies between countrymen crying for equality. What National Socialists hated in the Social Democrats was the latter's demand for equality. It was not equality as such that the Aryan nationalist hated but instead the fear that she would be nothing more special than anyone else in the crowd. Equality kills hierarchy. "The covetous mobs . . . have always been aware deep down that ultimately all they would get out of it themselves would be the pleasure of seeing others robbed of all they possessed."[46] Is this not what we call relative deprivation today? The racist doesn't directly hate equality as such. Instead, he feels indignant that a minority gains ground he considers rightfully his by birth.

---

43. For example, when the last president who actually practiced white evangelicalism, George W. Bush, invaded a nation and killed over a million people for no good reason, white evangelicalism felt little angst. This tells us something, just as the reaction to internment camps signals a desire. At this point, I don't think it's at all hyperbolic to suggest many millions of Americans would be perfectly fine with liquidating everyone left at Guantanamo. What percentage would be fine with the execution of adult undocumented immigrants now, and what will that percentage be with a few more years of lies and exhaustion?

44. "All the rational, economic, and political explanations and counter-arguments—however accurate they may be in part—cannot provide a justification, because the rationality associated with domination is also based on suffering. Attacking or defending blindly, the persecutor and his victim belong to the same sphere of evil." Horkheimer and Adorno, *Dialectic of Enlightenment*, 171.

45. Ibid., 168.

46. Ibid., 170.

Fascism is paranoia writ large. It hates with morbid, false projection. Rather than imitating the environment, the subject imagines an environment mirroring his own inner paranoia.[47] He thinks minorities are out to get him, because he desires to harm minorities. He can't imagine it any other way. Deviation from the madness gets treated like a neurotic malady, which we see today whenever one pleads for seeing the migrant as a human being. What happens at this point? The person crying "No person is illegal" gets ridiculed as desiring crime, demographic change, or various other things that signal "cultural suicide" to the white nationalist. Reasoning with the fascist cannot work. "Rationalization was a pretense . . . The person chosen as an enemy was already seen as an enemy."[48] Victims are interchangeable in the various times and places. It's a trap to imagine there's some good faith reason *this* particular victim was rationally chosen. In theological terms, whoever is damned now was always predestined by the fascist's god for damnation.

How effective are happy platitudes about seeking the common good to those feeding on cruelty? How effective is a plea to care for the poor or disadvantaged to those who see weakness at the very mention of privilege or structural oppression? It doesn't feel empathy. Even if leaders feel no genuine antipathy to the victim group, the mob and the masses enjoy the sadistic ritual and derive such deep pleasure. They'll abandon their economic interests for something more brutally imprinted on their psyche. Cruelty is a reward in itself.

> The true benefit for the *Volksgenosse* lies in collective approval of his anger. The smaller the actual advantages are, the more stubbornly he supports the movement against his better judgment. Antisemitism has proved immune to the argument of inadequate "profitability." It is a luxury for the masses . . . All the rational, economic, and political explanations and counter-arguments—however accurate they may be in part—cannot provide a justification, because the rationality associated with domination is also based on suffering.[49]

47. "Impulses which the subject will not admit as his own even though they are most assuredly so, are attributed to the object—the prospective victim." Ibid., 187.

48. Ibid.

49. Ibid., 170–71.

Hierarchies of Contempt

The most prominent influence in my theoretical repertoire on this topic is the political theorist Hannah Arendt, and I'll rely on her exposition of fascism for the remainder of this chapter. She is among the most important theorists for those who wish to understand the perilous times in which we live. Her book *The Origins of Totalitarianism* (1951) used the Dreyfus Affair as an early case study.[50]

The French officer Alfred Dreyfus was arrested on charges of espionage in 1894. The prosecution built its case on a single letter that was sent to a German military attaché. The handwriting was quickly attributed to Dreyfus, and they sentenced him to life imprisonment at Devil's Island. Two years later, the French intelligence officer Colonel Georges Picquart came to Dreyfus's defense when evidence began pointing to another character, Major Ferdinand Walsin Esterhazy, as the true culprit. After alerting his authorities, Picquart was reassigned and later arrested. The courts quickly acquitted the newly accused Esterhazy, but after a discharge due to embezzlement he confessed his guilt to a British journalist. Esterhazy claimed it was indeed his letter written under orders as part of a plot to frame Dreyfus. Esterhazy confessed in August 1898, which seemed to confirm a scandal printed in a Paris newspaper back in January of the same year. In that newspaper, Émile Zola's open letter *J'accuse* claimed the military had suppressed information on the true culprit. Indeed, it looked now like the French command was all too willing to ignore espionage in order to pin blame on Dreyfus for no other reason than that he was Jewish.

A court of appeal revisited the case in 1899. A series of legal skirmishes oscillated back and forth through the legal system until Dreyfus was exonerated in 1906. However, since the acquitting court technically overstepped its authority, the Dreyfus Affair was not quite settled. By that time, French society was split into the supportive Dreyfusards (largely on the Left) and the anti-Dreyfusards (mostly on the Right). One prominent anti-Dreyfusard, Charles Maurras, was a leading figure in Action Française, a movement some consider a first true iteration of fascism. Even after Dreyfus's death in 1935, and long after all the evidence was in the open, anti-Dreyfusards persisted in believing him guilty. Arendt described the Dreyfus Affair as a type of shibboleth in French society, since one's perspective on the case signaled a whole range of other sympathies or affiliations. The facts didn't matter so

---

50. See Arendt, *The Origins of Totalitarianism*, 89–95.

much to the French military command, but they didn't even matter to the public decades after the case had come and gone. Do facts ever matter to xenophobia?[51] It served as an ominous moment after a century of Jewish emancipation in Europe. In France, the French Revolution's emphasis on rights of man and equality had extended to Jewish communities a level of equity and privilege never before seen. However, legal emancipation was interrupted by the more clandestine anti-Semitism buried in the culture. Anti-Semitism was brewing, soon to erupt in the most grotesque machinations imaginable in the twentieth century.

The fascist then and now loves their conspiracy theories. The big question of the period was whether the world was controlled by the "secret Rome" or "secret Judah."[52] This type of tabloid conspiracy-mongering was going on long before the publication of the *Protocols of the Elders of Zion*. This faked document, originally fabricated in Russia around the turn of the twentieth century, described a road map for Jewish domination. It was translated and widely distributed in the United States and Europe. Nazis found it particularly helpful for amplifying anti-Semitism, but they took it less as a threat and more as a manual.[53] Hitler's famous slogan "Right is what is good for the German people" was copied from the fabricated *Protocols*: "Everything that benefits the Jewish people is morally right and sacred."[54] His inversion of a fabricated cabal into an actualized fascist ethic worked the same as his address to the Reichstag in early 1939, when he announced, "I want today once again to make a prophecy: In case the Jewish financiers . . . succeed once more in hurling the peoples into a world war, the result will be . . . the annihilation of the Jewish race in Europe."[55] Both in

---

51. We could examine the old anti-Semitic myths of Jews poisoning wells or the medieval and current myths of global domination. Compare these myths to the figure of the migrant who is at once lazily living off the dole and also working so much that they take the citizen's job. As with the anti-Dreyfusards, xenophobia signals one's affinity for a range of seemingly unrelated political commitments that cluster together. The myths never operate at the level of fact even for the bigot, who simply doesn't care whether the myth is true or false. If anything, the bigot prefers to justify himself with myths everyone knows to be false, because then he also gets to provoke the angst of anti-racists and laugh at their concern.

52. See Arendt, *The Origins of Totalitarianism*, 94.

53. Arendt speaks of Nazis reading this document with "admiration and eagerness to learn rather than on hatred." Ibid., 358.

54. As quoted in ibid.

55. Hitler, as quoted in ibid., 349.

this address and in the co-opted slogan from the *Protocols*, Hitler signaled violence was on the way and authorized as self-defense.

We find an example of this projection in the United States today with the way anti-Muslim bigots invoke the supposed doctrine *taqiyya*. This highly obscure concept isn't a common point of reference for Muslims, most of whom have probably never heard of the term unless it was thrown in their face out of hostility. Drawn from one particular interpretation of a small handful of verses in the Qur'an, the idea is that one can conceal her identity under duress, such as in cases of persecution or fear for one's life. Just as most any culture or faith condones lying to save one's life, the Qur'an acknowledges the practical realities of danger. It's not exactly the type of idea that needs a whole doctrinal support system, but this limited situation has been twisted by anti-Muslim nationalists, who choose to believe Muslims will lie to Christians at all times. Combined with the image of violence attributed to the very core of Islamic thought, the figure of the deceptive, violent extremist dehumanizes the victim of real, imperial violence. In effect, the American Christian nationalist sees herself always on the defense in her violence and never responsible for treating a Muslim's concerns in good faith. The neoconservative or the Christian nationalist becomes the perverse caricature they have invented for the Muslim. This is the reverse revenge fantasy in which the aggressor projects a mirror image of her own wish. Aiming to strip the Muslim of basic human rights, this is *Protocols* logic.

Another unnerving example stands out as patently absurd and closer to home. In 2015, there was a briefly popular conspiracy theory called Jade Helm 15. It drew its name from a real military training exercise involving over a thousand troops running from July 15 to September 15, 2015. In a panic lead by Alex Jones, conspiracy theorists feared President Obama was actually preparing to declare martial law in the American Southwest and round up conservatives in camps run by the Federal Emergency Management Agency. They believed Islamic State operatives were crossing the US-Mexico border and plotting attacks, which the federal government would use as a pretense to round up Americans under martial law. Several Walmart stores had recently closed, and conspiracy theorists believed these locations would be converted into internment camps. A man claiming to be a Texas Ranger said trains affixed with shackles were crossing the state in preparation for relocation. Texas Governor Greg Abbott lent support to the panic and requested the Texas State Guard to monitor the Jade Helm joint military operation in the area, which was the basis for the conspiracy theory. "It is important that Texans know their safety, constitutional rights, private property rights and civil liberties will not be infringed upon,"[56] he said. In a sense, this fantasy inverted and came true.

Three years later, camps would be opened for immigrant children forcibly separated from parents at the border. The largest of the early holding camps was Casa Padre in Brownsville, Texas. It was a converted Walmart.

Witness the impotence of "norm erosion" rhetoric. Totalitarianism requires masses with sufficient political appetite who are engaged and increasingly open to duplicitous propaganda from cynical ideologues. Arendt lists the ingredients of the masses, the mob, and the leader. The masses are those uncommitted to an organization or common interest, often due to indifference, and they exist everywhere. Communists and Nazis drew from this class, those ignored by the parties on the assumption that people were too stupid or apathetic, who were unsullied by traditional ideological dispositions and therefore more open to terror.[57] The activation of the masses dispelled the liberal illusion that the masses bought into the liberal parliamentarian order. The silence of the masses did not imply their consent to the norms they would soon happily discard. The critical miscalculation of the liberal bourgeoisie was that the totalitarian streak was displaying its inconsistency when, in fact, the totalitarians were convincing the masses that the norms were entirely irrelevant.[58] Out of the masses arises the smaller

56. Goodwyn, "Texas Governor Deploys State Guard To Stave Off Obama Takeover."

57. "It was characteristic of the rise of the Nazi movement in Germany and of the Communist movements in Europe after 1930 that they recruited their members from this mass of apparently indifferent people whom all other parties had given up as too apathetic or too stupid for their attention. The result was that the majority of their membership consisted of people who never before had appeared on the political scene. This permitted the introduction of entirely new methods into political propaganda, and indifference to the arguments of political opponents; these movements not only placed themselves outside and against the party system as a whole, they found a membership that had never been reached, never been 'spoiled' by the party system. Therefore they did not need to refute opposing arguments and consistently preferred methods which ended in death rather than persuasion, which spelled terror rather than conviction." Arendt, *The Origins of Totalitarianism*, 311–12.

58. "Now they made apparent what no other organ of public opinion had ever been able to show, namely, that democratic government had rested as much on the silent approbation and tolerance of the indifferent and inarticulate sections of the people as on the articulate and visible institutions and organizations of the country. Thus when the totalitarian movements invaded Parliament with their contempt for parliamentary government, they merely appeared inconsistent: actually, they succeeded in convincing the people at large that parliamentary majorities were spurious and did not necessarily correspond to the realities of the country, thereby undermining the self-respect and

group of the mob, those who share a perverted form of "the standards and attitudes of the dominating class, but reflect and somehow pervert the standards and attitudes toward public affairs for all classes."[59] While the mob is able to distinguish between its fascist-sympathetic (yet non-radicalized) "fellow travelers" from its anti-fascist opponents,[60] the mob is the aggressive residue of all classes. It desires the strong man.[61] The mob finds outward aggression and chauvinism spiritually appealing,[62] and its members conjoin the desire of the masses to be an anonymous cog in the glorious machine with the desire to be part of a movement signified by the leader.[63] The leader then must perform a double task: "to act as the magic defense of the movement against the outside world; and at the same time, to be the direct bridge by which the movement is connected with it."[64]

The leader does not hide his crimes but instead boasts of them. The leader curates passions. He's the crucial point of desire without which the movement crumbles, though the animus will remain in waiting for another. As Freud put long before the rise of fascism, the leader is the one who represents the ideal-ego of the people; they want to be strong like him, so they love him.[65] Followers excuse his flaws just as we look the other way on our own flaws—introspection is too painful for those who wish not to see.

The leader appoints subordinates who are his walking embodiment. Arendt saw this unification of responsibility—subordinates express the will of the leader, so the leader cannot tolerate criticism of subordinates—as the feature distinguishing totalitarian leaders from ordinary despots.[66] When the leader openly boasts of past crimes and plans for future crimes, it doesn't turn off the mob but instead invigorates their morbid attraction to his audacity.[67] He gets away with anything not only because they love him but because the leader and the mob feel no shame. For this reason, every

---

the confidence of governments which also believed in majority rule rather than in their constitutions." Ibid., 312.

59. Ibid., 314.

60. Ibid., 263

61. Ibid., 107.

62. Ibid., 226–27.

63. Ibid., 329.

64. Ibid., 374.

65. See Freud, *Group Psychology and the Analysis of the Ego.*

66. Arendt, *The Origins of Totalitarianism*, 374–75.

67. Ibid., 306.

ludicrous or hostile statement from the leader should be read as (1) a test for followers and (2) a declaration of intent toward opponents.[68]

Ideology is a murderous alphabet—once you give in to A, B, and C, the ideologue continues to the gruesome end.[69] Ideology promises to unveil the riddles of the universe, and its persuasion must speak to immediate experience and desire.[70] Ideology is the logic of an absurd idea. "Ideologies pretend to know the mystery of the whole historical process—the secrets of the past, the intricacies of the present, the uncertainties of the future—because of the logic inherent in their respective ideals," wrote Arendt. "Ideologies are never interested in the miracle of being."[71] Ideology is inevitable, not necessarily dangerous, but it's always potentially dangerous, and the first step of race-thinking ideology is the same as the first step of totalitarian ideology: kill off the juridical voice in society by normalizing the placement of persons outside the law.[72] The person who thinks highly of his political detective capacities—he who holds ideologically resistant clarity, he who always criticizes "both sides"—is probably less redeemable than the open fascist. At least the open fascist understands he's given in to the trap.

Propaganda is no longer necessary after the arrival of the camps.[73] If the *vermin* can be bloodied, the masses and the mob have a taste for blood. If propaganda gets replaced by indoctrination with the completion of rule, what then are the steps toward the loss of the juridical person?[74] That's our danger today. The teacher must not politicize the classroom with ethics or history. The minister loses a congregation if she preaches love of the neighbor or the alien, for she should "keep politics out of the pulpit." The anti-racist activist knows all too well who the police will protect at a march in a contest between them and the neo-Nazi. We increasingly see not only

68. Ibid., 385.

69. Ibid., 472.

70. "For an ideology differs from a simple opinion in that it claims to possess either the key to history, or the solution for all the 'riddles of the universe,' or intimate knowledge of the hidden universal laws which are supposed to rule nature and man. Few ideologies have won enough prominence to survive the hard competitive struggle of persuasion, and only two have come out on top and essentially defeated all others: the ideology which interprets history as an economic struggle of classes, and the other that interprets history as a natural fight of races." Ibid., 159.

71. Ibid., 469.

72. Ibid., 447.

73. Ibid., 344.

74. Ibid., 341.

the loss of the juridical subject in much of our society but also the loss of ability to respond. In our time, even the phrases "Nazis are bad" or "Love your neighbor" become a shibboleth. They hear the critique, know it to be true, and counterattack.

The leader's propaganda begins a chain reaction with a statement that seems incoherent or impossible and yet declares intent. When Goebbel's article "The Jews Are Guilty!" (1941) claimed the Jewish people wanted to violently wipe out Germans but didn't have the means to do so just yet, was this anything other than a declaration of intent? The masses must participate as the society proscribes thought and replaces the expert with the charlatan, the intellectual with the crackpot, the artist with the con artist, and the analyst with the propagandist.[75] Arguing against propaganda as if it can be swayed by logic in good faith—this is the trap into which liberals fall—makes as much sense as arguing metaphysics with a potential murderer over whether his intended victim is alive or deceased in the future.[76] Arguing is futile if someone's faith is built atop lies they actually, consciously recognize as lies, so don't give to the dogs what is sacred. Propaganda is predictive, and what matters is the intent.

The leader behind the propaganda does not desire society's insanity but only its bewilderment. Those who believe propaganda simply relays misinformation will debate the falsehoods and contradictions while the propaganda machine transforms the bureaucratic apparatuses before their eyes.[77]

---

75. "Intellectual, spiritual, and artistic initiative is as dangerous to totalitarianism as the gangster initiative of the mob, and both are more dangerous than mere political opposition. The consistent persecution of every higher form of intellectual activity by the new mass leaders springs from more than their natural resentment against everything they cannot understand. Total domination does not allow for free initiative in any field of life, for any activity that is not entirely predictable. Totalitarianism in power invariably replaces all first-rate talents, regardless of their sympathies, with those crackpots and fools whose lack of intelligence and creativity is still the best guarantee of their loyalty." Ibid., 339.

76. Ibid., 350.

77. When for example the Nazi party told its followers "What is right is what is good for the movement," it contradicted "What is right is what is good for Germany," since the two certainly did not align. Focusing on the contradiction of formulae does not help here, for the intent declared is that only a certain type of politically affiliated Aryan is a true Aryan, or only the SS member shall rule as the master race. Similarly, "America First" doesn't even mean "All Americans First" but instead only means a certain type of *real American* first. As Arendt explains, "To be sure, totalitarian dictators do not consciously embark upon the road to insanity. The point is rather that our bewilderment about the anti-utilitarian character of the totalitarian state structure springs from the

Propaganda excels at naming what the masses (and the mob in particular) see as ignored or covered over by traditional norms. Propaganda taps into the sense that "everyone knows" what "everyone's thinking" but can't say due to hypocrisy, corruption, or cowardice.[78] It's precisely because something is unacceptable to say that the mob finds it intriguing, exciting, and necessary to say. Arendt saw a chief characteristic of modern masses fine-tuned to deception: "They do not believe in anything visible, in the reality of their own experience; they do not trust their eyes and ears but only their imagination . . . What convinces the masses are not facts, and not even invented facts, but only the consistency of the system of which they are presumably part." Convincing comes from repetition of (mis)information. Don't look for what is most abhorrent or false but instead what is most repeated. That will be the end goal.

What the outside world never understands is the multiple vectors of propaganda. Propaganda sometimes aims for the masses, other times for the mob, sometimes for the fellow-travelers, other times for the convinced members. It is sometimes for the knave, sometimes for the fool, sometimes for the apathetic. Outsiders always think contradictions will need to get balanced out or accounted for, which is the fatal flaw in interpreting the fascist's speech.[79] Arendt calls these multiple vectors a "graduation of cynicism ex-

---

mistaken notion that we are dealing with a normal state after all—a bureaucracy, a tyranny, a dictatorship—from our overlooking the emphatic assertions by totalitarian rulers that they consider the country where they happened to seize power only the temporary headquarters of the international movement on the road to world conquest, that they reckon victories and defeats in terms of centuries or millennia, and that the global interests always overrule the local interests of their own territory. The famous 'Right is what is good for the German people' was meant only for mass propaganda; Nazis were told that 'Right is what is good for the movement,' and these two interests did by no means always coincide. The Nazis did not think that the Germans were a master race, to whom the world belonged, but that they should be led by a master race, as should all other nations, and that this race was only on the point of being born. Not the Germans were the dawn of the master race, but the SS." Ibid., 411–12.

78. "Totalitarian propaganda perfects the techniques of mass propaganda, but it neither invents them nor originates their themes. These are prepared for them by fifty years of the rise of imperialism and disintegration of the nation-state, when the mob entered the scene of European politics. Like the earlier mob leaders, the spokesmen for totalitarian movements possessed an unerring instinct for anything that ordinary party propaganda or public opinion did not care or dare to touch. Everything hidden, everything passed over in silence, became of major significance, regardless of its own intrinsic importance. The mob really believed that truth was whatever respectable society had hypocritically passed over, or covered up with corruption." Ibid., 351.

79. "It has been one of the chief handicaps of the outside world in dealing with

pressed in a hierarchy of contempt,"[80] for the cynicism of the masses is not the same as the cynicism of the true believer, and each will be ignited with specific codes. When discovering the lie, the masses will say they already knew it was a lie. The leader who gets away with constant deception has merely shown himself the superior tactician in his battle against society. No lie will prove too large. No contradiction will diminish the authority of the leader. The masses and the mob already expect contradictions.

It's at this point that the machine will radicalize or die from entropy, and it's here that our study concludes. What does it mean to see a movement thrive in struggles against future, against knowledge, against sexuality, against reality, and against society? We should consider these lessons carefully.

Why should they listen to the other if they feel they're the elect? Why preserve the society that is changing to deprive them of their hierarchy? Why preserve democracy when the goal is lordship? Why preserve the society that God will destroy? Such thinking will ready itself to "believe everything and nothing, think that everything was possible and nothing was true."[81] They are already forgiven for their sins, and you are not chosen.

---

totalitarian systems that it ignored this system and therefore trusted that, on one hand, the very enormity of totalitarian lies would be their undoing and that, on the other, it would be possible to take the Leader at his word and force him, regardless of his original intentions, to make it good." Ibid., 384.

80. Ibid.

81. Ibid., 382.

Epilogue

*Don't You See We Are
Short on Time?*

66 "Where id was, there ego will be." This was Freud's lesson, for where there is desire, there will follow the justification. This is what the young sect of white evangelicalism is perfectly suited to do. Those who believe themselves already forgiven can feel no shame at their sins. The faith is moralizing where it should be ethical, individual where it should be collective, hegemonic where it sees itself cornered, and demonic where it sees itself the savior. Its whiteness and chosenness are the gods it won't forsake. It's not hypocritical. The faith is doing what it's designed to do. This book was a warning.

Whatever comes of the cruelty of human suffering, the climate's collapse lies before us. The world is quite literally burning out, and we don't have much time. For those of us seeking to counter the resonances of capital, whiteness, and evangelicalism (among so many other resonance machines we must break), our task is not to see ourselves as the savior rescuing the duped. As Lacan taught, to see oneself as the non-duped already submits oneself to the same logic one seeks to critique. Do you think you simply see what another cannot due to intellectual blinders?[1] This is the fault of the

---

1. Lacan hints that the goal of understanding should actually be a refusal to be non-duped, to accept the existence of ideological blinders and see instead where this perverse logic ends up. "I know well that the way, the way that is at stake, the Tao, imagines itself as being in the structure. But is it quite sure that there is only one Way? Or even that the notion of the way, of the method, is worth anything at all? Might it not be in forging for ourselves a quite different ethic, an ethic that would be founded on the refusal of being *unduped*, on the way of being always more strongly the dupe of this knowledge, of this unconscious which, when all is said and done, is our only lot in terms of knowledge . . .

liberal criticizing the fascist, the intelligentsia criticizing folk religion, or even the true believer's conviction that we might rectify poor theology with better theology. We'd like things to run a bit more smoothly or at least less foolishly.[2] But ideological opponents are not simply the duped who must be rescued by the non-duped. Opponents desire just as we desire. What we need to recognize are the counterintuitive locations of enjoyment.

Society is repression. White evangelicalism is a symptom of repression in our time. After inhibition, the progression of difficulty and movement lead inexorably to turmoil or anxiety. It's a faith built upon acting-out for a big Other, for a community, for a politics, and so on. It sees itself as a Bonhoeffer while hanging on the every word of a Goebbels. And as Marx told us long ago, religion is both the expression of suffering and the protest against suffering. This project conjoined history and psychoanalysis to take seriously a symptom within civilization's most catastrophic hour. Let us hear Foucault's enjoinder to the intellectual:

> The intellectual no longer has to play the role of an advisor. The project, tactics and goals to be adopted are a matter for those who do the fighting. What the intellectual can do is to provide instruments of analysis, and at present this is the historian's essential role. What's effectively needed is a ramified, penetrative perception of the present, one that makes it possible to locate lines of weakness, strong points, positions where the instances of power have secured and implanted themselves by a system of organisation.[3]

We haven't the time to play games of interpretation. If we engage defense mechanisms in a test of strength, we will fail. The signifiers we interpret are already active, engaged in machinations and concealed in disguises. This is how Lacan so eloquently warned of the signifier's fate:

> You believe you are taking action when I am the one making you stir at the bidding of the bonds with which I weave your desires. Thus do the latter grow in strength and multiply in objects, bringing you back to the fragmentation of your rent childhood. That

---

And after all, behind what we choose to say about it, behind there is always a desire, an intention, as they say." Lacan, *Les Non Dupes Errent*, 35–36.

2. As Lacan put the turmoil of contradictions in society, "You would like for it to go differently. Obviously it could go better. What would be needed, would be for the master discourse to be a little less primary, and, to say it all, not so fucking stupid." Lacan, "On Psychoanalytic Discourse."

3. Foucault, *Power/Knowledge*, 62.

will be your feast until the return of the stone guest whom I shall be for you since you call me forth.[4]

Like in the book of Job, the master signifier gambles with their lives and yet demands fidelity, for it gives and takes away. In turn they shall say, "Blessed be the name." Blessed be the turmoil with which it curses the anxious creature. Blessed be the *jouissance* of knowing beyond all knowing, and cursed be humility. Blessed be rage and cruelty. Blessed be anything that might foreclose the mending of the world.

Our battle is not of information but of desire, and we are running out of time. Don't you see the world is burning?

4. Lacan, *Écrits*, 29.

Acknowledgements

So much of this book comes directly out of the conversations over the years with readers, friends, and family. Those conversations helped me see that I still had so many questions about the way this faith shaped me and how it continues to inflict such force in our culture. In a sense, this project is most indebted to you all who planted the idea with questions.

Thank you once again to Clayton Crockett not only for the introduction and scholarship underneath all I write but for the friendship and encouragement along the way. My thanks especially go out to Andrea, Randy, David, Larry, and Lauren for always letting me know how much my work is valued. A number of people ranging from friends to complete strangers went out of their way to provide resources and point my research in new directions, so I owe my thanks to Kirsten Gerdes, Scott Krzych, Chris Rodkey, Alan Jay Richard, Kevin Mequet, Paul Johnson, and Mason Inman. It's strange to realize in retrospect that I wasn't quite clear until very late in the writing process that my topic was fantasy. That realization came through conversation with Krzych, so my thanks go out to you for the feedback after reading an early version of the material. Since concepts were modified from my doctoral dissertation, I should also thank my committee, Henry Krips, Philip Clayton, and Ingolf Dalferth, whose comments enhanced the direction of this book. I apologize to anyone I may have missed. There are just so many to whom I'm indebted, because, in my experience, my research projects are always the culmination of catching up on recommendations from colleagues. One of my favorite parts of academia is knowing so many brilliant friends who can tell me what I don't know, so thanks to you all who have been a part of this academic journey so far.

Jesse Turri has produced the artwork on all of my books, and I'm deeply appreciative for his work once again. It is rare for authors of more academically oriented books to actually feel proud of the artwork, and Turri has been so gracious with his time and skill. I truly appreciate the photography by Elizabeth Colunga. Thank you to Zach Chrisman and Robin George for editing and for offering suggestions in the final busy weeks before publication. Thanks once again to the whole team at Cascade, especially my editor Rodney Clapp. My appreciation also goes out to my generous patrons. Being an independent scholar isn't easy, and I'm so deeply grateful for your support.

And to my wife, Deven, you know how much I love the process of writing, and, at the same time, you know how much it drives me to insanity. Your excitement about my excitement keeps me searching and moving forward. I remember exactly where we were on the day I told you, after months of derailed starts and aimless research, about this concept. You had this certainty about the idea, which told me I was on the right track. Your encouragement keeps me going when I'd rather quit. Your partnership reminds me that there are things worth fighting for and against, and education is one of those things worth fighting for. You are my best friend.

Author Photo

Tad DeLay, PhD, is the author of *The Cynic & the Fool* and *God Is Unconscious*.
He teaches philosophy and religious studies in Denver.

Photo by Elizabeth Colunga

Bibliography

Abbott, Elizabeth. *The History of Celibacy*. Cambridge, MA: Da Capo, 2001.

Adorno, Theodor W. "Education After Auschwitz." In *Critical Models: Interventions and Catchwords*, translated by Henry W. Pickford, 191–204. New York: Columbia University Press, 2005.

Althusser, Louis. "Ideology and Ideological State Apparatuses (Notes towards an Investigation)." In *Lenin and Philosophy and Other Essays*, translated by Ben Brewster, 127–86. New York: Monthly Review, 1971.

Anderegg, William R. L., James W. Prall, Jacob Harold, and Stephen H. Schneider. "Expert Credibility in Climate Change." *Proceedings of the National Academy of Sciences* 107, no. 27 (July 6, 2010) 12107–9. http://doi.org/10.1073/pnas.1003187107.

Answers in Genesis. "Statement of Faith." Accessed September 16, 2018. https://answersingenesis.org/about/faith/.

Arendt, Hannah. *The Origins of Totalitarianism*. New York: Harvest, 1976.

Associated Press. "Dempsey Hits Islamic State 'End-of-Days' Vision." *PBS*, August 21, 2014. https://www.pbs.org/newshour/world/dempsey-hits-islamic-militant-end-days-vision.

Augustine, "The Literal Meaning of Genesis, book I, chapter 19." In *Ancient Christian Writers*, no. 41, edited by Johannes Quasten, Walter J. Burghardt, and Thomas Comerford Lawler, 42–43. Mahwah, NJ: Paulist, 1982.

Ayers, Edward L. *The Promise of the New South: Life After Reconstruction*. New York: Oxford University Press, 2007.

Balmer, Randall. "The Real Origins of the Religious Right." *Politico*, May 27, 2014. https://www.politico.com/magazine/story/2014/05/religious-right-real-origins-107133?o=1.

———. *Thy Kingdom Come: How the Religious Right Distorts the Faith and Threatens America*. New York: Basic, 2006.

Baum, Dan. "Legalize It All: How to Win the War on Drugs." *Harpers*, April 2016. https://harpers.org/archive/2016/04/legalize-it-all/.

Bearman, Peter S., and Hannah Brückner. "Promising the Future: Virginity Pledges and First Intercourse." *American Journal of Sociology* 106, no. 4 (January 2001) 859–912. http://www.jstor.org/stable/10.1086/320295.

de Beauvoir, Simone. *The Second Sex*. Translated by H. M. Parshley. New York: Vintage, 1989.

Berkman, Michael B., Julianna Sandell Pacheco, and Eric Plutzer. "Evolution and Creationism in America's Classrooms: A National Portrait." *PLOS* 6, no. 5 (2008). https://doi.org/10.1371/journal.pbio.0060124.

BioLogos. "How have Christians responded to Darwin's 'Origin of Species'?" Accessed September 15, 2017. https://biologos.org/common-questions/christianity-and-science /christian-response-to-darwin.

BJU Press. *Life Science*. 3rd ed. Greenville, SC: Bob Jones University Press, 2007.

————. *United States History for Christian Schools*. 2nd ed. Greenville, SC: Bob Jones University Press, 1991.

Bowen, William, and Brian Ashbaugh. *American Government in Christian Perspective*. 2nd ed. Pensacola, FL: Abeka, 1997.

Boyd, James. "Nixon's Southern Strategy: 'It's All In the Charts.'" *The New York Times*. Accessed September 13, 2018. http://www.nytimes.com/packages/html/books/ phillips-southern.pdf.

Brückner, Hannah, and Peter Bearman. "After the Promise: The STD Consequences of Adolescent Virginity Pledges." *Journal of Adolescent Health* 36, no. 4 (April 2005) 271–78. https://doi.org/10.1016/j.jadohealth.2005.01.005.

Bryan, William J. "Life and Speeches of Hon. Wm. Jennings Bryan." Baltimore: Woodard, 1900.

Butler, Judith. *Gender Trouble: Feminism and the Subversion of Identity*. New York: Routledge, 2006.

Carmines, Edward G., and James Woods. "The Role of Party Activists in the Evolution of the Abortion Issue." *Political Behavior* 24, no. 4 (December 2002) 361–77. https:// www.jstor.org/stable/1558379.

Cassino, Dan, Peter Woolley, and Krista Jenkins. "What You Know Depends on What You Watch: Current Events Knowledge Across Popular News Sources." *Public Mind Poll*, May 3, 2012. http://publicmind.fdu.edu/2012/confirmed/.

Christianity Today. "Abortion Decision: A Death Blow?" February 16, 1973, 516.

CNN. "Surveyed Scientists Agree Global Warming Is Real." *CNN*, January 20, 2009. http:// www.cnn.com/2009/WORLD/americas/01/19/eco.globalwarmingsurvey/.

Cohen, Naomi W. "Antisemitism in the Gilded Age: The Jewish View." *Jewish Social Studies* 41, no. 3/4 (Summer-Autumn, 1979) 187–210. https://www.jstor.org/ stable/4467051.

Combee, Jerry H. *History of the World in Christian Perspective*. Pensacola, FL: Abeka, 1979.

Connolly, William E. *Capitalism and Christianity, American Style*. Durham, NC: Duke University Press, 2008.

Cook, John, Dana Nuccitelli, Sarah A. Green, Mark Richardson, Bärbel Winkler, Rob Painting, Robert Way, Peter Jacobs, and Andrew Skuce. "Quantifying the Consensus on Anthropogenic Global Warming in the Scientific Literature." *Environmental Research Letters* 8, no. 2 (May 15, 2013). http://iopscience.iop.org/ article/10.1088/1748-9326/8/2/024024.

Copjec, Joan. *Imagine There's No Woman: Ethics and Sublimation*. Cambridge, MA: MIT Press, 2002.

Cox, Daniel, Juhem Navarro-Rivera, and Robert P. Jones. "Americans More Likely to Attribute Increasingly Severe Weather to Climate Change, Not End Times." *Public Religion Research Institute*, December 13, 2012. https://www.prri.org/research/prri- rns-december-2012-survey/.

Cox, Daniel, Rachel Lienesch, and Robert P. Jones. "Who Sees Discrimination? Attitudes on Sexual Orientation, Gender Identity, Race, and Immigration Status." *Public Religion Research Institute*, June 21, 2017. https://www.prri.org/research/americans-views-discrimination-immigrants-blacks-lgbt-sex-marriage-immigration-reform/.

Cox, Daniel, and Robert P. Jones. "America's Changing Religious Identity." *Public Religion Research Institute*, September 6, 2017. https://www.prri.org/research/american-religious-landscape-christian-religiously-unaffiliated/.

————. "Majority of Americans Oppose Transgender Bathroom Restrictions." *Public Religion Research Institute*, March 10, 2017. https://www.prri.org/research/lgbt-transgender-bathroom-discrimination-religious-liberty/.

Crockett, Clayton, and Jeffrey W. Robbins. *Religion, Politics, and the Earth: The New Materialism*. New York: Palgrave Macmillan, 2012.

Dabney, Robert Lewis. "The Negro and the Common School." In *Discussions, Vol. IV*, edited by C. R. Vaughan, 176–90. Harrisburg, PA: Sprinkle, 1994.

Daly, Mary. *Beyond God the Father*. Boston: Beacon, 1973.

DC Talk and The Voice of Martyrs. *Jesus Freaks: Martyrs*. Grand Rapids: Bethany House, 1999.

DeLay, Tad. *The Cynic & the Fool: The Unconscious in Theology & Politics*. Eugene, OR: Cascade, 2017.

Deleuze, Gilles, and Félix Guattari. *Anti-Oedipus: Capitalism and Schizophrenia*. Translated by Robert Hurley. New York: Penguin, 2009.

Democracy Now! "Chomsky on the GOP: Has Any Organization Ever Been So Committed to Destruction of Life on Earth?" *Democracy Now!*, April 26, 2017. https://www.democracynow.org/2017/4/26/chomsky_on_the_gop_has_any.

Dickinson, Tim. "How Roger Ailes Built the Fox News Fear Factory." *Rolling Stone*, June 9, 2011. https://www.rollingstone.com/politics/news/how-roger-ailes-built-the-fox-news-fear-factory-20110525.

Dochuk, Darren. *From Bible Belt to Sunbelt: Plain-Folk Religion, Grassroots Politics, and the Rise of Evangelical Conservatism*. New York: Norton, 2011.

Du Bois, W. E. B. "The Souls of White People." In *Darkwater: Voices from Within the Veil*, 17–29. Mineola, NY: Dover, 1999.

Ducote, Nicholas. "For the Media: Former Homeschoolers Rally Against Abuse." *HARO*, March 16, 2013. "https://homeschoolersanonymous.org/2013/03/16/for-the-media-former-homeschoolers-rally-against-abuse/.

Dugan, Andrew. "More Americans Say Pornography Is Morally Acceptable." *Gallup*, June 5, 2018. https://news.gallup.com/poll/235280/americans-say-pornography-morally-acceptable.aspx.

Eckholm, Erik. "'Ex-Gay' Men Fight Back Against View That Homosexuality Can't Be Changed." *The New York Times*, October 31, 2012. https://www.nytimes.com/2012/11/01/us/ex-gay-men-fight-view-that-homosexuality-cant-be-changed.html.

Einstein, Albert. "Why War? A Letter from Albert Einstein to Sigmund Freud." Accessed September 14, 2018. https://en.unesco.org/courier/mayo-1985/why-war-letter-albert-einstein-sigmund-freud.

Falwell, Jerry. *Listen, America!* Garden City, NY: Doubleday, 1980.

Faubus, Orval E. "Speech on School Integration." Accessed September 15, 2018. http://www.blackpast.org/1958-governor-orval-e-faubus-speech-school-integration.

Federal Communications Commission. "Fifteenth Annual Report." Washington, DC: FCC, 1949. Accessed September 17, 2018. https://www.fcc.gov/reports-research/reports/annual-reports-congress/15th-annual-report-congress-1949.

———. "The Public and Broadcasting." Washington, DC: FCC, 2008. Accessed September 17, 2018. https://www.fcc.gov/media/radio/public-and-broadcasting.

Feldman, Lauren, Edward W. Maibach, Connie Roser-Renouf, and Anthony Leiserowitz."Climate on Cable: The Nature and Impact of Global Warming Coverage on Fox News, CNN, and MSNBC." *The International Journal of Press/Politics* 17, no. 1 (November 2, 2011) 3–31. https://doi.org/10.1177%2F1940161211425410.

Fineman, Howard. "Bush: What Bounce?" *Newsweek*, August 30, 1992. http://www.newsweek.com/bush-what-bounce-197918.

Finer, Lawrence B. "Trends in Premarital Sex in the United States, 1954–2003." *National Institutes of Health, Public Health Report* 122, no. 1 (February 2007) 73–78. https://www.ncbi.nlm.nih.gov/pmc/articles/PMC1802108/.

Finke, Roger, and Rodney Stark. *The Churching of America, 1776–2005: Winners and Losers in Our Religious Economy.* 2nd ed. New Brunswick, NJ: Rutgers University Press, 2005.

Foucault, Michel. *Discipline and Punish: The Birth of the Prison.* Translated by Alan Sheridan. New York: Vintage, 1995.

———. *The History of Sexuality, Volume 1: An Introduction.* Translated by Robert Hurley. New York: Vintage, 1990.

———. *Power/Knowledge: Selected Interviews and Other Writings, 1972–1977.* Edited by Colin Gordon. Translated by Colin Gordon, Leo Marshall, John Mepham, and Kate Soper. New York: Pantheon, 1980.

Fox New Channel. "A Megaphone for Their Master: Gutfeld Blasts Media's Climate Change Hysteria." *Fox News Insider*, May 7, 2014. http://insider.foxnews.com/2014/05/07/greg-gutfeld-blasts-media's-climate-change-hysteria.

———. "You're Out of Your Mind: Beckel Takes on Greenpeace Co-Founder Over Climate Change." *Fox News Insider*, March 12, 2014. http://insider.foxnews.com/2014/03/12/youre-out-your-mind-beckel-takes-greenpeace-co-founder-over-climate-change?page=2.

Friedman, Milton. "The Role of Government in Education." Originally in *Economics and the Public Interest*, edited by Robert A. Solo, 123–44. New Brunswick, NJ: Rutgers University Press, 1955. Accessed September 15, 2018. http://la.utexas.edu/users/hcleaver/330T/350kPEEFriedmanRoleOfGovttable.pdf.

Freud, Sigmund. *The Ego and the Id.* Edited by James Strachey. New York: Norton, 1960.

———. *Group Psychology and the Analysis of the Ego.* Translated by James Strachey. New York: Norton, 1959.

———. *Inhibitions, Symptoms, and Anxiety.* New York: Norton, 1959.

———. *Jokes and Their Relation to the Unconscious.* Translated by James Strachey. New York: Norton, 1960.

———. "Why War? A Letter from Freud to Einstein." Accessed September 14, 2018. https://en.unesco.org/courier/marzo-1993/why-war-letter-freud-einstein.

Gadsby, Hannah. *Nanette.* Directed by Jon Olb and Madeleine Parry. Los Gatos: Netflix, 2018.

Geiger, Abigail. "From Universities to Churches, Republicans and Democrats Differ in Views of Major Institutions." *Pew Research Center.* Accessed September 14, 2016. http://www.pewresearch.org/fact-tank/2016/09/26/from-universities-to-churches-republicans-and-democrats-differ-in-views-of-major-institutions/.

Gilman, Sander L., Helen King, Roy Porter, G. S. Rousseau, and Elaine Showalter. *Hysteria Beyond Freud*. Berkeley, CA: University of California Press, 1993.

Goldwater, Barry. *The Conscience of a Conservative*. Washington, DC: Regnery Gateway, 1990.

Goodwyn, Wade. "Texas Governor Deploys State Guard To Stave Off Obama Takeover." *NPR*, May 2, 2015. https://www.npr.org/sections/itsallpolitics/2015/05/02/403865824/texas-governor-deploys-state-guard-to-stave-off-obama-takeover.

Gottfried, Jeffrey, and Elisa Shearer. "Americans' Online News Use Is Closing in on TV News Use." *Pew Research Center*, September 7, 2017. http://www.pewresearch.org/fact-tank/2017/09/07/americans-online-news-use-vs-tv-news-use/.

Gottfried, Jeffrey, Michael Barthel, and Amy Mitchell. "Trump, Clinton Voters Divided in Their Main Source for Election News." *Pew Research Center*, January 18, 2017. http://www.journalism.org/2017/01/18/trump-clinton-voters-divided-in-their-main-source-for-election-news/.

Gramm, Marshall, and Phil Gramm. "The Free Silver Movement in America: A Reinterpretation." *The Journal of Economic History* 64, no. 4 (December 2004) 1108–29. http://www.jstor.org/stable/3874991.

Guilford, Megan C., Charles A. A. Hall, Peter O'Connor, and Cutler J. Cleveland. "A New Long Term Assessment of Energy Return on Investment (EROI) for U.S. Oil and Gas Discovery and Production." *Sustainability* 2011, 3: 1866-1887. http://www.mdpi.com/2071-1050/3/10/1866/htm.

Harris, Joshua. *I Kissed Dating Goodbye: A New Attitude Toward Romance and Relationships*. Colorado Springs: Multnomah, 2003.

Heaven's Gate. "Hale Bopp Brings Closure to Heaven's Gate." Accessed September 14, 2018. http://www.heavensgate.com.

Heimlich, Russell. "What Caused the Civil War?" *Pew Research Center*, May 18, 2011. http://www.pewresearch.org/fact-tank/2011/05/18/what-caused-the-civil-war/.

Hill, Jonathan P. "National Study of Religion & Human Origins." *Biologos* (2014). https://biologos.org/uploads/projects/nsrho-report.pdf.

Hodge, Archibald Alexander. *Public Lectures on Theological Themes*. Philadelphia: Presbyterian Board of Publication, 1887.

Horkheimer, Max, and Theodor W. Adorno. *Dialectic of Enlightenment*. Translated by John Cumming. New York: Herder and Herder, 1972.

Inman, Mason. "Behind the Numbers on Energy Return on Investment" *Scientific American*, April 1, 2013. https://www.scientificamerican.com/article/eroi-behind-numbers-energy-return-investment.

———. "The True Cost of Fossil Fuels." *Scientific American* 308 (2013) 58–61. http://doi.org/10.1038/scientificamerican0413-58.

IPSOS. "One in Seven (14%) Global Citizens Believe End of the World is Coming in Their Lifetime." Accessed September 14, 2018. https://www.ipsos.com/en-us/one-seven-14-global-citizens-believe-end-world-coming-their-lifetime.

Jehl, Douglas. "Surgeon General Forced to Resign by White House." *The New York Times*, December 10, 1994. https://www.nytimes.com/1994/12/10/us/surgeon-general-forced-to-resign-by-white-house.html.

Jesus Camp. Directed by Heidi Ewing and Rachel Grady. New York: Magnolia, 2006.

Johnson, Paul Elliott. "Imagining American Democracy: The Rhetoric of New Conservative Populism." PhD diss., University of Iowa, 2013. https://ir.uiowa.edu/etd/4996/.

Jones, Jo, William Mosher, and Kimberly Daniels. "Current Contraceptive Use in the United States, 2006–2010, and Changes in Patterns of Use Since 1995." *National Health Statistics Reports*, no. 60 (October 18, 2012). https://www.cdc.gov/nchs/data/nhsr/nhsr060.pdf.

Joyce, Kathryn. "Arrows for the War." *The Nation*, November 9, 2006. https://www.thenation.com/article/arrows-war/.

Keep, Stephanie. "Still Fighting for Evolution in Schools." *PBS*, December 1, 2015. http://www.pbs.org/wgbh/nova/blogs/education/2015/12/evolutionschools/.

Kirk, Russell. *Economics: Work and Prosperity in Christian Perspective*. 2nd ed. Pensacola, FL: Abeka, 1999.

Klein, Naomi. *This Changes Everything: Capitalism Vs. The Climate*. New York: Simon & Schuster, 2014.

Kolhatkar, Sheelah. "The Growth of Sinclair's Conservative Media Empire." *The New Yorker*, October 15, 2018. https://www.newyorker.com/magazine/2018/10/22/the-growth-of-sinclairs-conservative-media-empire/amp?__twitter_impression=true.

Kotsko, Adam. "On Having a Fake Culture." Accessed September 17, 2018. https://itself.blog/2018/03/22/on-having-a-fake-culture/.

Krips, Henry. *Fetish: An Erotics of Culture*. Ithaca, NY: Cornell University, 1999.

———. "Interpellation, Populism, and Perversion: Althusser, Laclau und Lacan." *Filozofski Vestnik* 27.2 (2006) 81–101. Accessed July 7, 2016. http://filozofskivestnikonline.com/index.php/journal/article/view/18/6.

Lacan, Jacques. *Anxiety: The Seminar of Jacques Lacan, Book X*. Edited by Jacques-Alain Miller and translated by A. R. Price. Malden, MA: Polity, 2014.

———. *Écrits: The First Complete Edition in English*. Translated by Bruce Fink. New York: Norton, 1996.

———. *Encore, 1972–1973, On Feminine Sexuality, the Limits of Love and Knowledge: The Seminar of Jacques Lacan, Book XX*. Edited by Jacques-Alain Miller. Translated by Bruce Fink. New York: Norton, 1998.

———. *The Four Fundamental Concepts of Psychoanalysis: The Seminar of Jacques Lacan, Book XI*. Edited by Jacques-Alain Miller. Translated by Alan Sheridan. New York: Norton, 1981.

———. *Freud's Papers on Technique, 1953–1954: The Seminar of Jacques Lacan, Book I*. Edited by Jacques-Alain Miller. Translated by John Forrester. New York: Norton, 1991.

———. *Les Non-Dupes Errent*. Translated by Cormac Gallagher. Accessed September 17, 2018. http://www.lacaninireland.com/web/wp-content/uploads/2010/06/Book-21-Les-Non-Dupes-Errent-Part-2.pdf.

———. "On Psychoanalytic Discourse." In *Lacan in Italia, 1953–1978*, translated by Jack W. Stone, 32–55. Milan: La Salmandra, 1978.

———. *The Other Side of Psychoanalysis: The Seminar of Jacques Lacan, Book XVII*. Edited by Jacques-Alain Miller. Translated by Russell Grigg. New York: Norton, 2007.

Laclau, Ernesto. *On Populist Reason*. New York: Verso, 2005.

LaHaye, Tim, and Beverley LaHaye. *The Act of Marriage: The Beauty of Sexual Love*. Grand Rapids, Zondervan, 1998.

LaHaye, Tim, and Jerry B. Jenkins. *The Indwelling: The Beast Takes Possession*. Carol Stream, IL: Tyndale, 2000.

Lewis, Andrew R. "Abortion Politics and the Decline of the Separation of Church and State: The Southern Baptist Case." Politics and Religion 7, no. 3 (July 18, 2014) 521–49. https://doi-org.ccl.idm.oclc.org/10.1017/S1755048314000492.

Lifeway Research. "Many Americans link U.S. military strike in Syria to end times." Accessed September 14, 2018. http://lifewayresearch.com/2013/09/13/many-americans-link-u-s-military-strike-in-syria-to-end-times/.

———. "Pastor Views on the End Times." Accessed September 14, 2018. http://lifewayresearch.com/wp-content/uploads/2016/04/Pastor-Views-on-the-End-Times-January-2016.pdf.

Mai, Lina. "'I Had a Right to Be at Central': Remembering Little Rock's Integration Battle." *Time*, September 22, 2017. http://time.com/4948704/little-rock-nine-anniversary/.

Maines, Rachel P. *The Technology of Orgasm: "Hysteria," the Vibrator, and Women's Sexual Satisfaction.* Baltimore: Johns Hopkins University Press, 1999.

Marist Poll. "Trust in Institutions Poll Findings." *NPR/PBS NewsHour/Marist Poll*, January 2018. http://maristpoll.marist.edu/wp-content/misc/usapolls/us180108_PBS_NPR/NPR_PBS%20NewsHour_Marist%20Poll_National%20Nature%20of%20the%20Sample%20and%20Tables_Institutions_January%202018.pdf#page=3.

Martin, Gregory J., and Ali Yurukoglu. "Bias in Cable News: Persuasion and Polarization." *American Economic Review* 107, no. 9 (September 2017). https://doi.org/10.1257/aer.20160812.

McGinniss, Joe. *The Selling of the President: The Classic Account of the Packaging of a Candidate.* New York: Penguin, 1988.

McGowan, Todd. *Enjoying What We Don't Have: The Political Project of Psychoanalysis.* Lincoln, NE: University of Nebraska, 2013.

McVicar, Michael J. *Christian Reconstruction: R. J. Rushdoony and American Religious Conservatism.* Chapel Hill, NC: University of North Carolina Press, 2015.

Media Matters. "Bill O'Reilly: Trump "Should Accept The Paris Treaty On Climate To Buy Some Goodwill Overseas." *Media Matters for America*, November 17, 2016. https://www.mediamatters.org/video/2016/11/17/bill-oreilly-trump-should-accept-paris-treaty-climate-buy-some-goodwill-overseas/214513.

———. "O'Reilly: Nobody Can Control The Climate But God, So Give A Little Extra At Mass Or Services." *Media Matters for America*, April 6, 2011. https://www.mediamatters.org/video/2011/04/06/oreilly-nobody-can-control-the-climate-but-god/178416.

National Center for Education Statistics. "Back to School Statistics." *U. S. Department of Education* (2018). Accessed September 16, 2018. https://nces.ed.gov/fastfacts/display.asp?id=372.

———. "National Household Education Surveys Program of 2016." *U. S. Department of Education* (2018). Accessed September 16, 2018. https://nces.ed.gov/pubs2018/2018100.pdf.

National Oceanic and Atmospheric Administration. "What percentage of the American population lives near the coast?" Accessed September 14, 2018. https://oceanservice.noaa.gov/facts/population.html.

Nietzsche, Friedrich. *On the Genealogy of Morals | Ecce Homo.* Translated by Walter Kaufmann and R. J. Hollingdale. New York: Vintage, 1989.

Noll, Mark A. *The Civil War as Theological Crisis.* Chapel Hill, NC: University of North Carolina Press, 2006.

———. *The Rise of Evangelicalism: The Age of Edwards, Whitefield and the Wesleys.* Downers Grove, IL: InterVarsity, 2010.

Paik, Anthony, Kenneth J. Sanchagrin, and Karen Heimer. "Broken Promises: Abstinence Pledging and Sexual and Reproductive Health." *Journal of Marriage and Family* 78 (January 4, 2016) 546–61. https://doi-org.ccl.idm.oclc.org/10.1111/jomf.12279.

Paxton, Robert. *The Anatomy of Fascism*. New York: Vintage, 2005.

Perlstein, Rick. "Exclusive: Lee Atwater's Infamous 1981 Interview on the Southern Strategy." *The Nation*, November 13, 2012. https://www.thenation.com/article/exclusive-lee-atwaters-infamous-1981-interview-southern-strategy/.

Pew Research Center. "Globally, People Point to ISIS and Climate Change as Leading Security Threats." Accessed September 14, 2018. http://www.pewglobal.org/2017/08/01/globally-people-point-to-isis-and-climate-change-as-leading-security-threats/.

———. "Jesus Christ Returns to Earth." Accessed September 14, 2018. http://www.pewresearch.org/fact-tank/2010/07/14/jesus-christs-return-to-earth/.

———. "The Partisan Divide on Political Values Grows Even Wider." Accessed September 14, 2018. http://www.people-press.org/2017/10/05/7-global-warming-and-environmental-regulation-personal-environmentalism/.

———. "Public Sees a Future Full of Promise and Peril." Accessed September 24, 2016. http://www.people-press.org/2010/06/22/section-3-war-terrorism-and-global-trends/.

———. "U.S. Christians' Views on the Return of Christ." Accessed September 14, 2018. http://www.pewforum.org/2013/03/26/us-christians-views-on-the-return-of-christ/.

———. "U.S. Public Becoming Less Religious." Accessed September 14, 2016. http://www.pewforum.org/2015/11/03/u-s-public-becoming-less-religious/.

Piper, John. "God Created Man Male and Female: What Does It Mean to Be Complementarian?" *Desiring God*. Accessed September 16, 2018. https://www.desiringgod.org/messages/god-created-man-male-and-female-what-does-it-mean-to-be-complementarian.

Plato. *The Republic*. Translated by Desmond Lee. New York: Penguin, 2003.

Polanyi, Karl. *The Great Transformation*. Boston: Beacon, 1957.

Politico. "Full Text: Trump's Comments on White Supremacists, 'Alt-left' in Charlottesville." *Politico*, August 15, 2017. https://www.politico.com/story/2017/08/15/full-text-trump-comments-white-supremacists-alt-left-transcript-241662.

Powell, James L. "Climate Scientists Virtually Unanimous: Anthropogenic Global Warming Is True." *Bulletin of Science, Technology & Society* 35, no. 5–6 (March 28, 2016) 121–24. https://doi.org/10.1177/0270467616634958.

Powers, Ashley. "Adam, Eve and T. Rex." *Los Angeles Times*, August 27, 2005. http://articles.latimes.com/2005/aug/27/local/me-dinosaurs27.

Pride, Mary. *The Way Home: Beyond Feminism, Back to Reality*. Fenton, MO: Home Life, 2010.

Public Religion Research Institute. "Backing Trump, White Evangelicals Flip Flop on Importance of Candidate Character." *Public Religion Research Institute/Brookings*, October 19, 2016. https://www.prri.org/research/prri-brookings-oct-19-poll-politics-election-clinton-double-digit-lead-trump/.

———. "Who Sees Discrimination? New Survey Shows Republicans and Democrats Perceive Two Different Realities." *Public Religion Research Institute*, June 21, 2017. https://www.prri.org/press-release/sees-discrimination-new-survey-shows-republicans-democrats-perceive-two-different-realities/.

Putnam, Robert D., and David E. Campbell. *American Grace: How Religion Divides and Unites Us*. New York: Simon & Schuster, 2010.

Reich, Wilhelm. *The Mass Psychology of Fascism*. Edited by Mary Higgins and Chester M. Raphael. New York: Farrar, Straus and Giroux, 1970.

Robin, Corey. *The Reactionary Mind: Conservatism from Edmund Burke to Sarah Palin*. New York: Oxford University Press, 2011.

Rodkey, Christopher. "God's Not Dead as Reverse Revenge Fantasy." Paper presented at Subverting the Norm, Springfield, Missouri, November 2015.

Rosin, Hanna. "Columbine Miracle: A Matter of Belief." *The Washington Post*, October 14, 1999. http://www.washingtonpost.com/wp-srv/WPcap/1999-10/14/026r-101499-idx.html.

Sandeen, Ernest R. *The Roots of Fundamentalism: British and American Millenarianism 1800–1930*. Chicago: University of Chicago Press, 1970.

Saul, Jennifer M. "On Treating Things as People: Objectification, Pornography, and the History of the Vibrator." *Hypatia* 21, no. 2 (2006) 45–61. https://www.jstor.org/stable/3810991.

Schmidt, Leigh Eric. "Is God Dead? A TIME Cover Turns 50." *Religion and Politics*. Accessed September 14, 2018. http://religionandpolitics.org/2016/04/05/is-god-dead-a-time-cover-turns-50/.

Schmitt, Carl. *Political Theology: Four Chapters on the Concept of Sovereignty*. Translated by George Schwab. Chicago: University of Chicago Press, 2005.

Scopes, John. *The World's Most Famous Court Trial: Tennessee Evolution Case*. Union: Lawbook Exchange, 1999.

Shabecoff, Philip. "Global Warming Has Begun, Expert Tells Senate." *The New York Times*, June 24, 1988. https://www.nytimes.com/1988/06/24/us/global-warming-has-begun-expert-tells-senate.html.

Silver, Nate. "The Mythology of Trump's 'Working Class' Support." *FiveThirtyEight*, May 3, 2018. https://fivethirtyeight.com/features/the-mythology-of-trumps-working-class-support/.

Socioeconomic Data and Applications Center. "Percentage of Total Population Living in Coastal Areas." Accessed September 14, 2018. http://sedac.ciesin.columbia.edu/es/papers/Coastal_Zone_Pop_Method.pdf.

Southern Baptist Convention. "Resolution on Abortion: St. Louis, Missouri—1971." Accessed September 16, 2018. http://www.sbc.net/resolutions/13/resolution-on-abortion.

Southern Education Foundation. "A History of Private Schools & Race in the American South." Accessed September 15, 2018. http://www.southerneducation.org/Our-Strategies/Research-and-Publications/Race-Ethnicity-Landing-Pages/A-History-of-Private-Schools-Race-in-the-American.aspx.

Stengel, Richard. "The Republicans: The Man Behind the Message." *Time*, August 22, 1988. http://content.time.com/time/subscriber/article/0,33009,968180-2,00.html.

Stoller, R. L. "The History of Homeschooling, 1904–Present." *HARO*, May 4, 2015. https://homeschoolersanonymous.org/2015/05/04/the-history-of-homeschooling-1904-present/#_edn254.

Stuehrenberg, Paul F. "Christian Responses to Charles Darwin, 1870–1900." *Yale Divinity School Library*. Accessed September 15, 2018. http://divinity-adhoc.library.yale.edu/Exhibits/Darwin.htm.

Suitts, Steve. "Race and Ethnicity in a New Era of Public Funding of Private Schools: Private School Enrollment in the South and the Nation." *Southern Education Foundation* (March 2016). Accessed September 15, 2018. http://www.southerneducation.org/getattachment/be785c57-6ce7-4682-b80d-04d89994a0b6/Race-and-Ethnicity-in-a-New-Era-of-Public-Funding.aspx.

Supran, Geoffrey, and Naomi Oreskes. "Assessing ExxonMobil's Climate Change Communications (1977–2014)." *Environmental Research Letters* 12, no. 8 (August 23, 2017). http://iopscience.iop.org/1748-9326/12/8/084019/.

Swift, Art. "In U.S., Belief in Creationist View of Humans at New Low." *Gallup*, May 22, 2017. https://news.gallup.com/poll/210956/belief-creationist-view-humans-new-low.aspx.

Telhami, Shibley. "American Attitudes Toward the Middle East and Israel." *Center for Middle East Policy at Brookings*. Accessed September 14, 2018. https://www.brookings.edu/wp-content/uploads/2016/07/2015-Poll-Key-Findings-Final.pdf.

Thornwell, James Henley. "Rights and Duties of Masters." In *A Documentary History of Religion in America to 1877*, edited by Edwin S. Gaustad and Mark A. Noll, 538–41. Grand Rapids: Eerdmans, 2003.

Time. "Education: Teaching Children at Home." *Time Magazine* 112, no. 23, December 4, 1978. http://content.time.com/time/magazine/article/0,9171,912280,00.html.

Toy, Eckard V., Jr. "Spiritual Mobilization: The Failure of an Ultraconservative Ideal in the 1950's." *The Pacific Northwest Quarterly* 61, no. 2 (April 1970) 77–86. https://www.jstor.org/stable/40488759.

United States Courts. "History—Brown v. Board of Education Re-enactment." Accessed September 15, 2018. http://www.uscourts.gov/educational-resources/educational-activities/history-brown-v-board-education-re-enactment.

US Holocaust Memorial Museum. "Charles E. Coughlin." Accessed September 17, 2018. https://www.ushmm.org/wlc/en/article.php?ModuleId=10005516.

US Mint. "Coinage Act of April 2, 1792." Accessed September 17, 2018. https://www.usmint.gov/learn/history/historical-documents/coinage-act-of-april-2-1792.

"'Welfare Queen' Becomes Issue in Reagan Campaign." *New York Times*. Accessed April 26, 2019. https://www.nytimes.com/1976/02/15/archives/welfare-queen-becomes-issue-in-reagan-campaign-hitting-a-nerve-now.html.

Wilkinson, Alissa. "After Columbine, Martyrdom Became a Powerful Fantasy for Christian Teenagers." *Vox*, April 20, 2017. https://www.vox.com/culture/2017/4/20/15369442/columbine-anniversary-cassie-bernall-rachel-scott-martyrdom.

Williams Institute. "More than 20,000 LGBT Teens in the US Will Be Subjected to Conversion Therapy." *UCLA School of Law*, January 24, 2018. https://williamsinstitute.law.ucla.edu/press/conversion-therapy-release/.

Wood, Thomas. "Racism Motivated Trump Voters More than Authoritarianism." *The Washington Post*, April 17, 2017. https://www.washingtonpost.com/news/monkey-cage/wp/2017/04/17/racism-motivated-trump-voters-more-than-authoritarianism-or-income-inequality/?utm_term=.e77cb5ebc793&wpisrc=nl_most-draw14&wpmm=1.

World Health Organization. "Climate Change and Health." Accessed September 14, 2018. http://www.who.int/news-room/fact-sheets/detail/climate-change-and-health.

Wyler, Rich. "A Change of Heart: My Two Years in Reparative Therapy." *Brothers Road*. Accessed September 16, 2018. http://www.brothersroad.org/stories/writtentestimonials/rich/.

Yale Program on Climate Change Communication. "Yale Climate Opinion Maps." Accessed September 14, 2018. http://climatecommunication.yale.edu/visualizations-data/ycom-us-2016/?est=happening&type=value&geo=county.

Made in the USA
Coppell, TX
09 December 2020